Mastery of the Financial Accounting Research System (FARS) Through Cases

Mastery of the Financial Accounting Research System (FARS) Through Cases

Wanda A. Wallace, Ph.D., CPA, CMA, CIA
The John N. Dalton Professor of Business Administration
College of William and Mary

John Wiley & Sons, Inc.

ACQUISITIONS EDITOR   Mark Bonadeo

MARKETING MANAGER   Keari Bedford

EDITORIAL ASSISTANT   Brian Kamins

This book contains citations from various FASB pronouncements. Copyright by Financial Accounting Standards Board, 401 Merritt 7, P.O. Box 5116, Norwalk, CT 06856.

This book was set in Times New Roman by Wanda A. Wallace and printed and bound by Hamilton Printing Company. The cover was printed by Phoenix Color Corporation.

This book is printed on acid-free paper. ∞

The paper in this book was manufactured by a mill whose forest management programs include sustained yield harvesting of its timberlands. Sustained yield harvesting principles ensure that the numbers of trees cut each year does not exceed the amount of new growth.

ISBN 0471-20073-5

Printed in the United States of America

10 9 8 7 6 5 4 3 2 1

Dedicated to
Alan Peterson

An avid reader, believer in lifelong learning,
and true investor in human capital

About the Author

Wanda A. Wallace, Ph.D., CPA, CMA, CIA is the John N. Dalton Professor of Business Administration at the College of William and Mary in Williamsburg, Virginia. She received her Ph.D. from the University of Florida, with an Accounting Major, Finance Minor, and Statistics Research Skill. Professor Wallace has been a member of the faculty at the University of Rochester, Southern Methodist University (as The Marilyn R. and Leo F. Corrigan, Jr. Trustee Professor), and Texas A & M University (as The Deborah D. Shelton Systems Professor of Accounting) before joining the College of William and Mary. Dr. Wallace has been the Associate Dean for Academic Affairs at the School of Business, College of William and Mary.

Dr. Wallace has received the Wildman Gold Medal awarded to the most significant literary contribution to the advancement of public accounting over a three-year period by the American Accounting Association (AAA) and Deloitte. She has been awarded a Certificate of Distinguished Performance on the Certified Management Accounting Examination and the Highest Achievement Award (Gold Medal) on the international Certified Internal Auditor Examination. Dr. Wallace was selected in 1998 to receive the Virginia Society of CPAs Outstanding Accounting Educator Award in recognition of excellence in classroom teaching and for active involvement in the accounting profession. She is extremely active in the academic profession, currently serving on the editorial board for nine national and/or international journals and in the past serving as AAA Vice President, an officer in the AAA's Auditing Section, Chair of the AAA's Government and Nonprofit section, a member of the Board of Regents of The Institute of Internal Auditors, and Visiting Distinguished Faculty member of the Doctoral Consortium, New Faculty Consortium, and Senior Faculty Consortium of the AAA. Dr. Wallace has been a visiting scholar at a number of domestic and international universities, including The University of Manchester in England and the Norwegian School of Economics and Business Administration in Bergen, Norway.

Dr. Wallace joined the Financial Accounting Standards Advisory Council (FASAC) that advises the Financial Accounting Standards Board (FASB) in 1991and served through 1995. At the invitation of Charles A. Bowsher, then Comptroller General of the United States, Dr. Wallace served on the Government Auditing Standards Advisory Council from 1991 through 1996. Dr. Wallace consults with national and international firms, ensuring up-to-date appreciation of current practice problems. Previous expert testimony has involved a number of areas including: statistical sampling; statistical analysis; surveys; research methods; auditing; market competition; modeling and econometrics; systems and control processes; accounting; finance and valuation; distribution systems; intellectual property; economics; and business operations. Dr. Wallace has authored over 40 books and monographs, and over 200 articles in such journals as the *Harvard Business Review, European Management Journal, Accounting Review, Journal of Accounting Research, Contemporary Accounting Research, CPA Journal, Government Finance Review, Financial Executive, Journal of Accounting, Auditing & Finance, Scandinavian Journal of Management, China Accounting and Finance Review, Accounting Today*, and *Wall Street Journal.* In 1990, she was identified as the "Most Prolific Author in the Past Decade (1979-88) in 24 academic accounting journals" in *The International Journal of Accounting*.

PREFACE

The Financial Accounting Research System (FARS) is a powerful tool for gaining an understanding of generally accepted accounting principles (GAAP). The ability to search the standards and associated guidance using Boolean logic, in addition to reasoning through indices as to where certain types of questions might be addressed, needs to be developed as an essential competency. This resource provides the rudiments, then develops application skills. Specifically, easy-to-assign introductory exercises, tied to topics common in financial accounting require accessing FARS to build business vocabulary. Then intermediate assignments appropriately called "Brain Teasers" use an active dialogue approach of individuals discussing a conceptual or practice problem that needs to be analyzed. Search phrases must be designed to identify the resources that can shed light on the issue at hand. In addition, you are asked to explore a number of resources beyond FARS. Responding to such requests is facilitated through a five-part case that draws upon interactive databases including resources for searching the literature, Internet, web sites, public filings, legal cases, and both financial statement and financial markets information.

GAAP are filled with areas of judgment that require a clear understanding of context in order to analyze the alternative reporting practices that are acceptable and their consequences. FARS is a powerful tool for gaining an understanding of how GAAP apply to a particular case setting. Cases draw on actual financial statements and events involving real companies and not-for-profit entities, to provide realistic applications of FARS. Particular case settings integrate requirements that call upon expertise in FARS, the Internet, and the general literature. Analytical abilities and reasoning processes are honed through consideration of real company events and reporting practices, as well as debates in the media.

By mastering the use of FARS, you will be better equipped to address the challenges that will arise in the course of your careers. All professions are affected by standard setting and regulation and call upon the individual to exercise judgment in their interpretation and application. An increasing number of databases are becoming available that use Boolean logic—the search infrastructure found in FARS. You can hone your ability to properly identify the scope of relevant guidance, the differences between a particular setting and the circumstances that may be illustrated in available guidance, and implied directions for 'uncharted territories.'

These resources in combination offer you the opportunity to be introduced to FARS in an effective and productive manner at the introductory level and then build on those skills to achieve mastery. Education in business is committed to building reasoning skills that facilitate the exercise of effective judgment when addressing unstructured problems. FARS provides a particularly appropriate resource for pedagogical use. Professionals in business are increasingly accessing multiple information bases using Boolean logic and coping with ever-changing guidance in regulation and business practices. The development of an appreciation of how to access, analyze, apply, and discern why contradictions might arise and be resolved will be an invaluable competency upon which to draw in the course of your professional career.

One of the opportunities with FARS that is taken advantage of in developing resource materials is the role of dissents in often highlighting the core conceptual issue on which decision makers disagreed, even as they moved forward to provide various forms of guidance. Among the lessons learned will be an appreciation for (1) the variety of pronouncements that speak to even basic accounting concepts and issues, just in different contexts, (2) the diversity of business transactions that must be accounted for in business settings, and (3) the nature of changes over time in guidance (highlighted as gray sections or superseded guidance within the FARS materials).

Every hard copy of the casebook includes a FARS CD-ROM. Installation instructions for FARS CD is included in the slipcase pocket containing the CD, found inside the front cover of the casebook. The CD is the academic version of FARS, which is updated once a year. Students gain automatic access to the online version with the purchase of a new casebook. The functionality of the online versions permit students to work entirely on the Internet. This eases access for use in a variety of courses throughout the curriculum. As an example, the Primer could be used to introduce the resource to entering business students, at both the undergraduate and graduate level, in tandem with the vocabulary assignments. The brain teasers can similarly be a focus in Intermediate Accounting and advanced graduate coursework—with some integration of the vocabulary assignments. The cases could be used in financial statement analysis courses at both the undergraduate and graduate levels. The Resources Beyond FARS is a case that facilitates integration of diverse research tools and is an invaluable beginning step in any course setting that calls upon students to perform research using a variety of technologically-based resources.

Many cases have discussions of related issues that span a variety of business topics associated with economics, finance, management, marketing, and analytics. Strategy courses and financial reporting courses, as one example, could coordinate the use of cases within a curriculum to revisit a familiar setting as a framework for exploring related business measurement and management dimensions. The courses interested in not-for-profit entities will find the comparison of Universal Health Services to St. Jude Children's Research Hospital/ALSAC to be an effective means of comparing sources of capital accessible to organizations of differing legal form. A tax class might want to explore more deeply the tax dimensions of the United Parcel Service case, integrating the actual tax court case findings, beyond the disclosure emphasis explored in an earlier financial accounting course. Internet-specific considerations such as the growing role of barter transactions might have relevance in an e-commerce or marketing course, and the case first discussed from an accounting perspective could be revisited to discuss marketing strategy implications. Similarly, a finance course on valuation will find the research and development cases of substantial relevance to acquainting students with the practice issues common in acquisitions.

I am committed to placing cases involving current practice developments into the classroom as expeditiously as possible. Hence, I will continuously author additional cases that will be added to the Web collection and made accessible for classroom use, while time elapses between editions of hard-bound case books. This takes advantage of three particularly unique aspects of the Internet: ease of accessibility, tailoring of that subset of cases you wish to use in a particular course, and timeliness of access without the common delay of the publication process. Yet, periodically, new cases will be folded into future editions of this bound casebook, for those preferring the published collection for classroom use. I welcome suggestions for areas in which you would like additional case materials developed.

Instructor resources include detailed instructor notes and Powerpoint slideshows, for each requirement, table, brain teaser, and case within chapters two through five. Condensed versions of Instructor Notes are provided for both Chapters 3 and 4 for ease of reference, in addition to longer versions that contain each of the FARS cites identified.

The support of the staffs of John Wiley & Sons is greatly appreciated. Mark Bonadeo and David Kear have worked toward the effective integration of this hard copy of the casebook with Internet capabilities. Cheryl Ferguson as copyeditor made a number of creative suggestions. The cooperation of the Financial Accounting Standards Board has permitted the development of this educational resource that is expressly designed to support the use of FARS.

My partner in life, James J. Wallace, has been, as usual, indispensable. A sounding board for ideas, first drafts, and multiple iterations, Jim has encouraged, improved upon, and selflessly contributed to this book.

Wanda A. Wallace
Williamsburg, Virginia
January 30, 2002

CONTENTS   PAGE

Chapter 4 – Brain Teasers: Using FARS to Untangle the Mystery 4-1

CHAPTER 1 – THE FINANCIAL ACCOUNTING RESEARCH SYSTEM (FARS) PRIMER

Getting Started With FARS: The Basics

Where Am I Going to Look?

The Financial Accounting Standards Board's (FASB's) Financial Accounting Research System (FARS) is a PC-based tool for accounting research that uses software for efficient and effective access to databases (infobases) of FASB literature. It is a research tool commonly used to identify guidance regarding how transactions and events are to be reported, in order for financial presentations to be in conformance with generally accepted accounting principles (GAAP).

The first question to answer as you access this PC-based tool is where should you look? Within the Financial Accounting Research System (FARS) are six major information bases from which to choose. These may differ over time, depending on the development of new types of guidance and the stage of completion at the point in time that a new version of FARS becomes available. In addition, the FARS Reference Guide contains an Overview of the PC-based tool, alongside files named: Getting Started, FARS Basics, Searching the Infobases, Printing and Exporting Text, and Glossary. That machine-readable resource, available by clicking on the menu of FARS, provides the basis for this description of FARS, complementing this PRIMER as you use the software. The FARS main menu acronyms for each of the six major information bases, with a description of the content of each follows:

FASB-OP   *Original Pronouncements*—All AICPA and FASB pronouncements, even if superseded (i.e., replaced by newer rulings): Accounting Research Bulletins (ARB), Accounting Principles Board Opinions (APB), AICPA Accounting Interpretations (AIN), Accounting Principles Board Statements (APS), Accounting Terminology Bulletins (ATB), FASB Statements (FAS), FASB Interpretations (FIN), FASB Technical Bulletins (FTB), and FASB Concepts Statements (CON). Note that superseded materials are shaded, with red diamonds that when clicked link to an explanation of what material applies in lieu of the superseded sections.

FASB-CT   *Current Text*—General Standards, Industry Standards, and the Current Text sections that have been superseded but are still applicable due to delays in effective dates: an appendix lists current AICPA Practice Bulletins, Statements of Position, and Audit and Accounting Guides.

EITF   *Abstracts*—The Emerging Issues Task Force infobase includes the full text of each abstract for every issue discussed by the EITF since its inception in 1984, the introduction to EITF Abstracts, a list of task force members (Appendix A), announcements of general and administrative matters (Appendix C), discussions of other technical matters (Appendix D), and the EITF topical index.

FASB-Q&A   *Implementation Guides*—The infobase contains staff special reports and other published implementation guidance on FAS 80 (Accounting for Futures Contracts); 86 (Accounting for the Costs of Computer Software to Be Sold, Leased, or Otherwise Marketed); 87 (Employers' Accounting for Pensions), 88 (Employers' Accounting for Settlements & Curtailments of Defined Benefit Pension Plans and for Termination Benefits), 91 (Nonrefundable Fees & Costs Associated with Originating or Acquiring Loans and Initial Direct Costs of Leases); 96 (Accounting for Income Taxes); 109 (Accounting for Income Taxes); 113 (Accounting and Reporting for Reinsurance of Short-Duration and Long-Duration Contracts); 116 (Accounting for Contributions Received and Contributions Made); and 117 (Financial Statements of Not-for-Profit Organizations). It also contains illustrations of financial instrument disclosure requirements in FAS 105 (Disclosure of Information about Financial Instruments with Off-Balance-Sheet Risk and Concentrations of Credit Risk), 107 (Disclosures about Fair Value of Financial Instruments), and 119 (Disclosure about Derivative Financial Instruments and Fair Value of Financial Instruments).

FASINDEX   *Topical Index*—This is the combined topical index for FASB-OP, FASB-CT, EITF, and FASB-Q&A infobases. Each reference in the index is linked to the appropriate paragraph(s), EITF issue, or questions in the relevant infobase. All "See" references (e.g., See Income Taxes) are linked to that section within the index.

DERIVCOD   *Derivative Instruments and Hedging Activities*—This is an aid to implementing FASB Statement 133 (Accounting for Derivative Instruments and Hedging Activities), amended by Statements 137 (Deferral of the Effective Date of FASB Statement No. 133) and 138 (Accounting for Certain Derivative Instruments and Certain Hedging. It also includes the full text of issues related to the implementation of Statement 133 that were discussed by the Derivatives Implementation Group and cleared by the FASB prior to September 25, 2000.

FARS is updated approximately five times a year, as appropriate, to ensure that the infobases contain the latest FASB pronouncements and abstracts of EITF issues.

Although you can look in multiple databases, it is probably preferable to learn FARS by accessing one infobase at a time and proceeding with your analysis. As you become more adept with the system, you can open multiple databases and apply your search to all of them at one time. However, you will find that a number of the FARS capabilities (such as *query templates* and clear query) are not applicable to multiple infobases and that the <u>Hits</u> button affects only the current view. Also, the tag function must be applied to each infobase separately. Given the cluttered display that can result from multiple open infobases, you may well find it more effective to work on a single infobase at a time.

Navigating in FARS

Select FARS from the <u>Start</u> menu to begin the program. You should see a screen with the following icon at the top and buttons corresponding to the infobases linked to the FARS Menu in Figure 1.1.

Financial Accounting Research System

Welcome to the FASB Financial Accounting Research System (FARS) which is current through
March 15, 2001.
Click on your desired selection below.

- Original Pronouncements
- Current Text
- EITF Abstracts
- Derivative Instruments and Hedging Activities
- Implementation Guides
- Topical Index
- FARS Reference Guide

Figure 1.1   Opening screen in FARS

Note that these buttons correspond to each of the infobases already described. If you click on any of the buttons, you will be connected with the respective infobase. For example, you can click the button beside <u>Original Pronouncements</u>, and the introductory screen in Figure 1.2 will appear.

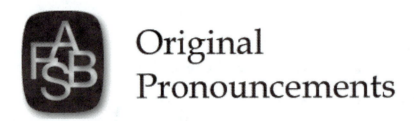

Figure 1.2   Icon for the Original Pronouncements infobase

If you click on <u>Window</u> at the top menu bar, you should see an indication that you are looking at the FASB-OP infobase. Any infobase can be opened by clicking your choice at the bottom of the FARS menu screen and then clicking <u>Go Back</u> on the toolbar or using the F6 key to permit clicking on more than a single infobase. Alternatively, to open the infobases on which you wish to search, click on the menu bar <u>File</u>, which will provide a pull-down menu, and click on <u>Open</u>. [In some settings, if FARS is on a network, you may need to click on <u>Programs</u> and <u>FARS</u> to reach the choice that presents Nfo.] Then click on the folder <u>Nfo</u>, and choose the infobase of interest by clicking on it. You can repeat the sequence to open multiple infobases. To check which are open, click <u>Window</u> on the menu bar and see what are listed as open infobases. If you have RAM constraints below 12 megabytes, the opening multiple infobases might cause your system to crash. This is one more reason to focus on one infobase at a time. The toolbar for FARS (which can vary across versions) is depicted in Figure 1.3.

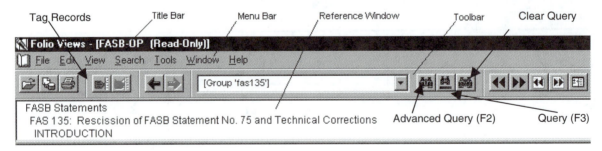

Figure 1.3   FARS toolbar

Linkages

Keep in mind that as you access an infobase, a number of embedded links are of interest. Specifically, you begin with *query* links from the FARS menu to the infobases connecting menu items, document references, and topical index references to the related information in the appropriate infobase. A query is a search for information within an infobase. Within infobases, you will find diamonds at the start of any superseded material (indicated by gray shading) that will link to explanations of what guidance applies in place of that material.

In other words, in FASB-OP links connect superseded or amended material in one document with the superseding or amending language in another document. At times you will find that materials you locate through a diamond will likewise include diamonds. That is because with the passage of time, amendments themselves may be amended or superseded. That is the nature of standard-setting activities. Within the text of both FASB-OP and FASB-CT, you will also notice diamonds to the left side of certain words; these will link glossary terms with their definitions. When footnotes appear, you can click on the number (the cursor will change to a hand image) and a pop-up screen will appear with the content of that footnote. This is known as a *pop-up link*. If you export text, remember that links may not be easily interpreted by the word-processing application selected. Reformatting may be required, and symbols relating to the links may be deleted.

How Do I Search?

You can search the infobases using any of three general techniques. One approach is to use the index, much as you would in a printed book. The second approach is to use a *query template*. The third is to query for particular words or phrases using either <u>Query</u> or <u>Advanced Query</u> capabilities.

Search Alternatives

To access the index, you may go to the FARS menu and click on *Topical Index*, which will link to the following screen. Alternatively, you can go to the menu bar and click <u>File</u>, select from the pull-down menu <u>Open</u>, select the <u>Nfo</u> folder, and then <u>Open</u> FASINDEX. Also note that the FARS toolbar, depicted in Figure 1.3, has an icon at the far left that appears as a folder and can be used to open a folder and infobase. Figure 1.4 shows what appears at the top of the screen of FASINDEX:

Figure 1.4 Icon for the Topical Index infobase

Red diamonds appear to the left of each letter. If clicked, a diamond will take you to an index of topics that begin with that letter of the alphabet. You will note that the cites appear in three columns, incorporating (1) the original pronouncements, (2) the current text, and (3) the EITF/Other infobases. The third column would include EITF abstracts, as well as the Staff

Implementation Guides. By clicking on the cite, the link will be made to the underlying pronouncement listed.

To use a *query template*, it is likewise necessary to open an infobase. This can be accomplished by selecting one of the buttons on the FARS menu (recall Figure 1.1). Alternatively, you can go to the menu bar and click on File, select Open from the pull-down menu, choose the folder Nfo, and then open an infobase. Either approach will have an open infobase on which you can search. Proceed to click on Search at the menu bar and select from among the *query template* alternatives in that pull-down menu: search by issue date; search only current documents; search within a single OP document title; or search within a single OP document type. The boxes that will be displayed guide you in requesting that you specify a date or range of dates, that you select from among a menu of titles or documents, and that you then proceed to specify your search in terms of words or phrases. If you select the *query template* to search within a single OP title, scroll through the choices in the Heading window and click to place the result in the document title. Then move to the Query window and type the search term and click OK. If you merely wanted to locate the document and not perform a search, then after selecting the document title, click OK and move to the Document pane.

To perform a search of a given infobase, once you click on File, Open, Nfo, and an infobase, you can click on Search and then select Query from the pull-down menu and enter a command. Query can be accessed by pressing F3, and Advanced Query can be accessed by pressing F2. Alternatively, you can click on the Query button on the toolbar, which is a set of binoculars icon (the smaller icon with the underscore is the simple query, whereas the larger binoculars on the icon represents the advanced query; the binoculars with a large red X through it is the Clear Query button). Figure 1.3 has these three icons shown to the right.

Words or phrases you type will be searched on the open infobase. If instead you choose to click on Advanced Query, you will obtain information on word counts that can assist your search. In addition, you will have the option of using the Apply to All capability that will search all open infobases, permitting multiple infobases to be concurrently searched. Note that multiple infobases when opened can be viewed by pressing Ctrl+Tab (in other words, hold the control key down and press the tab key to cycle through the views). Do not forget to clear the query when you are finished, before proceeding to the next search. Just click Search on the toolbar and then select Clear Query from the pull-down menu; this must be done per infobase.

Figures 1.5 and 1.6 show examples of the screens that appear when you click on Search and select Query or Advanced Query from the pull-down menu. Merely type in the search word or phrase and click OK.

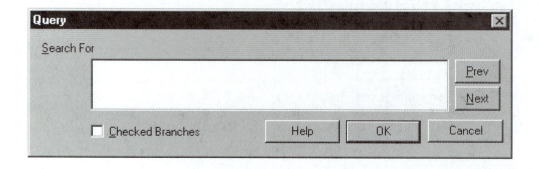

Figure 1.5 Query Screen

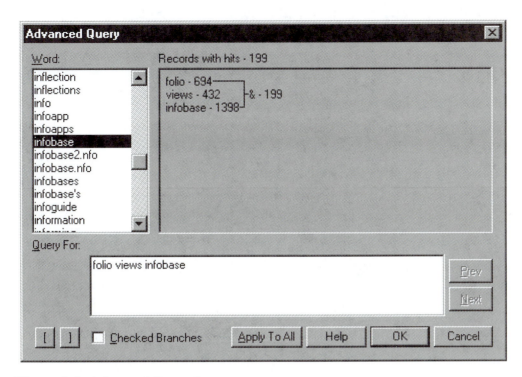

Figure 1.6 Advanced Query Screen

Boolean Logic

There are many ways to conduct a search. A *keyword search* finds all records that contain the word(s) you want to specify. If you search for more than one word, separate the words with a space. A *phrase search* finds all records that contain an exact phrase. This phrase must be enclosed in quotes. These two searches are the building blocks for all other types of searches. Table 1.1 lists search options available under Boolean logic. They are described in more detail in the following paragraphs.

Table 1.1 Search Options Using Boolean Logic

Option	Symbol	Example	Use
Precise quote	"*n*"	"current assets"	Find the exact phrase.
Proximity search			
Distance between words, order specific	/*n*	"current assets"/*n*	Find the word *assets* within *n* words of *current*, in order.
Distance between words, order not specific	@*n*	"current assets"@*n*	Find the word *assets* before or after *current*, within *n* words.
Across records	#*n*	"current assets"#*n*	Find the word assets within *n* records of current.

Option	Symbol	Example	Use
Wildcards			
Uncertain character	?	purch?se	Find any words that are spelled purch?se, with ? representing any letter.
Root word search	%	purchase%	Find words with the root word of *purchase*: purchasing, purchaser, purchased, purchases.
Letter pattern	*	purchas*	Find words that begin with the letters *purchas*: purchasing, purchaser, purchased. (Note that if purchase* were used, the word *purchasing* would not be a hit.)
Synonym	$	purchase$	Find synonyms: *buy*, *acquire*.
Boolean operators			
and	&	current&assets	Find records that contain both words.
		current and assets	Find records that contain both words.
or	|	current|assets	Find records that contain either word.
		current or assets	Find records that contain either word.
not	^	current^assets	Find records that contain the first word but not the second word.
		current not assets	Find records that contain the first word but not the second word.
exclusive or (xor)	~	current~assets	Find records that contain either word but not both.
		current xor assets	Find records that contain either word but not both

Search phrasing can be a precise quote, which means you enter the command in quotes and that is the exact phrasing to be identified. It does not matter whether something is capitalized or lower case. Alternatively, you can apply what are termed *proximity searches*. This requires that the search phrase be in quotes and then be followed by some symbols that instruct the software as to the distance between words and the order of the words required for a match to occur. Specifically, if you follow the quoted phrase with a forward slash and a number, then the words can appear anywhere within the specified number of words of each other but must be in the order you have indicated. Or you could follow the quoted words with @ and a number instead of a forward slash, and the words would have to appear within that specified number of word distance from one another, but they could appear in any order. The terms of /5 or @5 as examples are referred to as proximity conditions whereby the words are within five words of one another, with the first word in the quotes counting as a one and the other words having to appear before the sixth word. For example, you might specify "current assets"/5, which would mean these two words are within five words of one another in the order stated. Alternatively, if you indicated "current assets"@7, it would mean that the words *current* and *assets* appear within seven words of one another but may be in either order - *current assets* or *assets current*.

The search in the absence of a proximity indicator tends to be record based, which typically is defined as a paragraph. At times, you may wish the search process to consider more than a single record as the scope for the search. This can be accomplished by following the quotes of the search phrase with a # and a number representing the number of records you wish to consider as sufficient proximity. For example, "big business" on the FASB-OP infobase results in no hits. By adjusting the command to "big business"#3, it is possible to generate matches. Hence, rather than requiring two terms to be in the same record, one can tailor the search to finding the two terms within a certain number of records. Instead of constraining the space within a record as the scope of the search, this actually extends the search across records.

In addition to proximity conditions, Boolean logic permits the use of what are called wildcards, which facilitate more robust search phrasing. Specifically, if you were uncertain as to spelling, a question mark (?) could be inserted for any given letter. Then any word that has the letters you specified, along with any substitution of a letter for the question mark, would be selected. Multiple question marks for multiple letters can be used, but they must map one-to-one in terms of their number relative to the letters omitted. For example, if you were searching the word *uncollectible* and you were uncertain whether it should be spelled *uncollectable*, you could specify *uncollect?ble* and either spelling would be captured by the search.

A second wildcard capability is the percent sign, or % wildcard. This finds all forms of a specified root word. For example, if you are interested in variations of the root word purchase, such as *purchases*, *purchaser*, *purchasing*, and *purchased*, the search specification of *purchase%* would pick up all of these forms of that root word.

An alternative that is broader than the root word concept moves from guiding the search based on a root word to guiding the search based on the pattern of letters. Specifically, any multiple character substitution is captured by an asterisk. Note that if you specified *purchase** you would again obtain the *purchases*, *purchaser*, and *purchased*, but you would fail to access *purchasing* because the *e* is not found in the spelling and the asterisk only covers those letters omitted in the search. If instead you specified *purchas**, then the *purchasing* alternative spelling would be located. It should be apparent that you need to determine whether the better direction to your search can be gathered through root word guidance, or the pattern of letters. Then you can choose whether to use a % or an *.

One other wildcard capability can be particularly useful, and it is the synonym $. For example, you may wish to find any reference to synonyms of *purchase*. By using the command *purchase$* you will likewise find acquisition and buy among the search results - both synonyms for your specification.

Beyond direct quotes, proximity and ordering variation, and wildcards, Boolean logic permits the association among key words. These are referred to as *Boolean operators*. The term *and* can also be specified as &. This operator means that both terms must be contained in a record in order for it to be identified as a match. If two words appear side by side without typing any word in between, it will be presumed that the search is intended to be equivalent to inserting & in between the two words. The word *or* can also be specified as |. It means that all records containing any of the words will be matches. The term *not* can be specified as a caret, ^. It means that the first word would be included but the latter would not be included in the record. The *exclusive or* operator is abbreviated *xor* and can be specified as a tilde, ~. This is interpreted as either the first term or another but not both terms within a record.

Combinations of Boolean searches are helpful. When performing such a search, you can use parentheses. These define the order of operation similar to that which occurs in basic mathematics. In other words, the search within the parentheses is performed first and then the order of operations is from left to right. If no parentheses are used, then the order of operations is just left to right. Keep in mind that wildcards cannot be used with proximity searches because exact characters within the quotes are their focus. Hence, at times, you will need to perform multiple proximity searches if different word forms are of interest.

Remember to clear previous queries before beginning a new query. Click the <u>Clear Query</u> button to do this. As an example of the manner in which Boolean search operators can be combined, consider the following search phrasing entered after opening the FASB-OP infobase, clicking on the menu bar search, selecting advance query from the pull-down menu, and then resulting in a single match within the infobase:

current&assets$~liabilities^cash^(securities|investments) uncollect?ble

The term *assets$* includes the synonyms of property, capital, wealth, holdings, and liquid. Another example of a narrowing search phrase with a single match follows:

qualif*&securitization$&special&purpose&entit*&wash&sale*

An example of a broadened search would be a change from *wash transaction* which has one match, to *wash transaction$* having five matches. Such examples clearly reflect how Boolean operators and wildcards can either narrow or broaden a search of FARS, depending on their use.

What Results Can I Expect?

When you have completed a search, your results will be reported as *hits*. A match to a query is a hit and will appear in the infobase as highlighted text. Hits are usually reported as the number of records in the infobase that meets the search criteria (or it is the default number set, e.g., 50 hits, if that is a lower number than the actual matches). There are a variety of ways in which you can view those findings. The <u>Reference Window</u> pane is always connected to the top of the <u>Document</u> pane and is shown in Figure 1.3. This is the portion of the infobase window that displays the parent headings for a particular location within the infobase. It also appears with the <u>Contents/Document</u> pane. It identifies the document being viewed - both its title and paragraph. To change views of the infobase data, click on the tabs at the bottom of the infobase window, as shown in Figure 1.7.

Figure 1.7 Tabs to change views of infobase data

Views Available

After you do a search, five panes are accessible through clicking on tabs at the bottom of the infobase window. A pane is that region within a window that displays specific information, while a view is the current display of information in the infobase. Moving from left to right in Figure 1.7, the first pane is <u>Contents/Document</u>, the second is <u>Document</u>, the third is <u>Contents</u>, the fourth is <u>HitList</u>, and the fifth is <u>Object</u>. Note that multiple windows of the same infobase can be viewed by pressing Ctrl+Tab.

Contents/Documents	The first pane at the left identifies how many hits appear in each of the document types. By clicking on the + you are able to identify more details, such as in which Accounting Research Bulletin the hit was found. Another click on the + will identify the paragraph and subheads within the documents. The display of <u>Contents</u>, <u>Document</u>, and <u>Reference Window</u> panes permits browsing of the infobase for information related to the table of contents.
Documents	The <u>Document</u> pane is the actual document in FARS in which the hit appears. The <u>Document</u> pane is the primary pane for working with an infobase; all other panes provide navigational assistance or display other ancillary information. If you click on the bottom tab and open document, you will see both that display and the <u>Reference Window</u> pane. Keep in mind that FARS defaults to an "on" setting for those records with hits. As a result, the view is narrowed to those records with matches to your search and the text is seen out of the context of the original document. This should be apparent as you scroll down the screen, because the <u>Reference Window</u> pane will list different document titles and paragraphs as you scroll from hit to hit. If you wish to see the hits in context, select <u>All Records</u> from the view menu bar and choose the <u>HitList</u> tab.
Contents	The <u>Contents</u> pane displays the table of contents from the first pane. It permits a clear view for scanning the contents and full names that are headings in the table of contents. By double-clicking on a heading in the <u>Contents</u> pane, you will be taken to the appropriate section in the <u>Document</u> view. The table of contents may be expanded or collapsed by double-clicking on the plus or minus signs to the left of the headings.
HitList	The <u>HitList</u> pane permits the search results to be viewed. By double-clicking on a reference in the HitList, you are taken to the <u>Document</u> view of that section. If you have FARS set to its default, the hits are listed in order of relevancy.
Objects	The <u>Object</u> pane will display very large tables and exhibits too large to be displayed in line with the document text. These are displayed as objects when you follow an object link in the Document pane. To retun to the <u>Document</u> pane, click the tab at the bottom of the infobase view.

Tailoring Your Search and Results

In your search, the first fifty hits are displayed by default, unless there are fewer hits. If you want to consider means of tailoring the search, review the Boolean logic options. You can use the advanced query to review the counts of various searching approaches to better tailor the results. If you want to narrow the focus to a specific infobase, particular documents, or dates, consider using the *query template* options.

To move quickly between views and panes, try these shortcut keys.

Action	Shortcut Key
Next pane	F8
Next view	F7
Previous pane	SHIFT+F8
Previous view	SHIFT+F7

As you perform the word search, you will likely want to have your current view clicked onto the <u>Document</u> pane, since it will display the text and will provide a three-line source reference, the last of which is the important information necessary for definition of the full reference (e.g., CON6, Par. 234). To explore lower prioritized search results, you can click onto the <u>HitList</u> and peruse the sources, then click on the highlighted term and return to the <u>Document</u> screen to review further details.

<u>What Can I Do with the Results?</u>

As you click the <u>HitList</u> items and review the document, you will see the search terms highlighted. Then the <u>Next Partition Hit</u> and <u>Previous Partition Hit</u> buttons can assist you in navigating through the hits. *Partitions* are logical divisions of the infobase used to report hits. The default partition is called a *record* and, as mentioned earlier, is usually a numbered paragraph. (In FASINDEX, each reference is generally a record.) Partition icons are double arrowheads, as depicted to the right side of the toolbar shown in Figure 1.3 – note that screens may differ as to icons' location (e.g., they may appear as a second row to the left).

If you judge the record to be of use for your research purposes, a variety of options exist for marking and then exporting or printing those sections. The exporting can be to a file that is then retrievable by other software programs. Another alternative is to copy materials and paste them into a word-processing document.

Tagging

Select a hit that appears to be of use in your research, and that will bring you to the underlying document, click on the menu bar, and select the command <u>Edit</u> and then from the pull-down menu, select <u>Tag</u> in order to tag the record. The <u>Tag Record</u> function allows you to mark random records and collect them for subsequent actions. You can proceed through multiple hits, view the related document, and tag records as you analyze on the screen. The tagging will continue until you choose to clear the tags previously placed. The toolbar depicted in Figure 1.3 has an icon four from the far left that looks like a tag. By pressing that button, a record can be tagged. To the right of that icon is a <u>Clear All Tags</u> icon, which shows a tag with a large red X over it.

To collect all tagged records into a single view, tag the records you wish to collect. Then choose Tagged Records from the View menu. From here, they may be viewed, printed, exported, or formatted.

Exporting

Once you have tagged records of interest, you can export the collection of records to a separate file. Select File from the menu bar, select Export from the pull-down menu, and then type in the filename and select the type of file saved. For example, you can select such formats as a text file output, a Word or Wordperfect file, or a rich text format. The toolbar depicted in Figure 1.3 contains an icon, second from the left, that looks like a piece of paper linked to a disk, and it can be clicked to export.

Follow these steps to export records or text:

1. Select or tag the records you wish to export, choose the branches in the Contents pane that you wish to export, or narrow the view of the infobase to display what you wish to export.
   • To narrow the view, you may search the infobase and view records with hits, tag records and view tagged records, or select branches in the Contents pane and view selected branches.
   • If you are exporting the entire infobase, make sure that no text is selected.
   • Note that the entire record containing the selection is exported.
2. Choose Export from the File menu. The Export dialog box appears.
3. Choose Save as type and select the file format to which you want to export the infobase.
4. Type in the name of the new file. Change the drives and directories as needed.
5. Select the Export range. You may export the entire infobase (regardless of the current view), the current view, tagged records, selected text, or checked branches.
6. Choose Options and set any necessary options for the filter.
   • Not all filters have options for you to set.
   • Setting filter options is *not* supported on Windows 3.x.
7. Click OK.

Remember that links may not be interpretable by the word-processing application into which text is exported. Moreover, due to differences in font size, the numeric data in lists and tables might not appear as it did within FARS, requiring some reformatting. Generally, within a word processor, if you select the text in the table or listing and apply a Courier font that is either eight point or ten point, it will help you in aligning such lists and tables. If you export a table in text format, you may choose to import it into Excel, which will often achieve alignment and permit copying and pasting into a word processing document with ease.

If the delimited importing approach within Excel does not effectively achieve alignment, try the fixed width alternative and then click to create or delete the lines that separate the columns in the importing process. In this manner, it is often possible to achieve alignment of tabular information from text files.

Links contained in exported text may not be easily interpreted by your word-processing application. For example, some versions of MS-Word will display a question mark inside a yellow circle anywhere a link token appeared in the FARS document. Simply delete these "links" from your document. Additionally, some reformatting may be required for numeric data (lists and tables), and fonts may change, depending on your application's default settings.

To save your search results:
1. Perform your query on the infobase.
2. Verify that All Records is on. (To save only selected records within your search results, use the tag function.)
3. From the File menu, choose Export.
4. Pick a destination directory from the directory tree.
5. From the List Files of Type: window, choose the file format in which you would like to save your data. A number of word-processing programs are listed, along with ASCII and generic text.
6. Type a file name in the appropriate window.
7. Click OK.

Printing

If you wish to print the results of a search, click File on the menu bar and then click Print. The screen will permit you to choose among different panes that alternatively will print Document, Contents, HitList, or Object. If you are printing the table of contents, expand the table to show the branches you wish to print. To print a single branch, select that branch. You can specify that the printer prints tagged records, specific records, sections, or all. The toolbar in Figure 1.3 has an icon on which a picture of a printer appears (it is the third icon from the left). When clicked, it will generate a print command.

Before printing, consider clicking on Tools from the menu bar and selecting Options from the pull-down menu, then clicking on Print to consider other choices. You may wish for your results to use inline headings, thereby ensuring citations to the full source name, section, and paragraph reference. Note that interspersing of complete cites between records can be cumbersome in large excerpts, but they can be very useful for focused excerpts. If you want to highlight the words that were hit through your query, you may select Integrate Query. This results in words that were hit being boldfaced and underscored. In the absence of selecting this option, the text prints in regular format, without highlighting hits. After accessing Tools on the menu bar, click on Options. On the Print pane, click on the box beside Inline Headings and/or Query Results to print these options onto materials you generate.

Follow these steps to print:
1. Select the information you wish to print.
2. Choose Print from the File menu.
3. Set the print range for the job.
   • The print range options depend on the tab you use. Possible choices may include:
   • Choose All to print all of the records in the current view. (The current view of the Document control may be narrowed to only those records or partitions with search hits or tagged records. Otherwise, All prints the entire infobase.)
   • Choose Records: to print a specific range of records (you must also enter the first and last record to print).
   • Choose Selection to only print the selected portion of the infobase.
   • Choose Tagged Records to only print the tagged records in the infobase.
   • Choose Section to specify a section of the infobase to print based on the table of contents headings.
4. Specify the number of copies to make.
5. Specify the starting page number, if desired. Page specifies the starting page number to be printed in the header or footer for the print job (provided that the header or footer uses the Page # code). Use this when you do not want the first page to be numbered 1.

6. Specify the number of columns to print, if desired.
   • Folio Views can print information in one to five equal columns on a page. The columns flow like newspaper columns (top-to-bottom and left-to-right).
   • The default number of columns for all print jobs is set in the Print tab of the Options dialog box.
7. Choose OK.

Copying and Pasting

Rather than exporting or printing, the user can concurrently open the FARS program and another word-processing program and then mark the selections of interest and copy and paste the section onto the word processor's file. The advantage of this approach is its ease of integrating direct quotes from the FARS resources into formal reports or articles that are being prepared. The disadvantage is that gray coloring, formatting, and links will probably be lost. If this information is important, you will have to make the restorations individually afterward.

Follow these steps to paste text directly into other applications:
1. Block the FARS text you want to paste (use Shift-arrow keys).
2. Press Ctrl-C to copy the text or select Copy from the Edit menu.
3. Open the application you want to paste into. (Use Alt-Tab keys to toggle between applications.)
4. Position your insertion point where you want to paste the text and press Ctrl-V, or select Paste from your application's Edit menu.

Where Can I Go for Additional Direction?

This FARSPRIMER is intended to provide an overview to get you started. However, additional direction is provided within the FARS program. You can press the F1 key and use query to access help on any specific topic. A tutorial is likewise available online.

Help Capability: Online User's Guide

As you use FARS and have a question, access the OnLine User's Guide for assistance. If you click on Help, a menu appears. If you click on Overview a brief introduction to the software used in FARS, reinforcing points discussed herein, will be accessed. If you click on How Do I? you will see the following message:

For more information, click a topic below.
Folio Views Topics
Find Information
Annotate Infobases
Print & Export Information
Format Text
Incorporate Images
Edit Infobases
Organize Infobases
Customize Folio Views
Advanced Topics
Use Help

If you click on Use Help the following instructions appear:

Accessing Help

There are four primary methods for accessing Folio Help:

1.   Press F1. Help on the current dialog or menu item appears.

   • Use this method for quick help on a specific item or to open Help before performing a search.

2.   Choose Contents from the Help menu. The contents listing for Help appears.

   • Use this method to browse for the information you need.

3.   Choose How Do I? from the Help menu. The How Do I? list appears.

   • Use this method when you want a topical listing of tasks that you can perform in Folio Views.

4.   Open the FOLIOHLP.NFO infobase in Folio Views. Click on the Contents button to go to the contents listing, search this infobase using the *query templates*, or browse the infobase using the Contents pane.

   • Use this method when you want to take full advantage of the Folio Views interface while using the Help file.

FARS Reference Guide

When accessing FARS, click on File on the menu bar, and select Open from the pull-down menu, then click on Nfo folder and select the FARS Reference Guide. The result will be access to the online guide, which will detail materials that reinforce the discussion herein. Alternatively, use the FARS menu screen and click the button for the FARS Reference Guide.

Folio Views 4 Getting Started

Another approach to accessing guidance, besides through the Help menu bar already described, is through the file option. You can access File on the menu bar, select Open from the pull-down menu, and then select the Nfo folder and click Open, select Getstrt4, and click Open (Folio Views 4 Getting Started file will then open for use). Alternatively, the last selection could be made, clicking on Foliohlp and then a click on Open (Folio 4 Help Infobase will then open for use).

Self-Review and Cross-Checks

1. If you enter a search and are told there are zero hits, what is likely to be the problem?

You probably have not opened the infobase. In other words, there is nothing to search. (Another possibility is that you clicked the Checked Branches box in the query process and as a result are searching an empty set if the Contents pane does not have branches selected.)

2. What if you enter a search and get far fewer hits than you expected?

You are probably searching only the menu or some smaller subset of information than intended. Check to confirm which infobases are open by clicking Window on the menu bar. Proceed to open the infobase or multiple infobases you wish to search.

3. You specify a search and identify zero hits; you check Window on the menu bar and confirm that the appropriate infobase is open. How should you proceed?

If the search involves more than a single word, access Search on the menu bar and then select Advanced Query. This will allow you to check the word count of any item within your search phrasing and to see how the structure of your search may have limited your matches in an unintended fashion.

4. You perform a search and notice that most of the document you have accessed is shaded. What is meant by the shading, and how should you proceed?

The shading indicates superseded materials in FARS. There should be a red diamond at the beginning of the shaded material. Click that diamond to read what materials apply in place of the superseded section.

5. In the Document pane, a number of footnotes appear. How do you access the footnotes?

Click the footnote number, the cursor will take the form of a pointing hand, and a pop-up screen will appear. This will contain the text of the footnote.

6. You specify a word search in quotes that generates zero hits, even though you are certain that the phrase should be in the material. How might you proceed to explore the search phrasing?

The same phrasing might be attempted without the quotes. If that generates too many hits, then you might try with quotes but with a proximity delimiter such as /3. Another idea is to try a synonym command outside of quotes to see if a match can be achieved. As an example, if there are zero hits when you search "recording a deferred debit" but fifty hits if you remove the quotes, you might consider using such delimiters. If neither of those options produces the desired result, you might try using deferred debit$. The synonym command enlarges coverage to consider such phrases as deferred-charge account as one example of an additional hit identified.

7. You have performed a search using the FASB-OP infobase and prepared a related report on your findings. Upon reviewing the write-up, an associate points out that you have no references to the work of the Emerging Issues Task Force and wonders whether there might be some relevant EITF guidance. How should you proceed?

Your associate has pointed out that FARS only searches the infobases you indicate. Once you have completed a search on FASB-OP, you should check other infobases for relevant information regarding the issue being researched. In this case, you should access File on the menu bar, from the pull-down menu select Open, then apply that command to the folder Nfo, and click on EITF. Then you can proceed to search that infobase in the usual manner. Alternatively, you could have concurrently opened the FASB-OP and the EITF databases and accessed Search from the menu bar, selected Advanced Query, typed in the search phrasing, and then clicked Apply to All to trigger a search of all open infobases. Keep in mind that in order to view the HitList for each infobase, you need to access Window and switch among the infobases to which the search was applied. Alternatively, pressing Ctrl+Tab will cycle through the views. You might also consider searching other infobases. FASB-Q&A can be particularly helpful on some issues.

8. You perform an advanced query search of the FASB-Q&A and the FASB-OP infobases. Yet, when you view the results generated by the Advanced Query command to apply to all, your hits have no references to FASB-Q&A. Does that mean there are no hits within that infobase?

No, you have to move to the infobase FASB-Q&A to see the hits located, since they would not appear in the HitList for the FASB-OP infobase. In other words, you can use an Advanced Query to search multiple infobases, but you must switch to the respective infobase to view the results of that search for that particular resource.

9. You understand that links are connections between one point in an infobase and another. Distinguish the types of links within an infobase one from the other.

The links that arise include query links that connect menu items, document references, and topical index references to the related information in the appropriate infobase. Another type of link is the pop-up link that connects footnote references to the text of the footnote. In addition, in FASB-OP, links connect superseded or amended material in one document with the superseding or amending language in another document. Finally, both FASB-OP and FASB-CT link glossary terms with their definitions.

10. You export tagged records and import them into your wordprocessing software, but discover the listing is far longer than you expected. What might be the problem?

If you were searching more than one issue and forgot to clear the tags from the initial research, any records you had previously tagged would be exported, along with the last few that you really intended to bring into your software. Care must be taken to understand that a continuous session within FARS will keep all tagged records until you choose to clear them. Your tags remain until you clear them or exit the FARS system. This facilitates your performing multiple queries and tagging any and all records of use in your research, which is helpful when you want such a collection of cites.

11. You are performing an advanced query and your system crashes, triggering a general protection fault. What may be the cause of this crash?

If you open too many infobases at one time, such crashes are common, particularly if a system has less than twelve megabytes of RAM. Since FASB-OP and FASB-CT have essentially the same material, they would rarely need to be opened at the same time. Reconsider which infobases you really need to have opened and try again. Remember, you can always do a search on one infobase at a time and then combine such searches. Often it is easier to organize your results with such an approach. You merely need to keep track of which infobases you have searched and what your specific search phrasing was, so you can be consistent across the infobases.

12. Does it matter whether you query "Internal Revenue Service" or "internal revenue service"?

No, because queries are not case sensitive.

13. If you have more than a single infobase open and use the Search and Select a Query template, will it apply to all the opened infobases?

No, because query templates cannot be applied to multiple infobases. The Advanced Query dialog box is needed to consider multiple infobases with a single search.

14. How do you clear a query when you are analyzing multiple infobases through use of the advanced query capability?

You cannot use the Clear Query button, since it does not apply to multiple infobases. To clear a multiple infobase query, it is necessary to clear the query in each of the open infobases individually.

15. What is the logic of ordering of hits on the HitList?

The default is an ordering by relevance, with the first hit being deemed the most relevant to the search.

16. You wish to identify guidance related to corporate reorganization. What is the difference in the following approaches: "corporate reorganization"; "corporate reorganization"/3; "corporate reorganization"@4; corporate reorganization~bankruptcy; corporate reorganiz*^bankrupt%; corporate reorganization$; corporate reorgan*? Clearly describe the distinctions and identify the approximate number of hits that result from a search of the FASB-OP infobase.

The quoted search phrase matches every character of the terms and results in a single hit. The use of /3 means that the words must be within 3 records of one another and likewise results in one hit. The use of @4 permits the order of the terms to be reversed and increases the number of hits to nine. The removal of the quotes and the use of ~bankruptcy means that it can be either but not both terms in a record. The result is a total of seven hits. The use of the asterisk on reorganiz means that different endings to the word would be matched, such as reorganizing and reorganization. The ^ means not bankrupt% and the % permits consideration of words that are forms of the root word bankrupt, such as bankruptcy. The use of the dollar sign calls for* *synonyms. The last three searches all result in ten hits. Note the usefulness of the advanced query capability in understanding the structure of the various search commands.*

CHAPTER 2 – RESOURCES BEYOND THE FINANCIAL ACCOUNTING RESEARCH SYSTEM (FARS)

2

Researching Accounting and Business Issues

OUTLINE

Introduction
Literature Searches
    Interactive Databases
    Examples of Search Approaches
Internet Search Engines
Internet Resources
    Company Site
    Business Sites
    Popular Accounting Sites

EDGAR: http://www.sec.gov
Special Purpose Databases
    LEXIS/NEXIS
    COMPUSTAT
    CRSP
    FARS

Introduction

Assume you were in college in 1999. Spring break that year is the planned timing for a family reunion. Your uncle has been in Europe for the past year on a start-up venture with a large international corporation and is returning home. You view the event with mixed emotions. On the one hand, you look forward to seeing your uncle. On the other hand, you know your uncle well enough to expect that sometime in the course of the reunion, he will focus on you and inquire about your college education. In particular, he will likely ask: "Show us the return on our investment! What have you learned, and are you getting ahead?" As a business professional, he always uses business jargon and is especially keen on new technology and how well today's college students are mastering this information age.

You decide that this time, you'll be ready. As a result, you have been reading the news media with enthusiasm, looking for an idea for research that will show you are both up to date and lucid on technology's application to business. Since your uncle is particularly interested in accounting-associated matters and the financial services industry, those are the subject areas about which you are especially curious. You found an article in the February 4, 1999, issue of *The Wall Street Journal* called "SEC Probes Mutual Life of New York on Whether Surplus Was Manipulated" (page B16, by Michael Schroeder). As the title suggests, the article reported that the Securities and Exchange Commission (SEC) was investigating accounting practices of Mutual Life Insurance Co. of New York. The issue described involved whether that company, a unit of MONY Group Inc., had bolstered its surplus. Such inflation, the article explained, would not only strengthen the company but would likewise enhance sales to policy holders, improve the company's rating, and increase executives' compensation. Beyond this accounting issue, the article reported that the SEC was reviewing MONY's purchase of two third-party notes from PriceWaterhouseCoopers, LLP, its auditor, due to possible violations of independence standards.

The story seemed perfect, as it had business, accounting, auditing, and regulatory dimensions, while involving a familiar financial services company. The question was where to look for details, in order to prepare by Spring break for the questions that would likely come from introducing such a current event topic. For example, someone might ask what surplus meant, precisely. Someone else might inquire as to how the media learn about such an investigation in process. No doubt, your uncle will ask whether the company chose to respond to the story, and if so, how? Moreover, you have a very real opportunity to describe your mastery of technology by not only preparing your answers to such questions, but being ready to explain precisely how you found the answers. You have little doubt that broader business questions will follow, such as how investors reacted to the news and what are the findings to date of the regulators. Since compensation is one affect asserted of improved financial position, your uncle will pursue detailed follow-up questions, such as whether you happen to know anything about how well the company's managers are compensated or what the aftermath was of the bad press, including how MONY has performed relative to the industry and the overall market.

In short, your uncle is not going to meekly accept your pronouncement of knowledge. If you want to mount a credible defense against his inquisition, you are going to need more ammunition. It is time for a literature search.

Literature Searches

You decide to start by considering what you know about the company and related allegations based on the article read. The same article in *The Wall Street Journal* describes how MONY did an initial public offering (IPO) that began the insurer's trading on the New York Stock Exchange on November 11, 1998. Prior to that date, it was mutually owned by policy holders. The article alludes to different types of filings by MONY pre and post the IPO. Specifically, the article explains that pre-IPO, the company had filed financial reports with the SEC related to offerings of products such as annuities, as well as money-management activities. In order for MONY to have its IPO, a registration statement had been filed with the SEC. The article references a 1995 class-action lawsuit that has allegations related to 1982 through 1995. The article refers to the event in 1993 of New York state ordering $87 million in write-downs of foreclosed properties and $55 million reversal of sales commissions.

A few days after finding this article, you misplace it and decide you need to retrieve another copy in order to pursue your research. Now a literature search is more important than ever. Moreover, you need to explore stories from other sources that may have arisen in the same time frame, as well as gain a sense of the media coverage in the aftermath of the story of interest.

Interactive Databases

A number of interactive databases are available in the library at your university, and increasingly on the Web page for the library. Students at The College of William and Mary, for example, are able to access the Swem Library Information Gateway and find numerous resources. There, quick database links are available, as are digital collections, full-text journal collections, and instruction on searching and evaluating the Web through various search engines. The home page at http://www.swem.wm.edu/index.html shows available research tools and resources.

Dow Jones Interactive, First Search, InfoTrac WEB, Lexis-Nexis Academic Universe, Newsbank, and PCI (Periodicals Contents Index) are among the available resources. By accessing the Professional Resource Center (PRC) in the School of Business at the College of William and Mary through the Web, students can link to ProQuest Direct.

Examples of Search Approaches

Because your first interest is in an article in *The Wall Street Journal*, which you know is published by Dow Jones, you decide to begin with Dow Jones Interactive. You choose the Publications library and perform a search by using the term <u>MONY</u>, and you isolate the search of Dow Jones Selected Publications to the time frame from February 1 through February 28, 1999 (by clicking on <u>enter date frame</u>, then typing the dates), then you click on <u>Run Search</u>.

Another alternative is to access LEXIS-NEXIS Academic Universe and to select the <u>News Option</u>, then the <u>General News Option</u>, which will then present a screen that calls for keyword searches and also provides tips. You input the keywords "The MONY Group" and select the narrow search with the additional term of "investigation." You select the source as <u>Major Newspapers</u> and click on the date <u>From/To</u>, inputting 2/2/99 to 2/5/99 as the dates of interest. Click the <u>Search</u> button. This permits you to review the media coverage around the time of the article you first noticed in *The Wall Street Journal*.

A third alternative is InfoTrac, which has an option of "General Business File ASAP." When the keyword search is requested, you input "MONY GROUP" and indicate that you want to look at articles by date after 2/1/99 (i.e., you click on <u>After</u> and then scroll to select day 1, month <u>February</u>, and year <u>1999</u>), then click on the <u>Search</u> button. The result will be any articles to date that correspond to the MONY Group and have appeared since the first of February 1999.

Literature search bases are similar in their use. They access categories of subject matter, request a search by you, and return a list of citations, which can then be clicked on to read the underlying article or abstract, depending on the nature of the database. The keyword search formats vary, as described herein. Sometimes fields are required, and in other circumstances you can choose to use the field or to ignore that specification. For example, InfoTrac allows the search to be limited to articles with text, to refereed publications, or to particular journals, but this is optional. ProQuest Direct is a useful resource, providing full text access to articles.

Note that press releases and analyst information can be accessed on the Internet at http://www.infobeat.com and http://www.pointcast.com. Some articles can be located through http://www.findarticles.com. When interested in accounting topics, you will want to visit the site: http://www.cpaj.com. It has a searchable archive of *The CPA Journal*.

•Exercise A

1. Locate the article cited in *The Wall Street Journal*. Based on your reading of the article, explain the nature of the allegations that MONY has faced in the 1990s. What is the magnitude of the accounting abuse alleged in the early to mid-1990s according to the article?
2. Perform a literature search to identify related articles on MONY surrounding the events described, as well as related to performance by the company in the aftermath of this media coverage. Provide citations for what you deem to be particularly useful articles for your research effort.

Internet Search Engines

The Internet has a number of search engines available through which to perform keyword searches and identify resources. They include the following sites:

> http://www.altavista.com
> http://www.lycos.com
> http://www.yahoo.com
> http://www.excite.com
> http://www.webcrawler.com
> http://www.infoseek.com
> http://www.google.com
> http://www.deja.com
> http://www.hotbot.com

You can perform a word search, such as MONY and thereby identify Internet resources related to that topic. However, each engine will likely identify different resources due to its respective approach to searching the Web sites, classifying material, and presenting matches. Moreover, given estimates that fewer than one-third of available Web resources are captured by such search engines (*Wall Street Journal*, April 10, 1998, p.1), it is particularly prudent to access more than one such resource. You may also wish to visit http://www.northernlight.com.

Site-Specific Searches

Beyond general search engines, many Web sites have their own search mechanisms that help to identify information of interest on that site. These search assistants are often more tailored to context, such as requesting that the user read a site map, select a department, and then search content within that category. The box is frequently labeled Search This Site with a box provided in which to type your search, alongside a Go button.

•Exercise B

1. Access two different search engines and perform a word search on MONY. Indicate how many hits are identified. Peruse the identified links and discuss the extent to which the first ten sites identified prove to be relevant. Give a Web address for one source identified via the search engine that you find of relevance to your research.
2. Access the Independence Standards Board site (http://www.cpaindependence.org) and determine whether it provides any information of use in understanding the nature of the

allegations having to do with independence that are associated with MONY. (Note that the Independence Standards Board ended operations in the summer of 2001, per agreement between the Securities and Exchange Commission (SEC) and the American Institute of Certified Public Accountants (AICPA).)

3. Identify whether other sites are accessible that provide relevant information.

Internet Resources

The Internet is undergoing constant change; however, a number of sources can be counted on as providing both useful and relevant information when researching accounting and business issues. This exercise will assist you in gaining the ability to find your way on the information highway.

Reports from corporations, foundations, and public institutions from around the world can be found at http://www.zpub.com/sf/arl/. Access to current economic and social data in the United States is offered through Economic and Social Statistics briefing rooms that offer summary statistics and links to agencies responsible for the statistics, thereby permitting access to more detailed data. These sites available within the White House Web site include http://www.whitehouse.gov/fsbr/esbr.html, as well as http://www.whitehouse.gov/fsbr/ssbr.html. Another useful Web site in locating U.S. government information is http://www.fedworld.gov As an aside, you can design your own version of the U.S. budget, by your personal standards, and then analyze and graph the results, by accessing the following Web site on the Internet: http://garnet.berkeley.edu:3333/budget/budget.html.

Company Site

When interested in company-specific matters, you can use a search engine to locate that company's Web page. However, often the address is rather easy to deduce. Specifically, company Web sites tend to take the form of http://www.companyname.com. If you substitute MONY for company name, you will find yourself at the Web page of The MONY Group. Areas of the Web site include the Press Room and Investor Relations. In the latter category, you can access stock charts, historical prices, statistical supplements, SEC filings, fundamentals, and information on Wall Street analysts. MONY, as do many company sites, embed easy linkages to other Web sites that contain information concerning the entity. You will notice as you move around a site that the Web address will have words added behind the .com access you used. Such suffixes describe the file location within that site's server.

Business Sites

A number of sites provide information about companies. The Yahoo! Finance site is an example. Use this address: http://biz.yahoo.com/p/m/mny.html. Be certain to check out the 'more information' options that include quote, chart, news, research, SEC filings, messages, and financials. If you access historical quotes, you can elicit information for a specified time frame, including daily, weekly, monthly, and dividends information. Options are also available to explore news items and insider trading information. Company information likewise can be located at Web sites: http://www.hoovers.com, http://www.msn.com, http://www.quicken.com, http://www.spcomstock.com, and http://www.bloomberg.com.

On the MSN.com site, click <u>Money</u> on the menu, then <u>Investor</u> - stock research capabilities include quotes, charts & news, analyst ratings, advisor FYI, community, research wizard, and stock screener. In addition, information on IPOs (initial public offerings), up/downgrades, and mutual funds is provided. Charts and historical price information, along with financial highlights, some ratios, and selected news stories can be particularly useful.

For the Quicken.com site, click on <u>Investing</u> - the menu provides access to quotes, charts, intraday, news, one-click scorecard, evaluator, analyst ratings, research reports, message boards, compare companies (which highlights competitors), profile, insider trading, fundamentals, financial statements, and SEC filings. These are accessible by simply entering a company's symbol on the stock exchange. The Bloomberg.com site tracks information on regional indices and most active options, alongside news items, stocks, rates, and bond information. Both currency rates and commodity information is accessible. (*Caution*: Whenever downloading data, make note of how missing information is handled – if a resource uses a zero when no information is accessible, such values can be problematic when you attempt to analyze the information. If spreadsheet downloads are inaccessible, you can copy and paste into a spreadsheet. If that does not align well, you can copy and paste into a word-processing software, then save as a text file and import into Excel using either the delimited option or the fixed width option. For the latter, you can adjust the lines to create the desired demarcations between columns.)

Note that Web addresses are called URLs, or uniform resource locators. The standard formats of most sites are translated using hypertext transfer protocol, which is why the lead-in of http:// is needed. The second part of the address usually begins with www to represent World Wide Web. Beyond the .com for companies, .gov is used for government, .org for organizations, .edu for universities, and a number of international indicators are in use, such as .uk for United Kingdom.

Business-related sources of potential interest include

The Better Business Bureau	http://www.bbb.org
Federal Trade Commission	http://www.ftc.gov
U.S. Government Statistics	http://www.stat-usa.gov
S&P Bond Rating Criteria	http://www.standardpoor.com/ratings/index.htm
New York Stock Exchange	http://www.nyse.com
American Stock Exchange	http://www.amex.com
Chicago Berkeley Options Exchange	http://www.cboe.com
Business Week Online	http://www.businessweek.com
EconWPA	http://econwpa.wustl.edu
Econ Data & Links	http://www.csufresno.edu
Census	http://www.census.gov
FDIC	http://www.fdic.gov

A number of valuation-related Web sites are accessible to businesses and individuals. For example, when exploring the worth of vehicles or motorcycles, one can access http:///www.kbb.com or http://www.autopricing.com. The "value-at-risk" approach to measuring the risk of financial instruments developed by J.P. Morgan is described at http://www.jpmorgan.com, which includes information on a number of indices for the United States and a number of other countries. The Federal Reserve web site has such information as interest rates for treasury bills and bonds, foreign exchange rates, and statistics on consumer credit. It can be accessed at http://www.bog.frb.fed.us.

Proprietary services likewise provide information on companies. Returning to the Dow Jones Interactive Service (DJIA), you can select the option of <u>Company Information</u>, which will connect based on either the name of the company or its ticker symbol. Resources often available include Standard & Poor's Stock Reports and Net Advantage, Holt Stock Reports, Moody's Investor Service List, and Baseline equity research, among others. Standard & Poor's Corporation Records' Full Reports provide information on exchanges where companies trade, industry classifications in which they operate, business descriptions, recent financials, stock data, news digest, directors, history, subsidiaries and affiliates, and officers. You can try the site http://www.stock.basic.com for a description of economic earnings for 5,000 U.S. stocks.

DRI-WEFA provides economic and financial data, forecasting, consulting, and analytical software (as described at http://www.dri-wefa.com). Standard & Poor's Blue List relates to current municipal and corporate offerings (see http://www.bluelist.com). Morningstar is a provider of mutual fund analysis and tracks performance of variable annuities and variable life insurance products (see http://www.insure.com). Standard & Poor's Insurer Profile (e.g., for MONY Life Insurance Co.) is accessible through http://data.insure.com/ratings/reports. Primark Financial Information Division's Worldscope database, which tracks information from 1980, contains more than 22,000 active companies in developing and emerging markets, representing approximately 97 percent of global market capitalization in 53 countries – all countries in the World Bank's IFC Investables Index. Other Primark products include Global Access, Compustat, Datastream, I/B/E/S (which includes forecasts, revisions, consensus and analyst-by-analyst earnings estimates of both U.S. and international companies), New Issues (with coverage of all debt and equity offerings), and personalized research service – see http://www.primark.com. Other types of database resources are described at http://www.jolis.worldbankimflib.org.

The eXtensible Business Reporting Language XBRL is a free new XML-based specification that facilitates exchange of financial statements across all software and technologies, including the Internet. Related information can be found at http://www.xbrl.org.

Popular Accounting Sites

To identify current information and addresses to accounting resources, check one of the most popular accounting Web sites. Rutgers Accounting Web (RAW) International Accounting Network (http://www.rutgers.edu/accounting/) has links to numerous professional organizations, including the AAA, ACUA, AGA, FASB (e.g., http://www.fasb.org), GASB, IIA, and IMA. Click the Preview all the Websites on the RAW Link to Accounting Resources.

Direct Internet addresses for the Web sites of various professional and government organizations can also be helpful:

American Institute of Certified Public Accountants	http://www.aicpa.org
The Institute of Internal Auditors	http://www.theiia.org
The Institute of Management Accountants	http://www.imanet.org
National Association of State Boards of Accountancy	http://www.nasba.org
Association of Certified Fraud Examiners	http://www.cfenet.com
Certified Financial Planning Board	http://www.cfp-board.org
Association for Investment Management and Research (CFA)	http://www.aimr.org
Canadian Institute of Chartered Accountants	http://www.cica.ca/
International Accounting Standards Board	http://www.iasb.org.uk

(successor to International Accounting Standards Committee   http://www.iasc.org.uk
International Federation of Accountants   http://www.ifac.org

Public Oversight Board (search POB on AICPA site)   http://www.aicpa.org

Tax and Accounting Sites Directory can be found at: http://www.taxsites.com

A directory of accounting firms is accessible at: http://www.corpfinet.com
An example of a firm's portal site is that of PricewaterhouseCoopers, which has no fee for access at http://portal.pwcglobal.com; it contains volumes of content, including being an entry point to such online resources as CFOdirect (also accessible via http://www.cfodirect.com) – providing news items associated with accounting.

Independence Standards Board   http://www.cpaindependence.org
(operations were ended in the summer of 2001)

Federal Accounting
Standards Advisory Board   http://www.financenet.gov/financenet/fed/fasab/fasab.htm

Searchable links to federal, state, and international government   http://www.financenet.gov

Internal Revenue Service (includes income tax forms)   http://www.irs.com
    http://www.irs.ustreas.gov

Accounting research and career information   http://www.accountingnet.com
Auditing information   http://www.auditnet.org

•Exercise C

1. Access the company site for MONY and go to the press room. Determine if there are any relevant press releases for your research. Then proceed to use the other investor and financial information links to assess how MONY appears to be doing during and in the aftermath of this media event. Consider the level of executives' compensation as well as the types of compensation arrangements used by MONY. Such data can be accessed at http://yahoo.marketguide.com/mgi/compens.asp.
2. Identify the competitors of MONY. Give the names of the first five in the alphabetized list accessed on Yahoo! How are competitors defined? What is an effective way of defining competitors? Justify your position.
3. Access the Yahoo! site and generate a stock price chart that includes price information before and after the February 4, 1999, article. (Also see http://biz.yahoo.com/z/a/m/mny.html for EPS information, including estimates and recommendations.) Does the stock market appear to have reacted in any manner to *The Wall Street Journal* coverage?

EDGAR: http://www.sec.gov

Rather than use the company's site to link to the SEC filings, you can go directly to EDGAR, which stands for Electronic Data Gathering and Retrieval Service, a free Web site that permits you to search by company, type of filing, and read and/or download copies of such filings. The nature of the filings is described at the SEC site. The home page has a button on the left called EDGAR Database, which should be clicked. On the next screen, select Search the Edgar Database, and at the next screen, click Quick Forms Lookup. Enter the company name of interest, then click on the filing of interest. When saving a text file and trying to view in your word-processing package, you will likely find the columns align better if you use eight-point courier font boldface.

Beyond individual companies' information, EDGAR has details on regulators' proposals, such as *Staff Accounting Bulletins* (SABs) recently issued, and on its regulatory activities. The SEC's *Report to the President and Congress* are among the materials accessible.

•Exercise D

1. Access the SEC EDGAR site and identify all filings that are contained therein for MONY. Indicate the types of filings you find, the number, and the last filing listed on the date you check the filings – including the type of that last filing and the date it was made available on the Web.
2. Using the EDGAR site, explain what types of SEC filings exist and when they must be filed.

Special-Purpose Databases

Alternative sources of information include a number of special-purpose databases that may be available to you on CD-ROM resources or through various network interfaces. The subject matter of such databases varies widely. In this exercise, you will retrieve information regarding legal cases, financial statements, reporting practices, and the stock market.

For example, interest in legal cases can be explored in LEXIS/NEXIS. Financial databases would include COMPUSTAT-PC, which permits ease of downloading of a number of financial line items and ratios – not merely for particular companies but for sets of companies that meet selection criteria of interest, such as size or industry type. Stock price information is accessible through CRSP (Center for Research on Security Prices), a database accessible from the University of Chicago, which was initially a mainframe tape-based system but is increasingly being made accessible in various forms, including Intranet-site licensing interfaces. If one wishes to explore stock price movements relative to the market averages of particular companies or sets of companies, long-term trends can be analyzed. These can be evaluated, with corrections for stock splits and stock dividends. Details on generally accepted accounting practices (GAAP) can be accessed through the Financial Accounting Research System (FARS). It permits word searches using Boolean logic to explore accounting questions specific to industry settings and both practice and theory.

LEXIS/NEXIS

LEXIS/NEXIS is a full-text computer research database, with LEXIS representing the law libraries and NEXIS representing the business libraries. It maintains well over half a billion documents on line, with almost two million added weekly. The coverage includes such publications as *The New York Times*, *The Financial Times*, *Business Week*, and *Journal of Taxation*.

The legal libraries include M&A (Mergers and acquisitions library), UCC (Uniform Commercial Code library), BKRTCY (Federal Bankruptcy library), BANKNG (Federal Banking library), TRADE (Federal Trade Regulation library and International Trade library), REALTY (Real Estate library), GENFED (Federal Government Library), and STATES (States library).

The NEXIS libraries include NEWS (General News and Business library), LEXPAT (The U.S. Patent and Trademark Office library), MARKET (The Marketing Library, which covers advertising, marketing, market research, public relations, product announcements, and similar marketing-related items), PEOPLE (the People library), CMPCOM (the Computers and Communications Library), ACCTG (the Accounting Library), and COMPNY (the Company Library).

Once you access a library, you will be asked to narrow the search by specifying the names of additional file choices. For example, within the NEWS library, you can specify BUS, and all business-related stories from newspapers, magazines, wire services, and transcripts will be accessed. If within NEWS you select PERSON, biographical information can be accessed. Within ACCTG, examples of useful files would include AAER (the Accounting and Auditing Enforcement Releases from the SEC), TAXCFR (Tax Rules), PROSP (Prospectuses), EDGARP (EDGAR PLUS), ACCES (Access Disclosure), and PROXY (SEC Proxy Statements).

Within the EDGARP file, you can search for documents like the 10-K and proxy, then within the full text view of the documents, a table of contents is made available that permits you to pull only certain sections of the documents, such as the financial statements.

Examples of useful titles under the COMPNY library are DISCLO (disclosure), ALLMA (M&A Reports), SPCORP (Company profiles for both public and private firms), USPRIV (U.S. private companies), USPUB (U.S. public companies), and SKTRPT (Stock reports). Under either GENFED or STATES library, one can obtain cases under the COURTS file.

The search phrasing you can use within LEXIS and NEXIS includes *Or*, *And*, *W/n* (where *n* refers to the number of words within which you expect to find the words—*stock w/3 dividend* would mean that the cite would include anyplace these two words were within three words of one another), and *W/p* where articles with the two topics in the same paragraph are identified.

When the results are reported back, a toolbar permits you to select among the Full View, the Kwic View (providing an abstract including the sentence before and after that term specified), or a Cite View (bibliographical information).

When working on CD-ROM versions of LEXIS/NEXIS you typically cannot print your sessions or download your work to a disk in the usual fashion. Instead, to record your search on disk, you must first click on file. Then choose record session and hit start. This will record your entire search from choosing the libraries to article searches. If you do not want everything to be recorded, you can hit <u>Pause</u> and later <u>Start</u>, and there will be no recording of the interim actions. When you are finished with the session and log off, you can bring up your documents in Wordpad and then re-save the search as a Word file, aligning the margins to 7 inches when in Word to achieve realignment. Note that Wordpad can be found under your accessories section of your computer. The reason for using Wordpad rather than Word is that the latter will sometimes scramble your fonts.

If you are unable to identify the library.file to use for your search, you can conduct a search in the LEXIS/NEXIS online guide. If you would like to find a library/file on AAERs, you would type .gu AAER and the online service would then tell you that the library is ACCTNG and the file name is AAER. The LEXIS/NEXIS free help desk is available at 1-800-346-9759. Rather than the CD-ROM version, increasingly, universities are offering LEXIS/NEXIS Academic Universe on their intranets, with site license access by students and faculty.

Legal Information Institute is an Internet resource of related interest: http://www.law.cornell.edu has federal law materials searchable. Also see http://www.findlaw.com and http://www.refdesk.com. In addition, criminal justice links and other legal resource materials are accessible at the following Web site address: http://www.criminology.fsu.edu/cjlinks/default.htm. The Governmental Accounting Office (GAO) is a rich resource, including its publication "Investigator's Guide to Sources of Information," which can be found at http://www.gao.gov.

COMPUSTAT

Standard & Poor's PC Plus for Windows and the COMPUSTAT database are built into one system on CD-ROM, which provides financial and market data of U.S. and Canadian corporations, banks, savings and loans, business segments, geographic regions, industry information, indexes, and inactive companies. The system contains a collection of financial data from company annual and quarterly shareholders' reports and SEC 10-K and 10-Q reports. Although the details of any database change over time, the following instructions should be helpful in characterizing the types of commands that can be used to access information and generate analyses.

When accessing the screen showing COMPUSTAT moving horizontally across the screen, view the PC Plus desktop by pressing Enter and you will see some of your options represented by icons on the left border of the screen. These include abilities to find specific companies, create a single report or multiple reports for one or more companies, screen for particular companies, construct a set of companies, business segments, geographic areas, or issues, view a chart of COMPUSTAT data, and view a library of information about companies. To find a specific company, click on Company, click on Look Up. The $C CS Active category should be highlighted, and the available companies will then be listed in the Name List box. Hence, if you were looking for MONY, you would type *MONY* in the Name box in the upper right of the dialog box. Click on Paste and then the Close button. Click on View Data and then OK. You can choose what data you want to see by clicking on Look Up and then Item (the button on the left, second down). For example, if you wanted to find the price/earnings (PE) ratio for MONY, click on Name List and type in *price/ear*. The name list highlights the price/earnings item. Now double-click on Price/Earnings-Monthly and click on Close. Click on View data and on the up and down arrows to see the years you want. Click on New Item and repeat the process.

You can access business descriptions by clicking Library, entering the company's ticker symbol (MNY – which can be found by clicking the Look Up button if unknown), then clicking on OK.

To screen companies that meet your criteria, click on Screen and on New. The PC will show you a screen template with $C in the base set column and will highlight the Formula column. Type *sic* and hit Enter. The PC inserts what you have just typed into the formula bar and then into the Formula column. It highlights the Min column. The item shows a company's primary SIC code. Note that SIC stands for Standard Industrial Classification code. Until recently, it was the most commonly used in the United States (U.S.). In 1997, this framework was replaced by the North American Industrial Classification System (NAICS), which is intended to integrate Canada, Mexico, and the United States as part of the North American Free Trade Agreement. Systems will gradually transfer from SIC to NAICS. See http://www.osha.gov/oshstats/sicser.html for a search of SICs and related information. If SIC is in use, then type 6300 for insurance carriers and hit Enter. (You can also press the right arrow key to move to the Max column.) Type 6399 and hit Enter. The PC inserts what you have just typed into the Min and Max columns. These codes (6300 and 6399) tell the PC that you are screening for companies that list the insurance carrier industry as their primary SIC. Click on Formula column row 2, then click on the Look Up tool, a box with a pair of glasses. The PC shows the Look Up dialog box. Click on the Item button and click on Company in the Category List box. Type Return on Assets; ROA should be displayed on the screen. The ROA concept calculates a ratio. You can click on the Definition button. Click on Paste to insert the item into the formula bar. Click on the check mark to insert the item into the Formula column. The PC highlights the Min column. Type 1 and hit Enter. The Maximum column remains blank. This value tells the PC that you are screening for companies that have a return on assets value of at least 1 percent. Click on the Run button in the toolbar to evaluate the screen criteria. Note that you can screen from any field information in the COMPUSTAT system, including membership in an S&P Index, sales volume, number of employees, or other attributes of interest.

Compustat Research Insight's main menu has a Research Assistant icon that can be clicked; when the ticker symbol is placed in the field entitled companies, you can select from among the other options. For example, to generate a list of companies with the same SIC, click on find similar companies, then click company specifics, and choose an industry SIC designation. To customize a peer group for comparison, open Research Assistant, and click on Customize. To create a report, click the Open Report icon, select what you wish, and click Finish. From the Run Assistant screen, choose the desired company and click OK. You can customize your report within Report Assistant, including generating historical reports. The Chart Assistant icon can be useful in selecting a chart. To predefine charts, click on Open Chart, highlight the desired chart, click Finish, and when Run Assistant appears, select the desired company and click OK. Clicking on Open Set brings up four folders (Charts, Reports, Screens, and Sets) and uses predetermined sets of information, charts, estimates, comparisons, and similar information for analysis of a company. Click on the various charts to explore the resource.

Other sources for industry information on the Web include http://www.doc.gov and http://cnnfn.com, which are sites for the Department of Commerce and CNN Financial network, respectively. Industry information with company data (as cited earlier), as well as links to corporate Web sites can be located at http://www.hoovers.com.

Company-specific information can be accessed at http://www.pointcast.com (which provides free software for customizing your search), http://www.cnn.com, http://www.dbc.com, http://www.stockmaster.com/ and http://moneypages.com/syndicate.

CRSP

CRSP has traditionally been accessed through FORTRAN programming on mainframe systems. However, the tape-based data are increasingly being transferred onto intranet sites, with friendly interfaces. Explore whether your university has CRSP and whether students have access. Find out whether user manuals or other tutorials are available. Since the interface can vary widely, no further details on use are included herein.

Daily stock market quotes are accessible at numerous Web sites, including:

http://stockmaster.com
http://www.pcquote.com
http://finance.yahoo.com
http://www.msn.com
http://www.bloomberg.com and

http://www.quicken.com/investments/quotes.

The stockmaster web site provides current information and summarizes stock-price performance of a company for the last year, providing a graph charting this information relative to the S&P 500. Links are provided at that site to other information associated with the company, including a link to EDGAR. Indices are accessible at http://www.spglobal.com, and the site explains the composition of indices (e.g., the weight placed on different sectors of the economy, the sizes of entities included, and the weights on various countries within global indices). Excel worksheets can be downloaded. Similarly, http://www.russell.com has indices available on a number of countries, and it explains the approach to forming its indices.

FARS

When you access FARS, whether it is on a CD-ROM, through your library, or through the network, the basic system is well described by the following overview (Figure 2.1) presented within the software of the database.

Figure 2.1 Overview of FARS (quoted from software)

Overview

Welcome to the FASB's Financial Accounting Research System (FARS) for Windows.

Welcome to the FASB's Financial Accounting Research System (FARS) for Windows. FARS is a PC-based tool for accounting research that uses Folio VIEWS 4.2 software for efficient and effective access to databases *(infobases)* of FASB literature.

FARS is made up of six major infobases, each of which is designed to resemble the printed version of the original documents as much as possible:

Original Pronouncements	**(FASB-OP)**
Current Text	**(FASB-CT)**
EITF Abstracts	**(EITF)**
Staff Implementation Guides	**(FASB-Q&A)**
Comprehensive Topical Index	**(FASINDEX)**
Derivative Instruments and Hedging Activities	**(DERIVCOD)**

FASB-OP infobase contains all AICPA and FASB pronouncements in chronological order, including totally superseded pronouncements. This includes:

Accounting Research Bulletins (ARB)
Accounting Principles Board Opinions (APB)
AICPA Accounting Interpretations (AIN)
Accounting Principles Board Statements (APS)
Accounting Terminology Bulletins (ATB)

FASB Statements (FAS)
FASB Interpretations (FIN)
FASB Technical Bulletins (FTB)
FASB Concepts Statements (CON)

Amended or superseded material has been shaded in the same manner as in the printed version. Amended or superseded material is **linked** to the appropriate language in the amending pronouncement. In some instances, several links will have to be followed to determine the current guidance.

FASB-CT infobase contains the General Standards, Industry Standards, and the *Current Text* sections that have been superseded but are still applicable due to a significantly delayed effective date. Those sections are shaded to indicate that they have been superseded. This infobase also contains an appendix listing current AICPA Practice Bulletins, Statements of Position, and Audit and Accounting Guides.

EITF infobase includes the full text of each abstract for every issue discussed by the Emerging Issues Task Force since its inception in 1984, the introduction to *EITF Abstracts,* a list of Task Force members (Appendix A), announcements of general and administrative matters (Appendix C), discussions of other technical matters (Appendix D), and the EITF topical index.

FASB-Q&A infobase contains staff Special Reports and other published implementation guidance on FAS 80, 86, 87, 88, 91, 96, 109, 113, 116, 117. It also contains illustrations of financial instrument disclosure requirements in FAS 105, 107, and 119.

FASINDEX infobase is the combined topical index for FASB-OP, FASB-CT, EITF, and FASB-Q&A infobases. Each reference in the index is linked to the appropriate paragraph(s), EITF issue, or question(s) in the relevant infobase. All "See" references (for example, See *Income Taxes*) are linked to that section within the index.

DERIVCOD infobase is an aid to implementing FASB Statement 133 which presents Statement 133 as amended by Statements 137 and 138. It also includes the full text of issues related to the implementation of Statement 133 that were discussed by the Derivatives Implementation Group and cleared by the FASB prior to September 25, 2000.

FARS is updated approximately five times a year, as appropriate, to ensure that the infobases contain the latest FASB pronouncements and abstracts of EITF issues.

Features of the Financial Accounting Research System

FARS was designed to be flexible and easy to use. The accounting literature within the infobases can be accessed in three different ways—through the Contents view tab, through the Topical Index references that link to the appropriate text in the infobases, and, finally, through predefined *query templates* and user-defined *queries*.

The graphical interface of FARS for Windows has a look that will be familiar to MS-Word users. Flexible printing functions, simple text *exporting*, a true WYSIWYG text display, and easy-to-follow navigational tools combine to make FARS for Windows an indispensable system for GAAP research.

You have a curiosity about two basic issues at this point. The first relates to the nature of extraordinary items (referred to as the nature of demutualization expenses in 1998 and of expenses associated with the commission-free sale and purchase program offered to odd-lot shareholders) and the nonrecurring restructuring charges associated with voluntary retirement and realignment program. The second involves the term *surplus* which is being applied in *The*

Wall Street Journal article to describe the difference in MONY's assets and liabilities. Indeed, you have an impression from past coursework that the term *surplus* was not supposed to be used.

•Exercise E (depending on which databases are accessible)

1. Access the LEXIS/NEXIS Academic Universe or CD-ROM version, if it is available. Consider the original article's reference to a class action suit. Perform a search of the LEXIS portion of LEXIS/NEXIS to identify the case and its general nature.

   To do so using LEXIS/NEXIS Academic Universe, access Legal Research and a descriptive screen on Basic Legal Research will show subheads of Secondary Literature, Case Law, Codes & Regulations, Patent Research, and Career Information. If you select <u>Get a Case</u>, the first bullet under Case Law, then a screen will appear offering the option to retrieve a case by citation or by party name. From the article posted in the Press Room of the MONY Web site, dated December 20, 1999, on the Business Wire, you can locate the *caption Goshen vs. The Mutual Life Insurance Company of New York*. Hence, when the LEXIS/NEXIS Academic Universe asks for input, type *Goshen* as Party One and *The Mutual Life Insurance Company of New York* as Party Two. You need not have the legal citation requested. Hit the <u>Search</u> button and under the document list will be the citations, any of which you can choose to review.

   If LEXIS/NEXIS is unavailable, check the Internet resources described herein. Note that the http://www.hoovers.com has added to its company information a subhead titled "recent federal litigation." Since you have an interest in a particular case, you could also seek information in hard-copy form from a law library. Moreover, SEC filings will contain descriptions of litigation.

   Compare the description you access from SEC filings to that found in the LEXIS/NEXIS or similar data source. If you were responsible for drafting the disclosure found in the SEC filing, what adjustments to its content would you recommend?

2. Using the COMPUSTAT database, download a report on the information available for MONY, as well as a similar report for the key competitors within their industry.

   If COMPUSTAT is unavailable, check to see what resources with company financial information are available at your library. Compare the ease of use, quality of information, and relative advantages and disadvantages of these resources, relative to the Internet sources described herein.

3. Using CRSP, download all information available for MONY (i.e., all stock prices since its IPO). Also download a market index accessible through CRSP.

   If CRSP is unavailable, check to see what resources with companies' stock price data are available at your library and how they compare to the information accessible on the Internet. You should be able to locate both a time-series database of the stock prices of MONY since its IPO and a market index for the same time frame on the Internet.

4. Access FARS.

Open the Financial Accounting Research System (FARS) main menu. If you click on <u>the Topical Index</u>, you gain access to the following screen:

Topical Index

Copyright 2001 Financial Accounting Standards Board

*To search the entire infobase, click the **Query** button on the **Toolbar**. To directly access a segment of the infobase, click on any link token (◆) in the menu below. Links to referenced material are indicated with text which is colored according to the type of reference as follows: See Amortization, FAS19, ¶30, Oi5.121, and EITF.93-1. To follow a link, click with the mouse on the text of the reference.*

◆A	◆B	◆C	◆D
◆E	◆F	◆G	◆H
◆I	◆J	◆K	◆L
◆M	◆N	◆O	◆P
◆Q	◆R	◆S	◆T
◆U	◆V	◆W	◆XYZ

You can proceed to use this index for extraordinary items.

Topical Index

The Topical Index has references to material contained in all of the FARS infobases. Each reference in the index is linked with the appropriate paragraph(s), EITF issue, or question(s) in the relevant infobase. All "See" references (for example, See Income Taxes) are linked with that section within the index. From the main menu, click on Topical Index to view the screen with diamonds corresponding to letter(s). For ease of use, the index has been segmented into alphabetical groups. Also, the Table of Contents function will display a handy list of all the topics in the index.

Click on the first letter of the term of interest, and that will link to a listing of terms that begin with the letter chosen, with detailed links to underlying cites. Within topics, references are sorted into three columns, as in the following example:

	OP	CT	EITF/Other
FUTURES CONTRACTS			
Hedges			
Ongoing Assessment of Correlation	FAS80, ¶11	F80.111	EITF.85-6
			Q&A.80 #20-21

In this example, FAS80, 11 indicates paragraph 11 of FASB Statement No. 80, Accounting for Futures Contracts. F80.111 indicates paragraph .111 of the Current Text Section F80, "Futures Contracts." EITF.85-6 indicates EITF Issue No. 85-6, "Futures Implementation Questions." Q&A.80 #20-21 refers to questions 20 and 21 of the FASB Highlights, "Futures Contracts: Guidance on Applying Statement 80." This should be helpful to you when interpreting what you find on extraordinary items.

Alternatively, use the search capabilities. Specifically, click on <u>Open</u>, <u>FARS</u>, <u>Open</u>, <u>Nfo</u>, <u>Open</u>, <u>FASB-OP</u>, and click <u>Search</u> at the top of the toolbar. Select <u>Query</u> and then type *extraordinary items criteria* and click on <u>OK</u>. Select the <u>Document</u> view (using the tabs toward the bottom of the screen).

(a)   Identify the relevant guidance, as cited in the top bar of the view, and describe what must be the criteria met for both the 1998 and 1999 items described as extraordinary in MONY's new releases.

(b)   Describe how you would suggest finding accounting guidance within FARS relative to the restructuring charges described in the media coverage of MONY. Be specific. Do likewise for *surplus*. Be specific as to the search your perform and what you locate in terms of guidance.

(c)   To further consider the meaning of extraordinary, access *The Wall Street Journal* article appearing on October 1, 2001, on pages C1 and C2 in the "Heard on the Street" column—authored by Steve Liesman and titled "Accountants, in a Reversal, Say Costs from the Attack Aren't 'Extraordinary'." The technical issue is entitled "Accounting for the Impact of the Terrorist Attacks of September 11, 2001" Issue No. 01-10, reflecting discussions on both September 20 and 28, 2001 in the EITF Meeting Minutes. Check both FARS and http://www.fasb.org for associated materials. Does the decision and/or related discussion and guidelines influence your evaluation of MONY's reporting practices?

CHAPTER 3 – BUILDING YOUR BUSINESS VOCABULARY:

Defining Terms and Solving Problems Through FARS

Going Straight to the Source

Have you wondered if parenthood comes with a manual of required phrases? For example, "Do you live in a barn?" whenever the door is left ajar and phrases intended to break the bad habits of saying "well," "you know," or "like"— such as "a well is a hole in the ground," "no, we don't know," or "like what?" Moreover, there's the popular rhetorical question: "If all your friends jumped off a bridge, would you?" And then there is this exchange: "Dad, what does affinity mean?" "There's the dictionary. Look it up!" Pause. "But Dad, why can't you just tell me?" With a grin, Dad might say, "Go straight to the source; why take my word for it?"

In a similar vein, in building your mastery of the language of business, you can go to the source: the Financial Accounting Research System (FARS). Every source outside of the pronouncements has less authoritative weight. An opportunity is at hand to gain familiarity with the standards that describe the language of business. In addition to building your vocabulary, you can compare this authoritative definition to other explanations of the term or concept that have been offered in conversation and in your readings. Are the differences important? As you use FARS, you will gain familiarity with how to perform searches on information databases that are becoming increasingly important tools for all professionals to master. These skills will serve you well in your career. This chapter includes separate FARS-directed problems (Tables 3.1 – 3.38) for each of the main subject areas in an introduction to the language of business.

Using FARS to Master Business Terminology

The remainder of this chapter consists of thirty-eight tables for you to complete, along with problems that can be solved based on the information you will uncover as you complete the tables.

For each of the following topics, assignments include a table of terms for which you are to check the original source for its definition. The term and a suggested search approach are provided. You are asked to apply these instructions to FARS, complete each table, and respond to the related questions per topic.

The citation expected should include a reference to the document type, number, and paragraph. As an example, assume that you access FARS, click on File, Open, select Nfo, Open, select FASB-OP, click Open, and click Search. Then you type in the query *vocabulary*. If you view the Document pane, it will have a clear reference at the top of the screen that reads ATB-1, Par. 1. This is what you need to complete the next to last column of each table (i.e., the column labeled "Citation for Definition: Provide Full Reference." The actual content shown in the window has the phrase:

> "1. The committee on terminology was constituted in 1920 and assigned the task of compiling a vocabulary of words and expressions used peculiarly in accounting and of gradually preparing definitions thereof."

Reading the content for the prioritized search will not only prepare you to define each term but will also provide the background for solving the problems associated with each table. Keep in mind that the citations you provide may well reference more than a single paragraph, as you deem best describes the concept or term of interest.

FARS does not always give a specific definition for each term. However, the meanings of the terms usually can be inferred from the context in which they are used. Analyze the surrounding words or sentences to deduce terms' meanings. You are also asked to suggest other searches of relevance for each of the terms in the table. Your suggestions will likely involve exploring alternative Boolean operators, proximity adjustments, and synonyms for the concepts or terms cited. Be creative in exploring and suggesting other searches. The Appendix to this chapter will be of use, in tandem with the Primer (Chapter 1), in completing the tables and associated questions.

You may find additional searches of FARS to be useful in responding to the questions, beyond those required for completion of the table. In responding to the problems, highlight the specific citation you believe ties to your solution. You are encouraged to experiment and gain improved skill at finding the answers to various questions likely to arise in practice and theory.

■ ACCOUNTING STANDARDS

Table 3.1   Accounting Standards COMPLETE THIS TABLE

Terms	Search Recommended* (Semicolons are not part of the search but are used as separators.)	Citation for Definition: Provide Full Reference	Other Searches You Would Suggest
Financial reporting	Financial reporting defin*		
Financial statements	Financial statements of business		
Generally accepted accounting principles (GAAP)	GAAP hierarchy for financial statements		
Emerging Issues Task Force (EITF)	**		
Financial Accounting Standards Board (FASB)	Financial Accounting Standards Board Mission		
Interpretations***	Interpretation and mission and accounting		
Technical bulletins****	Purpose of Technical Bulletins		
International Accounting Standards	International Accounting Standards		
Tax Policy	"tax policy";		
	"tax-planning strategy";		
	tax$ strategy$		

Table 3.1 Accounting Standards   Page **3-5**

Terms	Search Recommended* (Semicolons are not part of the search but are used as separators.)	Citation for Definition: Provide Full Reference	Other Searches You Would Suggest
Statements of Financial Accounting Concepts*****	Statements of Financial Accounting Concepts are intended		
Governmental Accounting Standards Board (GASB)	Government Accounting Standards Board		

*Access FARS, click on File, Open, Nfo, Open, and select FASB-OP, click Search, enter query.

**After selecting FASB-OP, on the menu presented, click on EITF Abstracts and then Introduction.

***After selecting FASB-OP, on the menu presented, click on AICPA Accounting Interpretations (AIN) and peruse the topics; then return to the FASB-OP menu and click on Interpretations (FIN) and peruse the topic.

****After selecting FASB-OP, on the menu presented, click on Technical Bulletins(FTB) and peruse the topics.

*****Also, select Statements of Financial Accounting Concepts (CON) from menu and read topics covered.

Problems

1. In what sense does the FASB influence trend analysis (i.e., the ability to compare and analyze information over time)?

2. Why do generally accepted accounting principles diverge among companies at an international level?

3. How might tax policy influence decision making in Germany and Japan, compared to the same dynamic in the United States?

4. What is the difference between financial statements and financial reporting? What are the objectives of financial reporting?

5. Describe the GAAP hierarchy.

■ CONCEPTS

Table 3.2 Concepts COMPLETE THIS TABLE

Concepts	Are these assumptions (A), principles (P), or constraints (C)? Classify each concept.	Search Recommended *	Citation for Definition: Provide Full Reference	Other Searches You Would Suggest
Historical cost		Historical cost principle		
Cost benefit		"cost benefit constraints"		
Monetary unit		Monetary unit		
Going concern		Going concern		
Industry practice		Specialized industry practice		
Materiality		Materiality		
Matching		Matching		
Full disclosure		Objective of full disclosure		
Economic entity		Economic entity		
Conservatism		Conservatism		
Periodicity		Period*		
		reporting period		
Revenue Recognition		Recogniz* revenue*		

*Access FARS, click on File, Open, Nfo, Open, and select FASB-OP, click Search, enter query.

Table 3.3 The Accounting Information System   Page **3-7**

Problems

1. An individual who is also a partner in a CPA firm is expected to maintain his or her personal checking account separate from the business checking account based on what fundamental concept? Explain.

2. A business, Diehl Incorporated, has operated for ten years. In its first year of operations, it acquired a tract of land for $30,000. Since that date, the market value has fluctuated significantly. By the fifth year of operation, the value had reached $100,000, and by the tenth year, market value for the tract of land was $200,000. How should this land be recorded on the balance sheet of Diehl Incorporated in the (a) first year of operations? (b) fifth year of operations? (c) tenth year of operations?

3. A company purchased an electric pencil sharpener that is estimated to have a useful life of five years. Nonetheless, the company is considering expensing the pencil sharpener rather than recording it as an asset. What concept must justify such an action?

THE ACCOUNTING INFORMATION SYSTEM

Table 3.3   The Accounting Information System COMPLETE THIS TABLE

Terms	Search Recommended* (Semicolons are not part of the search but are used as separators.)	Citation for Definition: Provide Full Reference	Other Searches You Would Suggest
Double entry accounting	Double entry accounting		
Cash basis accounting	"cash basis accounting"		
Net cash flow	"net cash flow is" defin*; computation of net cash flow		
Net income	Net income defin*		
Accrual accounting	Accrual accounting defin*		
Collections	Collection* of receiv*; Journal entry for collection of receivable		
Balance sheet equation	Double entry accounting balance sheet		
Balancing the books	Balancing the books trial balance		
Miscellaneous account	Caption line item immaterial miscellaneous; "miscellaneous income"		

*Access FARS, click on File, Open, Nfo, Open, and select FASB-OP, click Search, enter query.

Table 3.3 The Accounting Information System   Page **3-9**

Problems

1. What are the advantages of double-entry accounting?

2. Lancione Incorporated purchased $30,000 of goods for cash and an additional $20,000 on credit. It made cash sales of $40,000 and credit sales of $70,000. The cost of the goods sold was $45,000. The company paid off $12,000 of the balance owed to suppliers. What would be the net cash flow using cash basis accounting? What would be the net income if accrual accounting were used?

3. When asked to explain the economic transaction that led to the journal entry below, a new accounting student responded: "Cash was debited $30 and Accounts Receivable was credited $30." Has the student responded correctly? Explain your answer.

    Cash   30

        Accounts Receivable 30

4. During a review of a new client who was considering issuing securities, an accountant ran across a "miscellaneous account" on the books. It seemed particularly unusual because every month it was charged, sometimes with a debit and sometimes with a credit. Moreover, the magnitude of the adjustment ranged from pennies to thousands of dollars. Bewildered, the accountant asked the client's bookkeeper what had been recorded in the account. The bookkeeper responded that every time the trial balance was run, whatever amount was needed to make it balance had been charged to the "miscellaneous account." The accountant called his partner and said "We've got a problem here." Explain what he meant. What is the scope of the problem?

■ INCOME STATEMENTS

Table 3.4   Income Statements COMPLETE THIS TABLE

Terms	Search Recommended* (Semicolons are not part of the search but are used as separators.)	Citation for Definition: Provide Full Reference	Other Searches You Would Suggest
Income statement	"income statement is"		
Natural business year	Operating cycle natural business year		
Unusual items	Unusual items defin*		
Extraordinary items	Criteria for extraordinary items		
Income from continuing operations	Income for continuing operations line caption		
Discontinued operations	Discontinued operations defin*		
Divestiture	"divestiture of assets"		
Loss from operations	Defin* loss from operations		
Allocation of overhead	Allocation of overhead		
Proceeds from sale of operations	Proceeds from sale of operations; proceeds from sale of property		

*Access FARS, click on File, Open, Nfo, Open, and select FASB-OP, click Search, enter query.

Table 3.4 Income Statements   Page **3-11**

Problems

1. What is meant by a natural business year?

2. How do unusual items differ from extraordinary items?

3. Why is income from continuing operations typically reported as a subtotal on the income statement?

4. A segment of business is being disposed of (i.e., discontinued), with divestiture expected. While an interim loss from operations is incurred, the disposal of the line of business will result in a gain. Explain how the measurement date influences income statement presentation. What types of costs and expenses are permitted to be associated with the determination of the gain or loss on disposal? How much time can elapse between the measurement date and the disposal date, in order for the presentation in accordance with the discontinued operations of a segment of business to apply?

■ BALANCE SHEETS

Table 3.5   Balance Sheets COMPLETE THIS TABLE

Terms	Search Recommended* (Semicolons are not part of the search but are used as separators.)	Citation for Definition: Provide Full Reference	Other Searches You Would Suggest
Balance Sheet	"statement of financial position"		
Assets	"the definition of an asset"		
Entity principle	Economic entity		
Line items	Specif* line items statement of financial position		
Order of line items	Order of presentation statement of financial position line items		
Prepaid advertising	Prepaid advertising		
Earned subscriber revenue	Earned subscriber revenue		
In construction	In construction		
Prematurity period	Prematurity period		
Partially in service	Partially in service		
Subscriber related costs	Subscriber related costs		
Organization costs	Start up organization costs		
Capitalization	"capitalization of costs"		

*Access FARS, click on File, Open, Nfo, Open, and select FASB-OP, click Search, enter query.

Table 3.5 Balance Sheets   Page **3-13**

Problems

1. Two students of financial accounting are reviewing their understanding of assets. John asserts, "Football teams record players' contracts as assets." Cynthia asks, "How can they? Most assuredly, people can't be owned, and how can they possibly be quantified in dollar terms?" Explain to the two students why the contracts of professional athletes, in fact, can be recorded as assets.

2. A businesswoman who sells a line of cosmetics part-time has a Cadillac, which she uses for business purposes as well as for personal errands. How should the automobile be recorded on the books maintained for the cosmetics business, and why?

3. What determines the order in which line items are arranged on a balance sheet?

4. When asked to explain the economic transaction that led to the journal entry below, a new accounting student responded, "Prepaid advertising has been used up." Has the student responded correctly? Why or why not?

   Prepaid Advertising   800

      Cash   800

5. Cable television companies experience what is termed a prematurity period which is expected not to exceed two years and may be shorter. During this period, the cable television system is partially under construction and partially in service. Its beginning will be with the first earned subscriber revenue and its end will be determined according to plans for completion of the first major construction period. During this period, a number of costs are likely to be incurred related to the costs of cable television plant, materials, direct labor, and construction overhead. In addition, subscriber-related costs will be incurred, as will general and administrative expenses. Subscriber-related costs include costs to obtain and retain subscribers, costs of billing and collection, bad debts and mailings, repairs and maintenance of taps and connections, franchise fees related to revenues, or number of subscribers, and programming costs as well as direct selling costs. Another type of cost is that related to initial subscriber installation costs, for which initial hookup revenue is generated. Do you believe such costs should be accumulated and reported in the financial statements? If so, why? Respond to each of the types of costs described.

■ CASH FLOWS

Table 3.6   Cash Flows COMPLETE THIS TABLE

Terms	Search Recommended* (Semicolons are not part of the search but are used as separators.)	Citation for Definition: Provide Full Reference	Other Searches You Would Suggest
Statement of Cash Flows	"statement of cash flows is"		
Operating activities	Operating activities		
Investing activities	Investing activities defin*;		
	"investing activities include"		
Financing activities	"financing activities include"		
Cash outflows for income tax paid	Cash outflows for income tax paid		
Liquidity	Liquidity		
Income statement classifications	Income statement classifications		
Noncash investing and financing activities	Noncash investing and financing activities		
Direct method	Direct method cash flow defin*		
Indirect method	Indirect method operating cash flow		

*Access FARS, click on File, Open, Nfo, Open, and select FASB-OP, click Search, enter query.

Table 3.6 Cash Flows   Page **3-15**

Problems

1. What is the purpose of a statement of cash flows?

2. What classifications are used for the statement of cash flows, and how do they compare to classifications used on the face of the income statement?

3. Describe the type of noncash investing and financing activities that are required to be disclosed with statements of cash flows.

4. The FASB mentions that cash outflows for income taxes paid cannot be allocated to operating, investing, and financing activities. Do you agree? Why or why not?

5. State the principal advantage of (a) the direct method of reporting net cash flow from operating activities and (b) the indirect method.

■ **TIME VALUE OF MONEY**

Table 3.7   Time Value of Money COMPLETE THIS TABLE

Terms	Search Recommended* (Semicolons are not part of the search but are used as separators.)	Citation for Definition: Provide Full Reference	Other Searches You Would Suggest
Time value of money	Time value of money		
Present value	Applications of present value		
Future value	"future value"		
Compounding	Compounding;		
	Compounding of interest		
Interest rate	Interest rate		
Return on investment	Return on investment		
Discounting the note	Discounting the note;		
	Interest on receivables		
Negative loan amortization	Negative loan amortization**		

*Access FARS, click on File, Open, Nfo, Open, and select FASB-OP, click Search, enter query.

**Access FARS, click on File, Open, Nfo, Open, and select EITF, Search, enter query, and then click on link to access EITF.

Table 3.7 Time Value of Money   Page **3-17**

Problems

1. Real estate sales in the 1980s frequently involved graduated payment and insured mortgages, with negative loan amortization, meaning that principal could actually increase over the life of the obligation (because the cash payment was insufficient to cover interest). How should these attributes influence revenue recognition?

2. The federal consumer Truth-in-Lending law requires that interest rates on consumer loans be stated in annual percentage terms. Why do you think this provision is required?

3. Assume that LeeVan Company makes a 120-day 9 percent $20,000 note on January 3, 20x1. All interest is payable at maturity. On February 1, 20x1, the note was discounted at a 10 percent rate. Record the discounting of the note. How would the discounting be recorded if the note was not discounted until March 1, 20x1?

4. You are offered a chance in one of three lotteries, which have the following related prizes: (1) an annuity of $1,000 a year for 20 years, (2) an annuity of $1,500 a year for 15 years, beginning after 5 years have elapsed, (3) a lump sum of $50,000 at the end of 18 years. Rank these three lottery prizes by value from highest to lowest. Quantify the basis for your ranking, assuming you demand a 10 percent return on your investments. [*Hint*: You can use spreadsheet software to compute present value; for example, EXCEL has the command available of PV to compute a present value of an annuity, using the command =PV(rate, nper,pmt,fv,type) in which nper is the number of periods that an equal amount is paid and type is 0 if payment is at the end of the period and 1 if the payment is at the beginning of the period, with 0 as a default. Note that the command can be entered with only the first three terms specified.]

5. On the Public Broadcasting System, December 27, 1987, Adam Smith's "Money World" reported that had the Indians invested the $28 received for Manhattan, at a 12 percent rate of return, the 1987 value would be far more than the value of New York City. In fact, the amount to which the $28 would have grown would exceed the total 1987 gross national product. To demonstrate how quickly compounding can earn a return, assume that you decide to save $100 a quarter for seven years, earning 12 percent a year. What amount would you have saved by the end of the seven-year period?

6. Your younger brother wants to attend a university in Paris to major in art. He asks you to lend him $100 a month for the next two years. In return, he promises to repay $3,500 at the end of the second year. He is certain by that date he will be selling his paintings. (a) If you demand a 30 percent return on risky investments, should you agree to lend the money? (b) What rate of return would you earn on the lending arrangement? (c) Would your return increase or decrease if instead you commit to lend $200 every two months for two years? Why?

■ CASH

Table 3.8   Cash   COMPLETE THIS TABLE

Terms	Search Recommended* (Semicolons are not part of the search but are used as separators.)	Citation for Definition: Provide Full Reference	Other Searches You Would Suggest
Cash	"cash includes"; cash currency bank accounts		
Cash equivalents	"cash and cash equivalents"		
Bank Overdrafts	Bank overdrafts		
Compensating balance	Compensating balance		
Restricted Cash	Restricted cash xor donations		

*Access FARS, click on File, Open, Nfo, Open, and select FASB-OP, click Search, enter query.

Problems

1. What is included in the definition of cash? Distinguish between cash and cash equivalents.
2. Can two companies, Busbee Corporation and Hawthorne Company, with identical assets differ in their presentation of cash and cash equivalents? Explain.
3. What is the purpose of a compensating balance?
4. Give an example of a restricted cash balance. How should such a balance be presented in the financial statements?

Table 3.9 Short-Term Investments   Page **3-19**

■ SHORT-TERM INVESTMENTS

Table 3.9   Short-Term Investments COMPLETE THIS TABLE

Terms	Search Recommended* (Semicolons are not part of the search but are used as separators.)	Citation for Definition: Provide Full Reference	Other Searches You Would Suggest
Short-term investments	"short-term investments";		
	"classification fair value financial instrument"		
Marketable securities	Marketable securities line item;		
	"equity securities"		
Investment in Equity and Debt Securities	Accounting guidance investment* in equity and debt securities		
Impairment of securities	Impairment of securities;		
	Impair* and sec*		
Market value accounting	Market value accounting for short-term investments		

Terms	Search Recommended* (Semicolons are not part of the search but are used as separators.)	Citation for Definition: Provide Full Reference	Other Searches You Would Suggest
Fair value	"fair value of a financial instrument is";		
	fair value defin* glossary;		
	"fair value" and "financial instruments"		
Relevance	Relevance		
Reliability	Reliability;		
	Reliability defin*		
Portfolio basis	Portfolio basis;		
	"Portfolio basis" and "financial instrument"		

*Access FARS, click on File, Open, Nfo, Open, and select FASB-OP, click Search, enter query.

Problems

1. How are impairments in short-term investments reported?

2. What are the categories into which debt and equity securities are to be classified?

3. In examining international accounting standards, through the 1980s, the United Kingdom, France, Germany, the Netherlands, Sweden, Switzerland, and Japan all reported short-term marketable securities at the lower of cost or market value. This was a time when much diversity existed internationally. Why do you believe these countries were reasonably homogeneous in their choice of accounting for short-term marketable securities?

4. On November 15, 1991, the United States Securities and Exchange Commission sponsored a market value conference titled "Relevance in Financial Reporting: Moving toward Market Value Accounting." In announcing the conference, the brochure explained that the discussion

Table 3.9 Short-Term Investments   Page **3-21**

would focus on whether market-based measures would be a useful and relevant alternative to historical cost information for decision makers, including investors, analysts, regulators, creditors, and management. Opponents of the market value accounting frequently cited lack of reliability, excessive cost, and an expected increase in reported volatility as insurmountable obstacles to market value accounting. Explain what discussion points you would expect to have raised regarding (a) relevancy, (b) reliability, (c) cost, and (d) volatility? [*Hint*: Search FARS using the phrase dissent management intent and consider implications of the associated discussion identified.]

■ **RECEIVABLES**

Table 3.10   Receivables COMPLETE THIS TABLE

Terms	Search Recommended* (Semicolons are not part of the search but are used as separators.)	Citation for Definition: Provide Full Reference	Other Searches You Would Suggest
Net realizable value	Net realizable value		
Trade receivables	Trade accounts and notes receivable*;		
	"trade receivables are";		
	Receivables from customers separate		
Nontrade receivables	Receivable* xor trade;		
	"receivables from"		
Factoring with recourse	Factoring with recourse;		
	Transfers of receivables with recourse		
Factoring without recourse	Factoring without recourse		

Table 3.11 Inventories   Page **3-23**

Terms	Search Recommended* (Semicolons are not part of the search but are used as separators.)	Citation for Definition: Provide Full Reference	Other Searches You Would Suggest
Note receivable	"notes receivable";		
	secured and unsecured notes		
Installment receivable	Installment receivable from installment sale		

*Access FARS, click on File, Open, Nfo, Open, and select FASB-OP, click Search, enter query.

Problems

1. How do you compute the net realizable value of receivables?

2. What is the difference between trade and nontrade receivables, and how should they be presented on a balance sheet?

3. Would you expect the charge for factoring with recourse to be higher or lower than the charge of factoring without recourse? Why?

4. Define an installment receivable.

INVENTORIES

Table 3.11   Inventories COMPLETE THIS TABLE

Terms	Search Recommended* (Semicolons are not part of the search but are used as separators.)	Citation for Definition: Provide Full Reference	Other Searches You Would Suggest
Inventory	Inventory defin* goods		
Periodic inventory	Periodic inventory relative to perpetual inventory		
Perpetual inventory	"perpetual inventory"		
Pilferage expense	Pilferage expense		
Cost flow assumptions	Cost flow assumptions inventory		
Physical flow of goods	Physical flow of goods		
Inventory Method	Choice of inventory method;		
	"first-in-first-out";		
	inventory is accounted for first-in-first-out		
Matching	Matching;		
	cost of goods sold determination		
Retail method	Retail method of estimating inventory		

*Access FARS, click on File, Open, Nfo, Open, and select FASB-OP, click Search, enter query.

Table 3.11 Inventories   Page **3-25**

Problems

1. Which system provides the more accurate estimate of pilferage expense: periodic or perpetual? Why?

2. How does a cost flow assumption relate to the physical flow of goods?

3. In what sense is LIFO said to produce better matching? What do you suspect was the reason claimed by the media for a number of companies changing to LIFO in the late 1970s and early 1980s?

4. Can selling expenses be made a part of inventory costs?

■ INVENTORY VALUATION

Table 3.12 Inventory Valuation COMPLETE THIS TABLE

Terms	Search Recommended* (Semicolons are not part of the search but are used as separators.)	Citation for Definition: Provide Full Reference	Other Searches You Would Suggest
Fair market value	Fair market value of inventory		
Cost principles	Cost principles inventory valuation		
Writedowns	Writedowns inventory		
Price recovery	"price recovery"		
Trade discounts	"trade discount"		
Inflation	Inflation		
Net realizable value	Appl* net realizable valu* of inventory defin*		

*Access FARS, click on File, Open, Nfo, Open, and select FASB-OP, click Search, enter query.

Problems

1. Declines in the fair market value of inventory below cost principle at the date of interim financial statements require writedowns of assets to lower of cost or market when near-term price recovery is uncertain. Does this appear to be consistent or at odds with the historical cost or periodicity concept?

2. What are trade discounts?

3. In a period of inflation, how would we expect inventory values to compare if the same company makes calculations using FIFO, LIFO, and weighted-average cost-flow assumptions?

4. When using the lower of cost or market method, how is market defined?

5. Define net realizable value.

Table 3.13 Property Plant and Equipment   Page **3-27**

■ **PROPERTY PLANT AND EQUIPMENT**

Table 3.13   Property Plant and Equipment COMPLETE THIS TABLE

Terms	Search Recommended* (Semicolons are not part of the search but are used as separators.)	Citation for Definition: Provide Full Reference	Other Searches You Would Suggest
Property plant and equipment	Property plant and equipment classif* statement of financial position		
Land	"land"		
Investment in land	"investment in land"		
Equipment	"equipment"		
Capitalized interest	"capitalization of interest"; accounting treatment of interest capitalization on fixed assets		
Interest expense	"interest expense include"; recording of interest incurred when purchasing fixed assets		
Pledged asset	"pledged asset"		

Terms	Search Recommended* (Semicolons are not part of the search but are used as separators.)	Citation for Definition: Provide Full Reference	Other Searches You Would Suggest
Self-constructed asset	Self-constructed asset under construction; Self-constructed asset under construction interest incurred capitalization		
Cost of equity capital	"cost of equity capital"		
Exchange of assets	"exchange of assets"; accounting for nonmonetary exchange		
Book value	"book value"		

*Access FARS, click on File, Open, Nfo, Open, and select FASB-OP, click Search, enter query.

Problems

1. What is the distinction between land as a noncurrent asset and land held by a real estate company?

2. If a company purchases a piece of equipment on credit, is the interest capitalized? Why or why not?

3. Do pledged assets differ in value from assets that are not pledged?

4. When the amount of interest to capitalize on self-constructed assets is determined, how is the cost of equity capital reflected?

5. If two assets are exchanged without any cash changing hands, will the new asset be recorded at the book value of the asset given up? Explain your reply.

6. Three of the seven members of the Financial Accounting Standards Board dissented to the final FASB Statement No. 34, "Capitalization of Interest Cost." What do you think their reasons were for dissenting?

Table 3.14 Depreciation   Page **3-29**

■ DEPRECIATION

Table 3.14   Depreciation COMPLETE THIS TABLE

Terms	Search Recommended* (Semicolons are not part of the search but are used as separators.)	Citation for Definition: Provide Full Reference	Other Searches You Would Suggest
Depreciation	Depreciation defin*		
Units of production	Units of production		
Straight line	"straight line depreciation"		
Depreciable basis	"depreciable basis"; depreciable basis is computed as		
Sum of the years' digits	"Sum of the years digits method"		
Double declining balance	"declining balance depreciation"		
Accelerated depreciation	Accelerated depreciation		
Group depreciation	"group depreciation"		
Risk of computation with software	Risk of depreciation computation with software		

*Access FARS, click on File, Open, Nfo, Open, and select FASB-OP, click Search, enter query.

Problems

1. Will the units-of-production method result in a write-off patttern similar to the pattern produced by the straight-line method?

2. How does the depreciable basis calculation apply to the straight-line, sum-of-the-years'-digits, and double-declining-balance methods?

3. What is meant by the term *accelerated depreciation*?

4. What is the most distinctive aspect of group depreciation?

5. What types of risks arise from the use of software to compute depreciation?

Table 3.15 Depletion   Page **3-31**

■ **DEPLETION**

Table 3.15   Depletion COMPLETE THIS TABLE

Terms	Search Recommended* (Semicolons are not part of the search but are used as separators.)	Citation for Definition: Provide Full Reference	Other Searches You Would Suggest
Depletion	Depletion of property		
Successful efforts	Successful efforts accounting framework		
Full cost accounting	Full cost accounting framework		
Natural resources	Natural resources		
Extraction	"extraction"		
Reserves	"reserves"		
Legal life of intangibles	Legal life of intangibles		
Useful life of intangibles	Useful life of intangibles		

*Access FARS, click on File, Open, Nfo, Open, and select FASB-OP, click Search, enter query.

Problems

1. Distinguish between successful efforts and full cost accounting.
2. If an oil well costing $60,000 is expected to produce 500,000 barrels and 100,000 barrels have been extracted, what is the depletion expense?
3. The debate over successful efforts and full cost accounting has been both heated and affected by political intervention. Use FARS to describe the evolution of current accounting practices as they relate to oil and gas.

■ IMPAIRMENTS

Table 3.16   Impairments COMPLETE THIS TABLE

Terms	Search Recommended* (Semicolons are not part of the search but are used as separators.)	Citation for Definition: Provide Full Reference	Other Searches You Would Suggest
Impairment	Impairment defin*		
Idle property	"idle facility"		
Permanent improvement	"term property improvements";		
	"property improvements"		
Asset writeoffs	Asset writeoffs		
Writedowns of assets	Writedowns of assets		
Involuntary conversion	Involuntary conversion		
Uninsured	"uninsured";		
	self-insured loss		

Table 3.16 Impairments   Page **3-33**

Terms	Search Recommended* (Semicolons are not part of the search but are used as separators.)	Citation for Definition: Provide Full Reference	Other Searches You Would Suggest
Insured	Recording insured losses;		
	Insurance proceeds for loss;		
	Measuring and recording insured loss on property;		
	Loss on fire		

*Access FARS, click on File, Open, Nfo, Open, and select FASB-OP, click Search, enter query.

Problems

1. If property is idle, should depreciation be recorded? Should permanent impairment be recorded? Are writedowns of assets appropriate in such a setting?

2. What is a common source of asset write-offs?

3. How does the recording of an insured involuntary conversion differ from that of an uninsured involuntary conversion?

4. Writedowns have been criticized in the literature. What is the nature of such criticism?

■ INTANGIBLE ASSETS

Table 3.17   Intangible Assets COMPLETE THIS TABLE

Terms	Search Recommended* (Semicolons are not part of the search but are used as separators.)	Citation for Definition: Provide Full Reference	Other Searches You Would Suggest
Intangible assets	"intangible assets"		
Tangible assets	"tangible assets"		
Patents	Patents received or applied for;		
	Patents are intangible		
Research and development	Research and development		
Pledged asset	"pledged asset"		
Defense cost of patent	Patent litigation;		
	Cost of successfully defending a patent infringement		
Goodwill	Valu* called goodwill is recorded defin*;		
	Goodwill is recorded defin*;		
	Goodwill defin*		
Negative goodwill	"called negative goodwill"		

Table 3.17 Intangible Assets   Page **3-35**

Terms	Search Recommended* (Semicolons are not part of the search but are used as separators.)	Citation for Definition: Provide Full Reference	Other Searches You Would Suggest
Amortization of intangibles	Amortization of intangible assets		
Period of amortization	Period of amortization for intangible assets		
Capitalization	Capitalization intangible assets;		
	Purchased intangibles capitalizable		
Patent dispute	Patent dispute		

*Access FARS, click on File, Open, Nfo, Open, and select FASB-OP, click Search, enter query.

Problems

1. How do tangible assets differ from intangible assets?

2. Since research and development costs are intended to result in a new product on which a patent will be granted, they are capitalized as an asset in the patent account. Is this statement true or false? Explain.

3. Do pledged assets differ in value from assets that are not pledged?

4. If patent rights are disputed, how are the costs of defending the patent handled in the accounting records?

5. Define the terms (a) goodwill and (b) negative goodwill.

6. Over what period should intangibles be amortized?

■ CURRENT LIABILITIES

Table 3.18   Current Liabilities COMPLETE THIS TABLE

Terms	Search Recommended* (Semicolons are not part of the search but are used as separators.)	Citation for Definition: Provide Full Reference	Other Searches You Would Suggest
Current liabilities	"current liabilities"		
Accounts payable	Accounts payable defin*		
Notes payable	"notes payable";		
	distinction in notes and accounts payable		
Utility bills	Utility bills;		
	Electricity used to light;		
	Obligations for electricity used		
Payroll	Payroll expense and obligations defin*		
Property taxes	Property taxes		

Table 3.18 Current Liabilities   Page **3-37**

Terms	Search Recommended* (Semicolons are not part of the search but are used as separators.)	Citation for Definition: Provide Full Reference	Other Searches You Would Suggest
Interim financial statements	Interim financial statements defin*;		
	Interim financial reporting;		
	Integral interim statements		
Deferred taxes	Deferred taxes		

*Access FARS, click on File, Open, Nfo, Open, and select FASB-OP, click Search, enter query.

Problems

1. How do accounts payable differ from notes payable?
2. Utility bills are typically recorded by a company upon payment, as is payroll. If the fiscal year-end precedes a monthly utility bill's payment by one week and payday by two days, how are such obligations commonly recorded?
3. In January, Kiernan Company paid $24,000 of property taxes. The company prepares interim financial statements. What should be reflected as property tax expense for the first quarter?
4. Describe the circumstance that results in a current liability for deferred taxes.

■ CONTINGENCIES

Table 3.19   Contingencies COMPLETE THIS TABLE

Terms	Search Recommended* (Semicolons are not part of the search but are used as separators.)	Citation for Definition: Provide Full Reference	Other Searches You Would Suggest
Contingencies	"a contingency is defined"		
Warranty obligations	Warranty obligations		
Retroactive adjustment	Retroactive adjustment reversal of revenue or billings		
Probable	Probable		
Range	Range of estimated contingency		
Litigation	Litigation		

*Access FARS, click on File, Open, Nfo, Open, and select FASB-OP, click Search, enter query.

Problems

1. Under what conditions must liabilities be accrued on the books of a company for contingencies?

2. Wagih Dafashy Company has estimated its long-term warranty obligations to range from $500,000 to $700,000 on product A. Its new product B also has a warranty, but the company has no basis for quantifying the amount of customers' potential claims. How would these long-term warranty obligations be reported in the financial statements, and why?

3. The health care industry has been affected by the existence of predefined procedures and related cost-reimbursement formulas for physicians' services. Insurers regularly audit the billings received for their compliance with guidelines on appropriate procedures, as well as for the reasonableness of the time charges. Medicare diagnostic related group (DRG) payment rates for wages often result in retroactive adjustment. An example of a retroactive adjustment would be where a billing by a physician was considered to be too high for the procedure performed, or the procedure was deemed unnecessary for the circumstances at hand. How should this affect accounting (i.e., how would you expect the anticipation of retroactive adjustments to be captured by the information system)?

Table 3.19 Contingencies   Page **3-39**

4. A suit for breach of contract seeking damages of $1,000,000 was filed against a company on July 1, 20x1. The company's legal counsel believes that an unfavorable outcome is probable. A reasonable estimate of the court's award to the plaintiff is in the range of $100,000 to $500,000. No amount within this range is a better estimate of potential damages than any other amount. What should be recorded in the financial statements?

■ LONG-TERM LIABILITIES

Table 3.20   Long-Term Liabilities COMPLETE THIS TABLE

Terms	Search Recommended* (Semicolons are not part of the search but are used as separators.)	Citation for Definition: Provide Full Reference	Other Searches You Would Suggest
Long-term liability	Long-term liability balance sheet classification; Definitions debt security		
Face value	Face value of liability is defined as glossary		
Interest rate	"interest rate is"		
Coupon rate	"coupon rate"		
Real rate	Real versus nominal rate of interest		
Effective rate	Effective rate of interest is defin* glossary		
Nominal rate	"nominal rate"		
Stated rates	"stated rate"		
Rates incurred	Interest rate incurred		
Rate paid	Interest rate paid on liability		
Market rates	"market rates"		

Table 3.20 Long-Term Liabilities   Page **3-41**

Terms	Search Recommended* (Semicolons are not part of the search but are used as separators.)	Citation for Definition: Provide Full Reference	Other Searches You Would Suggest
Unsecured debt	Unsecured debt;		
	Collateral		
Subordinated debt	Subordinated debt defin* glossary		
Callable convertible debt	Callable convertible debt defin* glossary		
Term bond	Fixed term of existence for bonds;		
	Example bond liabilities financial instrument		
Serial bond	"serial bonds"		
Debt swaps	Debt swap* transaction* defin*		
Defeasance	Defeasance defin* glossary;		
	Accounting treatment for defeasance		
Amortization	Recording amortization of debt liabilities defin*		
Straight-line amortization	"straight-line amortization"		
Premium	"bond premium"@		
Discount	Bond discount defin*		

Terms	Search Recommended* (Semicolons are not part of the search but are used as separators.)	Citation for Definition: Provide Full Reference	Other Searches You Would Suggest
Imputed rate	Imputation of interest defin*;		
	How to imput* interest		
Implicit rate	"implicit rate"		
Subjective acceleration clause	"subjective acceleration clause"		

*Access FARS, click on File, Open, Nfo, Open, and select FASB-OP, click Search, enter query.

Problems

1. Practitioners have posed the following question to those who set the standards: Should long-term debt be classified as a current liability if the long-term debt agreement contains a subjective acceleration clause that may accelerate the due date? How do you believe the standard-setters responded? Why? (*Hint*: Examine the FASB Technical Bulletins.)

2. If a 10-percent, $100,000 bond is issued in each of the following markets, would the proceeds be greater than, equal to, or less than the face value? (a) 15 percent market (b) 8 percent market (c) 10 percent market.

3. Interest rates are referred to as coupon rates, real rates, effective rates, nominal rates, stated rates, rates incurred, rates paid, and market rates. Which of these terms are synonymous and which differ from each other?

4. Define the following terms: (a) unsecured debt, (b) subordinated debt, (c) callable convertible debt, (d) term bond, (e) serial bond, (f) debt swaps, (g) defeasance.

5. Peterson Incorporated issued a $500,000, 10 percent, 20-year bond at 97. Record the issuance of the bond and amortization for the first year using the straight-line method.

6. You want to furnish your dormitory room. A local furniture store advertises that you can buy any desk in the store on September 1, 20x1, and not pay the bill for two years (i.e., not until September 1, 20x3). No interest will be charged. You buy a desk for $300. (a) What is the stated interest on this transaction? Is this the interest you incurred? Why or why not? (b) Assume you determine that the value of the desk is $270. What was the implicit interest rate? (c) Assume that you cannot determine the value of either the desk or the note, but you have an imputed borrowing rate of 10 percent. What should the recorded value of the desk be?

Table V.21 Stockholders' Equity   Page **3-43**

■ **STOCKHOLDERS' EQUITY**

Table 3.21   Stockholders' Equity COMPLETE THIS TABLE

Terms	Search Recommended* (Semicolons are not part of the search but are used as separators.)	Citation for Definition: Provide Full Reference	Other Searches You Would Suggest
Stockholders' equity	"balance-sheet presentation of stockholders' equity"		
Par value	"par value"		
Market value	"market value"		
Owners' equity	Owners' equity defin*		
Proprietorship	"proprietorship"		
Partnership	"partner"		
Convertible debt	"convertible debt"		
Common stock	"common stock"; capital stock		
Preferred stock	Preferred stock defin* shareholders rights and privileges		
Voting rights	"voting rights"		
Cumulative	"cumulative preferred stock"		
Preemptive	"preemptive"		
Participating	"participating preferred stock"		
Convertible	"convertible"		
Treasury stock	Treasury stock defin*		

Terms	Search Recommended* (Semicolons are not part of the search but are used as separators.)	Citation for Definition: Provide Full Reference	Other Searches You Would Suggest
Cost method	Stock buybacks recorded as treasury stock cost basis and reissuance		

*Access FARS, click on File, Open, Nfo, Open, and select FASB-OP, click Search, enter query.

Problems

1. Are par value and market value synonymous? What purpose do they serve?

2. How do owners' equity accounts for a proprietorship differ from those of a partnership?

3. A company issues straight debt (bonds) with a 5 percent stated rate, convertible debt A with a 4.5 percent stated rate, and convertible debt B with a 2 percent stated rate. Common stock yields approximately an 8 percent return. Describe the promises granted by convertible debt and their relative value to the bondholder and explain how, if at all, they influence the accounting treatment.

4. Outline the principal types of transactions that can influence stockholders' equity.

5. What rights are typically granted to common stockholders? Briefly describe the nature of each right. Describe the typical differences between preferred stock and common stock.

6. Indicate whether the following attributes commonly apply to common stock (C) or preferred stock (P): (1) Voting rights, (2) Participative, (3) Cumulative, (4) Preemptive, (5) Convertible.

7. Smith, Inc. issued 500,000 shares of stock for $20 a share. The par value of the stock was $10 a share. It concurrently reissued 1,000 shares of treasury stock, previously purchased for $15,000, at the same $20-per-share market price. The corporation uses the cost method of accounting for treasury stock. Record the necessary journal entries.

Table 3.22 Contributed Capital   Page **3-45**

■ CONTRIBUTED CAPITAL

Table 3.22   Contributed Capital COMPLETE THIS TABLE

Terms	Search Recommended* (Semicolons are not part of the search but are used as separators.)	Citation for Definition: Provide Full Reference	Other Searches You Would Suggest
Contributed capital	Invested and earned contributed capital;		
	The contributed portion of capital		
Gifts	Gifts by owners to corporations;		
	Recording of gifts to not-for-profit organizations		
Paid-in capital in excess of par	Stated capital paid-in capital in excess of par		

*Access FARS, click on File, Open, Nfo, Open, and select FASB-OP, click Search, enter query.

Problems

1. Define contributed capital.
2. A gift of land worth $50,000 was granted to a corporation by a municipality. How would this be recorded?

■ RETAINED EARNINGS

Table 3.23   Retained Earnings COMPLETE THIS TABLE

Terms	Search Recommended* (Semicolons are not part of the search but are used as separators.)	Citation for Definition: Provide Full Reference	Other Searches You Would Suggest
Retained earnings	Presentation of retained earnings		
Dividend	"dividend";		
	definition of dividends;		
	interest$ dividends$		
Cumulative preferred stock	Cumulative preferred stock		
Date of declaration	Date of declaration		
Stock split	"stock split";		
	stock split		
Plant expansion	Appropriat* of retained earnings for plant expansion		
Appropriations	Appropriations		

*Access FARS, click on File, Open, Nfo, Open, and select FASB-OP, click Search, enter query.

Table 3.23 Retained Earnings   Page **3-47**

Problems

1. Is a dividend analogous to interest expense? Explain your response.

2. Bill Geary, Inc. has not declared dividends on its $100 par-value 6 percent preferred stock for two years. This year there are 40,000 shares outstanding, and dividends are declared for $2 million. If the preferred stock is cumulative, what journal entry will be recorded as of the date of declaration?

3. One thousand shares of an $18 par value stock of Tom White Corporation was subjected to a three-for-one stock split. Prior to the stock split, the market value of the shares was $54. Describe the effects of the stock split in specific terms.

4. Aamer Sheikh Corporation with $90,000 retained earnings wishes to earmark $10,000 for an intended purchase of land for plant expansion. Record the necessary journal entry. How does this entry affect total earnings?

■ **DILUTIVE SECURITIES**

Table 3.24   Dilutive Securities COMPLETE THIS TABLE

Terms	Search Recommended* (Semicolons are not part of the search but are used as separators.)	Citation for Definition: Provide Full Reference	Other Searches You Would Suggest
Dilutive securities	"dilutive securities"		
Stock options	Stock options		
Stock appreciation rights	"stock appreciation rights are awards"		
Warrants	"stock purchase warrants"		

*Access FARS, click on File, Open, Nfo, Open, and select FASB-OP, click Search, enter query.

Problems

1. What is the key advantage of stock appreciation rights over stock options from the perspective of the holder?
2. What is a warrant?

Table 3.25 Earnings Per Share   Page **3-49**

■ **EARNINGS PER SHARE**

Table 3.25   Earnings Per Share COMPLETE THIS TABLE

Terms	Search Recommended* (Semicolons are not part of the search but are used as separators.)	Citation for Definition: Provide Full Reference	Other Searches You Would Suggest
Earnings per share	Simplifies standards for computing earnings per share		
Per share computations	Required disclosure of per share information;		
	Cash flow per share earnings per share;		
	"computing basic eps"		
Fully diluted earnings per share	Simplify compute fully diluted EPS		

*Access FARS, click on File, Open, Nfo, Open, and select FASB-OP, click Search, enter query.

Problems

1. What is typically reported in per-share terms on the statement of earnings?
2. What is the difference between earnings per share and fully diluted earnings per share?

■ INVESTMENTS

Table 3.26   Investments COMPLETE THIS TABLE

Terms	Search Recommended* (Semicolons are not part of the search but are used as separators.)	Citation for Definition: Provide Full Reference	Other Searches You Would Suggest
Investment	Accounting for investments in stock$ other companies		
Pooling of interests	"pooling of interests"		
Purchase	"purchase of a company"		
Marketable securities	"equity securities"		
Cost method	Certain equity securities cost method		
Equity method	"the equity method of accounting for investments in common stock";		
	certain equity securities equity method		
Control	Control		
Consolidated financial statements	"consolidated financial statements are required";		
	consolidation means		

*Access FARS, click on File, Open, Nfo, Open, and select FASB-OP, click Search, enter query.

Problems

1. Distinguish between pooling of interests and purchase-based consolidations.

2. If an investor holds 15 percent of a stock or 25 percent of a stock, does that difference in holdings have an effect on the accounting treatment of the investor? Be specific. What if that same investor held 60 percent of a company's stock?

■ REVENUE RECOGNITION

Table 3.27   Revenue Recognition COMPLETE THIS TABLE

Terms	Search Recommended* (Semicolons are not part of the search but are used as separators.)	Citation for Definition: Provide Full Reference	Other Searches You Would Suggest
Revenue recognition	Revenue recognition occurs;		
	Realization and recognition		
Line items	Line items def*;		
	Sequence of line items assets liquidity		
Advances from customers	"advances from customers"		
Unearned revenue	"unearned revenue"		
Revenue realization	"revenue realization";		
	revenue realization def*		
Completed-contract method	"completed contract method"		
Percentage of completion method	"Percentage of completion method"		
Cash basis accounting	"cash basis accounting"		

Table 3.27 Revenue Recognition   Page **3-53**

Terms	Search Recommended* (Semicolons are not part of the search but are used as separators.)	Citation for Definition: Provide Full Reference	Other Searches You Would Suggest
Installment sales	"installment sales"; "installment method"; revenue recognition installment sales method retail land sales		
Substance versus form	Substance versus form		

*Access FARS, click on File, Open, Nfo, Open, and select FASB-OP, click Search, enter query.

Problems

1. What type of line item is "advances from customers"? Is this type of line item the same as "unearned revenue"? Why?

2. Distinguish between revenue realization and recognition.

3. How does the completed-contract method differ from the percentage-of-completion approach to income recognition for a long-term construction contractor?

4. Given an example of when a type of cash-basis accounting is prescribed by generally accepted accounting principles and why this is the case.

5. How does the idea of substance over form relate to revenue recognition?

■ ACCOUNTING FOR INCOME TAXES

Table 3.28   Accounting For Income Taxes COMPLETE THIS TABLE

Terms	Search Recommended* (Semicolons are not part of the search but are used as separators.)	Citation for Definition: Provide Full Reference	Other Searches You Would Suggest
Income taxes	Income taxes def*		
Deferred charges	"deferred charges";		
	"Deferred tax assets"		
Deferred taxes	deferred taxes defin*		
ACRS	"acrs guidelines";		
	acrs rollover effect		
Rollover effect	Tax strategy of rolling over equipment before reversal of timing effects;		
	Rollover effect		
Payroll withholding taxes	"payroll withholding";		
	payroll withholding tax		
Taxation of partnerships	Taxation of partnerships		
Timing differences	"timing differences"		

Table 3.28 Accounting for Income Taxes   Page **3-55**

Terms	Search Recommended* (Semicolons are not part of the search but are used as separators.)	Citation for Definition: Provide Full Reference	Other Searches You Would Suggest
Permanent differences	"permanent differences"		
Liability method	"liability method"		
Deferred method	"deferred method"; fas 109 accounting for income tax		
Expected tax rate	Expected tax rate		
More likely than not	"more likely than not"; more likely than not		
Discounting	Discount* of tax liabilit*		
Tax asset	"tax asset"		

*Access FARS, click on File, Open, Nfo, Open, and select FASB-OP, click Search, enter query.

Problems

1. A common line item in financial statements is "deferred charges," as is "deferred taxes." Does the accounting framework provide clear direction as to whether such balances are likely to be debits or credits? Why or why not? Do you believe this somehow detracts from the elegance of double-entry accounting? Why or why not?

2. Is the ACRS method for tax purposes more analogous to the straight-line or accelerated method of depreciation? Explain your response.

3. What is a sign that James Smith Corporation, or any other company, is effectively using the rollover effect to its advantage?

4. How do payroll withholding taxes affect a company's recorded income?

5. How are partnerships taxed?

6. The Financial Accounting Standards Board on April 8, 1985, presented its tentative conclusion that the effects of tax timing diffferences are assets and liabilities (liability method), rather than deferred debits and credits (deferred method). While the deferred method does not adjust balances to reflect a subsequent change in taxes, the proposed liability method uses expected tax rates and adjusts balances for future changes. (a) Under

the new tax rates applied in 1988, what would be the expected change in deferred tax balances under the liability method when compared with those of 1987? Would there be a predictable income effect? (b) If discounting is applied to deferred taxes, what are the expected effects on reported liabilities? [*Hint*: An excellent resource regarding tax rates at different points in time is "Instructional Resource: Using Tax History to Teach the Concepts of Tax Planning," by William D. Samson, *Issues in Accounting Education* (13, no. 3, August 1998), pp. 655-692 – especially Table 1, pp. 679-681.]

7. In letters responding to the Financial Accounting Standards Board's discussion memorandum entitled "An Analysis of the Issues Related to Accounting for Income Taxes," approximately 88 percent opposed discounting of deferred taxes. (a) What do you believe are the reasons for this opposition? (b) Do you personally favor or oppose the discounting of deferred taxes? Why?

Table 3.29 Accounting for Pensions   Page **3-57**

■ ACCOUNTING FOR PENSIONS

Table 3.29   Accounting For Pensions COMPLETE THIS TABLE

Terms	Search Recommended* (Semicolons are not part of the search but are used as separators.)	Citation for Definition: Provide Full Reference	Other Searches You Would Suggest
Pensions	"pensions are"		
Service costs	"service costs"		
Prior service costs	"prior service costs"		
Assumed rate of return	"assumed rate of return"		
Defined benefit	"defined benefit pension plans"		
Defined contribution	"defined contribution pension plans"		
Pension benefits	"pension benefits"; benefits glossary defin*		
Actuarial present value of pension plan benefits	Actuarial present value of pension plan benefits		
Vesting	"vested benefits are"; "vested benefits are defined"		

*Access FARS, click on File, Open, Nfo, Open, and select FASB-OP, click Search, enter query.

Problems

1. Define the following pension-related terms: (a) service cost, (b) prior service costs, (c) vesting.

2. Pension funds use an assumed rate of return in computing the actuarial present value of pension plan benefits. What is the nature of an assumed rate of return and what would happen to the pension liability as the percentage moves up, for example by 4 percent?

3. Distinguish between a defined benefit and a defined contribution plan.

Table 3.30 Postretirement Benefits   Page **3-59**

■ **POSTRETIREMENT BENEFITS**

Table 3.30   Postretirement Benefits COMPLETE THIS TABLE

Terms	Search Recommended* (Semicolons are not part of the search but are used as separators.)	Citation for Definition: Provide Full Reference	Other Searches You Would Suggest
Postretirement benefits	"postretirement benefits";		
	postretirement benefit defin*		
Matching	"matching"		
Obligations related to employees	"obligations related to employees"		

*Access FARS, click on File, Open, Nfo, Open, and select FASB-OP, click Search, enter query.

Problems

1. Define postretirement benefits.
2. When the FASB passed the related pronouncement, there was a "Gray Panthers" protest. Why do you believe this was a controversial proposal?

■ LEASES

Table 3.31   Leases COMPLETE THIS TABLE

Terms	Search Recommended* (Semicolons are not part of the search but are used as separators.)	Citation for Definition: Provide Full Reference	Other Searches You Would Suggest
Leases	Lease* agreements defin*		
Operating lease	Criteria for classification as operating lease		
Capital lease	Original classification as a capital lease criteria;		
	"the lease shall be classified as a capital lease"		
Sale-leasebacks	"sale-leasebacks are"		
Residual value	"residual value"		
Guaranteed residual value	"guaranteed residual value is"		
Bargain purchase	"bargain purchase option"		
Initial direct costs	"initial direct costs"		
Minimum lease payments	"minimum lease payments over the lease term"		

Table 3.31 Leases   Page **3-61**

Terms	Search Recommended* (Semicolons are not part of the search but are used as separators.)	Citation for Definition: Provide Full Reference	Other Searches You Would Suggest
Penalty for failure to renew	"penalty for failure to renew";		
	penalty for failure to renew defin*		
Lease commitments	"lease commitments are"		
Blindpool syndication	Blindpool syndication def*		
Lease note disclosures	Disclosure in notes of lease agreements		
Incremental borrowing rate	"incremental borrowing rate";		
	"lessee's incremental borrowing rate"		
Economic life test	Economic life test		
Transfer of ownership	"transfer of ownership"		
Implicit interest	"implicit interest";		
	implicit interest rate lease*		
Leaseholds	"leasehold improvements"		
Bargain renewal option	"bargain renewal option"		

*Access FARS, click on File, Open, Nfo, Open, and select FASB-OP, click Search, enter query.

Problems

1. Real estate developers sold an office building to a public real estate blindpool syndication. Then, a sale and leaseback arrangement was reached. How should this be recorded?

2. Why do leaseholds sometimes appear as long-term assets?

3. What is the typical content of notes to financial statements that relate to lease commitments?

4. What are the criteria used to distinguish a capital lease from an operating lease?

Table 3.32 Accounting Changes   Page **3-63**

■ **ACCOUNTING CHANGES**

Table 3.32   Accounting Changes COMPLETE THIS TABLE

Terms	Search Recommended* (Semicolons are not part of the search but are used as separators.)	Citation for Definition: Provide Full Reference	Other Searches You Would Suggest
Accounting changes	Accounting changes defin*;		
	"change in depreciation method for plant equipment"		
Change in estimates	"Change in estimate";		
	"changes in estimates used"		
Cumulative effect of an accounting change	"cumulative effect of an accounting change is"		

*Access FARS, click on File, Open, Nfo, Open, and select FASB-OP, click Search, enter query.

Problems

1. Do differences exist in the depreciation accounting for (a) changes in estimates and (b) changes in accounting method? Explain your response in detail.

2. Denise Jones's High Tech corporation purchased 100 personal computers on January 2, 20x1, estimating five-year useful lives and a salvage value of $1,000 per computer. A straight-line method of depreciation was applied to the $500,000 purchase price. However, by 20x3, the company determined that technology had advanced to such a degree, that the terminals would need to be replaced by the end of 20x4. Moreover, due to tax law changes that made it attractive to decrease reported net income, per books, the corporation switched to the sum-of-the-years'-digits method of depreciation in 20x3. The tax law change

determined the alternative minimum tax on reported net income, creating an influence by tax law on financial statement presentation. Make all necessary journal entries to reflect the personal computers in the company's books over their useful life to the corporation.

Table 3.33 Error Analysis   Page **3-65**

■ ERROR ANALYSIS

Table 3.33   Error Analysis COMPLETE THIS TABLE

Terms	Search Recommended* (Semicolons are not part of the search but are used as separators.)	Citation for Definition: Provide Full Reference	Other Searches You Would Suggest
Error	"error"		
Irregularity	"irregularity";		
	misstatement		
Correction	"correction of error"		

*Access FARS, click on File, Open, Nfo, Open, and select FASB-OP, click Search, enter query.

Problems

1. An insurance premium of $1,600 was prepaid in 20x1 covering the years 20x1, 20x2, 20x3, and 20x4. The entire amount was recorded as an expense in 20x1. No other errors occurred during 20x1 and no corrections were made for the error. Ignoring any tax considerations: (a) What was the effect on net income in 20x1? (b) What was the effect on net income in 20x2? (c) What was the effect on retained earnings as of the end of 20x1? (d) What was the effect on assets as of the end of 20x1? (e) What was the effect on retained earnings as of the end of 20x2? (f) As of what date will retained earnings be accurately reported?

2. A customer called and complained that an order for 15,000 parts, serial number A278, had been filled with 15,000 parts, serial number B278. The customer noted that although a check had been mailed three days before, a stop-payment was being issued. The parts would be returned within the week. The customer requested that the actual order be filled immediately and that your company incur the costs of express transit to ensure delivery by the next day. Following the phone call, you wish to investigate the accuracy of the complaint. Moreover, you need to decide how to proceed, including what actions to take and what journal entries to record. Explain what steps are appropriate and why.

■ **STATEMENT OF CASH FLOWS REVISITED**

Table 3.34   Statement of Cash Flows Revisited COMPLETE THIS TABLE

Terms	Search Recommended* (Semicolons are not part of the search but are used as separators.)	Citation for Definition: Provide Full Reference	Other Searches You Would Suggest
Statement of cash flows	"statement of cash flows";		
	defin* statement of cash flows;		
	"a statement of cash flows as part of a full set of financial statements"		
Cash management	"cash management";		
	objective of enterprises' cash management programs		
Family loans	loans to family members		
Related parties	"related parties"		
Concessions to creditors	concessions to creditors		
Small business	"small business"		

Table 3.34 Statement of Cash Flows Revisited   Page **3-67**

Terms	Search Recommended* (Semicolons are not part of the search but are used as separators.)	Citation for Definition: Provide Full Reference	Other Searches You Would Suggest
Charge-offs of loans	write-offs and charge-offs of loans		
Cash equivalents	"cash and cash equivalents"		
Investing activities	"investing activities"		
Net cash flows	net cash flows within the statement of cash flows defin*		
Gross cash flows	gross cash flows in statement of cash flows defin*		
Indirect method	"indirect method"		
Reconciliation to net income	"reconciliation to net income";		
	adjusting net income to net cash flow remove		
Write-offs of receivables	"write-offs of receivables"		
Internal control	"internal control"		

*Access FARS, click on File, Open, Nfo, Open, and select FASB-OP, click Search, enter query.

Problems

1. It has been asserted that one of the cheapest ways for companies to finance themselves is to take control of the cash they already have. Many claim that U.S. corporations are "quite primitive" in their cash management. What do you believe are the problems? How would you quantify the related costs? What steps might be taken to make cash management more effective?

2. In the 1980s, it was observed that the 14 million small businesses in the United States provided about half of all private sector jobs and generated almost 40 percent of the gross national product; the role of small business in the economy has been growing. Yet, money

for such businesses has been represented to be a nightmarish experience. About three-quarters of new businesses are reported to get at least part of their financing from friends and relatives. What types of concessions can small businesses grant to providers of capital to obtain the cash resources they need? Be specific.

3. A very real control problem relates to write-offs of accounts receivable and charge-offs of loans. Numerous cases are available in which officers and employees systematically diverted written-off accounts or charged-off loan recoveries to their own use. Clearly, controls must be established over such recoveries. Accounts written off or loans charged off are potential assets. In fact, member banks of the Federal Reserve Bank are able to recover over a quarter of their charged-off loans. As it turns out, they were not entirely uncollectible. How would you establish control over accounts written off and loans charged off? Why do you think these types of transactions are difficult to control?

4. If items meet the definition of cash equivalents that are part of a larger pool of investments, they are properly considered investing activities. The FASB allows these items not to be segregated and treated as cash equivalents. What desirable attribute of accounting information seems to be lacking as a result of this decision? How is this problem addressed by the FASB?

5. What is the general requirement for reporting of cash receipts and payment – gross or net? Why? Provide an example of an exception to such a requirement.

6. The indirect method of presenting a statement of cash flows requires that net income be reconciled to net cash flow from operating activities. To do so, what must be removed from net income?

Table 3.35 Full Disclosure   Page **3-69**

■ **FULL DISCLOSURE**

Table 3.35   Full Disclosure COMPLETE THIS TABLE

Terms	Search Recommended* (Semicolons are not part of the search but are used as separators.)	Citation for Definition: Provide Full Reference	Other Searches You Would Suggest
Full disclosure	"full disclosure";		
	transparency		
Materiality	"materiality"		
MD&A	MD&A		
General purpose financial statements	"general purpose financial statements"		
Notes to the financial statements	required notes to the financial statements		
Offsets	offset* defin* permitted;		
	general principle that offsetting is improper statement of financial position		
Concentration	"concentration"		
Off-balance sheet financing	"off-balance sheet financing"@		

*Access FARS, click on File, Open, Nfo, Open, and select FASB-OP, click Search, enter query.

Problems

1. The SEC requires disclosures in SEC filings only for material items (SEC SX 210.4-02). What are the pros and cons of such a policy?

2. What is the general purpose financial statement beyond the income statement, balance sheet, and statement of retained earnings?

3. How can notes to the financial statements be of use?

4. In reviewing a company's detailed journals and subsidiary ledgers, you note that a single company is both a supplier and a customer. It seems to you rather strange that this entity's balance represents 20 percent of outstanding receivables and likewise represents about 15 percent of outstanding payables. Is it appropriate for such a situation to arise? Can the receivables and payables be offset? Why or why not? Would the net amount be important information? Why or why not? Is there any disclosure you would recommend to such a company?

5. Give an example of a possible source of off-balance-sheet financing.

Table 3.36 Not-For-Profit Considerations   Page **3-71**

■ **NOT-FOR-PROFIT CONSIDERATIONS**

Table 3.36   Not-For-Profit Considerations COMPLETE THIS TABLE

Terms	Search Recommended* (Semicolons are not part of the search but are used as separators.)	Citation for Definition: Provide Full Reference	Other Searches You Would Suggest
Not-for-profit organization	"not-for-profit organization is"		
Investment objective of not-for-profit organizations	investment objective of not-for-profit organizations		
Restricted by donor	"restricted by donor"		
Pledges	"pledges"		
Endowment fund presentation	Endowment fund presentation		
Contributions	"contributions to not-for-profit"		

*Access FARS, click on File, Open, Nfo, Open, and select FASB-OP, click Search, enter query.

Problems

1. What are the investment objectives of a not-for-profit organization?

2. How should an endowment fund be presented in financial statements? When a restriction by donor applies, how is it accounted for in the not-for-profit setting?

3. When a not-for-profit organization receives a pledge of support, how is this accounted for relative to contributions?

4. How are investments held by not-for-profit organizations to be recorded?

■ FINANCIAL STATEMENT ANALYSIS

Table 3.37   Financial Statement Analysis COMPLETE THIS TABLE

Terms	Search Recommended* (Semicolons are not part of the search but are used as separators.)	Citation for Definition: Provide Full Reference	Other Searches You Would Suggest
Financial statement analysis	"financial statement analysis"		
Line items	selection of line items relationship to financial analysis and comparability		
Classes of current assets	"current assets"; "classes of current assets are"		
FIFO	FIFO financial statement analysis		
Inflation	"inflation"		
Dividends	"dividends"; dividends financial statement analysis		
Declaration of a dividend	"declaration of a dividend"		
Payment of a dividend	payment of a dividend		
100 percent payout	paying out all earnings in the form of dividends		

Table 3.37 Financial Statement Analysis   Page **3-73**

Terms	Search Recommended* (Semicolons are not part of the search but are used as separators.)	Citation for Definition: Provide Full Reference	Other Searches You Would Suggest
Working capital	"working capital" and defin*		
Cash flow per share	"cash flow per share"		
Ratio analysis	analysis with ratios		
Stock dividend	"stock dividend"		
Treasury stock	treasury stock is def*		
Stock split	"stock split"		
Debt to equity ratio	"debt to equity ratio"		
Interim financial statements	"interim financial statements"; "interim financial reporting"		
Discrete view	"discrete approach"		
Integral view	integral approach interim reporting		
Segment disclosures	"segment disclosures"; "operating segment disclosures"; segment$ disclosure*$		

Terms	Search Recommended* (Semicolons are not part of the search but are used as separators.)	Citation for Definition: Provide Full Reference	Other Searches You Would Suggest
Back orders	sales orders unfulfilled; "unfulfilled commitments"		

*Access FARS, click on File, Open, Nfo, Open, and select FASB-OP, click Search, enter query.

Problems

1. Although a number of line items may appear in the current section of a balance sheet, what are the four general classes of current assets into which these items can be categorized?

2. Kimberly Smith Enterprises has used the FIFO method of inventory over a period of rapid inflation. The corporation has a policy of 100 percent payout of net income in the form of dividends. Recently, the company has noticed a steep decline in net income and in volume of sales. Back orders have climbed. What is the probable problem?

3. Does each of the following transactions increase (I), decrease (D), or have no effect (N) on the ratio of debt to equity (i.e., total liabilities divided by the sum of total liabilities and total stockholders' equity)? (1) a two-for-one stock split, (2) the declaration and payment of a cash dividend, (3) the declaration of a 5 percent stock dividend, (4) issuance of stock, (5) purchased treasury stock.

4. Why doesn't the FASB permit cash flow per share to be reported? Note that some respondents to the exposure draft for the statement of cash flows asked if the board intended to preclude the reporting of per-unit amounts of cash flow that were distributable under the terms of a partnership agreement or other agreement between an enterprise and its owner. How do you believe the FASB responded to this question? Explain.

5. Many respondents to the statement of cash flow exposure draft commented negatively as to the usefulness of working capital as a concept of funds. They questioned its relevance, since positive working capital was not necessarily an indication of liquidity and negative working capital was not necessarily an indication of illiquidity. Do you agree with this overwhelming majority view of responses? Why or why not?

6. What are the major classes of ratios and what is the information content of each class?

7. Distinguish between the discrete and the integral method to interim reporting. Which is the approach embraced by generally accepted accounting principles? Do you agree with GAAP?

8. Describe the reporting requirements for segment operations and how they might be used by an investor.

Table 3.38 Internal Control Design and Evaluation   Page **3-75**

■ INTERNAL CONTROL DESIGN AND EVALUATION

Table 3.38   Internal Control Design and Evaluation COMPLETE THIS TABLE

Terms	Search Recommended* (Semicolons are not part of the search but are used as separators.)	Citation for Definition: Provide Full Reference	Other Searches You Would Suggest
Internal control	"internal control"		
Sequence checks	completeness;		
	counting documents sequence		
Receiving reports	receiving goods		
Small business	"small business"		
Vacation	"vacation"		
Bank checks	"checks"		
Paid invoices	paid invoices		
Control risk	control risk		
Board of directors	board of directors		
Situation pressures	situation pressures legal;		
	economic or legal pressure		
fraud	fraud$		

*Access FARS, click on File, Open, Nfo, Open, and select FASB-OP, click Search, enter query.

Problems

1. A manager was asked whether periodic sequence checks were made of receiving reports. The manager responded, "No, but the receiving reports are prenumbered." Evaluate the control implications of this verbal exchange.

2. A friend of yours has a small business. Her CPA asked her the following questions: (a) What is done when employees are on vacation? (b) What is done when one employee goes to lunch? She asks you why the CPA made these inquiries. How would you respond? What are desirable responses to these questions from a control standpoint?

3. In your review of a company's internal controls, the following practices were observed. (a) Whenever one of the two normal check signers plans to be out of the office for a day, he will sign a set of twenty blank checks to ensure that his absence won't hinder business operations. (b) When payments are made, original invoices from suppliers are filed; no notation is made on these invoices to indicate that they have been paid. Comment on the risks posed by these practices.

4. The concept of corporate governance has long been debated, particularly in terms of who should serve on the board of directors. Some contend that representatives of labor, owners, suppliers, customers, the community, and management should be a part of the board. What do you think is a desirable composition of a board of directors, and why? What are the implications for internal control of your recommendations for membership?

5. What types of situational pressures do you believe might motivate individuals to commit fraud against a company?

APPENDIX: ADVANCED SEARCH
CAPABILITIES OF FARS

The following materials describe how the advanced search options can be accessed and applied with the Financial Accounting Research System (FARS). The advanced capabilities can be helpful in crafting searches. For example, the frequency count for each of the words included in a search command can help tailor the Boolean logic to better address the issue of interest. This resource is available within FARS.

Advanced Query

Search, Advanced Query

Purpose
Use the advanced query to unleash the full power of the Folio Views query syntax.
Advanced query gives you complete access to the Folio Views query syntax. This syntax helps you focus and refine your searches through the use of Boolean operators, wildcards, proximity operators, and scope limitations.

See also query (in the Primer—Chapter 1) for more information on performing simple searches.

> *Note:* Folio Views 4.x can open and search on Folio Views 3.x infobases. However, the query syntax and options for the two are different. Basic Boolean, phrase, and wildcard queries should work fine on both. For advanced searches, there are some differences you need to be aware of. See "Differences Between the Folio Views 4.x and 3.x Query Syntaxes" for more information.

¹See Table 3.A-1 at the end of this Appendix for a summary chart of the query syntax.

Steps
The following procedures are detailed in this section:
- Searching the infobase
- Searching a subset of the infobase
- Performing a relevancy ranked search
- Performing a heading search
- Changing the view of your search results

Searching the Infobase
To search all text in the infobase:
1. Choose **Advanced Query** from the **Search** menu. Figure 3.A-1 shows the dialog box.

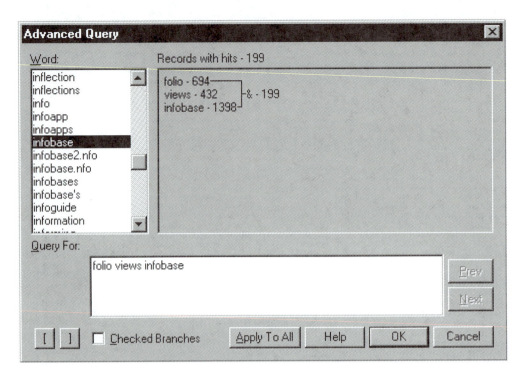

Figure 3.A-1 Advanced Query dialog box

2.   Type the words you wish to search for, separated by a space or the appropriate operator.

•You may search by keyword (not using any specific operators). For example:

paragraph formatting options

•You may search for an exact phrase. Enclose the phrase in quotation marks. For example:

"searching the infobase"

•You may use Boolean operators (and, or, not, exclusive or). For example:

search and help
search or help
search not help
search xor help

•You may use wildcards (single character, multiple character, word form, synonym). For example:

run?
run*
run%
run$

•You may use proximity operators to specify how close terms must be. For example:

"phrase search"/5

•If you wish to modify a previous query, click the **Prev** button next to the **Query For** box to display the previous query.

•Note that as you type, the Query dialog attempts to complete the word you are typing with a word contained in the infobase. If the word is correct, press the Enter key and type the next term.

•Queries may be up to 2048 characters in length.

3.   If desired, choose **Checked Branches** at the bottom of the dialog to search only the checked branches of the table of contents.

•If you have not selected any branches in the <u>Contents</u> pane, do not select this option. Doing so will result in zero hits (you will be searching an empty set).

•To select branches in the <u>Contents</u> pane, click in the <u>Contents</u> pane, choose <u>Show Check Boxes</u> from the <u>View</u> menu, and then click in the checkboxes next to the headings in the <u>Contents</u> pane.

4.   Choose **OK** to apply the search to the current infobase. Choose **Apply to All** to apply the search to all open infobases.

For more information on selecting branches in the **Contents** pane, see **Show Check Boxes**.

Note: Depending on how the infobase was created, a simple search may or may not search in pop-ups and notes within the infobase. The infobase author may specify whether pop-ups and notes are searched by default. See New for additional information on setting the options for infobase creation. See the <u>Misc</u> tab in the <u>Properties</u> dialog for the settings for the infobase.

Searching a Subset of the Infobase

Changing the scope of your search allows you to focus on a particular subset of the infobase. <u>Views</u> defaults to searching the entire infobase unless a specific scope is selected.

You may limit the scope of your search to a particular contents heading, level, field, highlighter, note, group, or pop-up. To set the scope of your search:

1.   Choose **Advanced Query** from the **Search** menu.

2.   Click the left bracket [at the bottom of the dialog (or type in a left square bracket). The Word list changes to display the general search Scopes in the infobase.

3.   Select the general scope you wish to search (contents, field, group, headings, highlighter, level, note, partition, or pop-up).

    •The Scope list changes to display the names of the available specific scopes (the names of the levels, fields, highlighters, or groups, etc.)

    •Notes and pop-ups are not named for searching purposes. Skip to step 5 if searching in notes or pop-ups.

    •Some query options are not displayed in the dialog but are still valid (such as rank and heading). See Advanced Query Constructions for more information.

4.   Double-click the specific scope you wish to search.

    •You can also scroll to the name using the up and down arrows and then press CTRL+Enter.

5.   Select the **Query For** box and move the insertion point after the colon or the right bracket]. Type the words, phrases, or patterns you wish to search for.

    •Field, Headings, Highlighter, and Level searches require the search terms to follow a colon.

    •Contents and Group searches require the search terms to follow the right bracket; no colon is used. Skip step 6 for these scope searches.

    •You may use Boolean operators (and, or, not, exclusive or), wildcards, and proximity operators, and may perform phrase searches.

6.   Click the right bracket] (or type a right square bracket), if you did not in step 5. This closes the current scope.

7.   If desired, choose **Checked Branches** at the bottom of the dialog to search only the checked branches of the table of contents.

    •If you have not selected any branches in the <u>Contents</u> pane, do not select this option. Doing so will result in zero hits (you will be searching an empty set).

    •To select branches in the <u>Contents</u>, click in the <u>Contents</u> pane, choose <u>Show Check Boxes</u> from the <u>View</u> menu, and then click in the checkboxes next to the headings in the <u>Contents</u> pane.

8.   Choose **OK** or **Apply to All**.

    •**OK** applies the query to the current infobase.

    •**Apply to All** applies the query to all open infobases.

For more information on selecting branches in the **Contents** pane, see <u>Show Check Boxes</u>.

Performing a Relevancy Ranked Search

The simplest way to perform a relevancy ranked search is to use the Query dialog or the Query toolbar. You, however, also may construct a ranked query in the Advanced Query dialog or use this syntax to create a ranked search in a custom query template. (The Query Template Editor is included with the Folio Builder product.) To find a specified number of records most relevant to your search topic (rather than all records having anything at all to do with your search topic):

1.   Choose Advanced Query from the Search menu. The Advanced Query dialog appears.
2.   Type

     [Rank

3.   Enter the number of items you want ranked, followed by a closing bracket.

     [Rank 10]

     •Think of this as the top ten list. If you want to the see the ten most relevant items, enter 10. If you want to see the one hundred most relevant items, enter 100.

     •You must enter a whole number (no fractions or decimal values permitted).

4.   Enter the query you wish to perform.

     •*Note:* If you wish to specify a partition, you must do so before the rank. For example:

     [Partition Chapter][Rank 15]

5.   Choose **OK** to apply the query to the infobase.

     •See Query for information on how Folio Views determines relevance.

     •See Ranking Queries for additional ranking options.

Performing a Heading Search

Heading searches allow you to specify a subsection of the infobase to search without having to specify the entire heading structure (as is required with the Contents search).

> *Note:* This option is not available for all infobases. A special index must be created when the infobase is built for heading searches to work. This option may be set in the New dialog (choose Options).

To perform a heading search:

1.   Choose Advanced Query from the Search menu. The Advanced Query dialog appears.
2.   Type

     [Headings

     •Note that this option is not available for all infobases. The infobase must have a special option set when it is created for this to work.

3.   Enter the level name for the headings you wish to search.

     •The level name must be one of the levels in the infobase. Usually, it is not the first level.

     •For example:

     [Headings Chapter

4.   If desired, enter the specific heading name you wish to search. End the scope with a closed bracket,].

     •The heading name corresponds to an actual heading in the infobase, such as Advanced Query or Chapter 12 - Horticulture and You.

     •The level name and heading name must be separated by commas.

     •Subheadings may also be listed. Separate subheadings by commas.

     •For example:

[Headings Chapter, Advanced Query]

[Headings Chapter, Advanced Query,Purpose]

[Headings Chapter, Chapter 12 - Horticulture and You,Overview]

5.   After the closing bracket, enter any terms or other query constructs that you wish to
     search for. You may enter any other query constructs except partition or rank.
See Headings for more information.

Changing the View of Your Search Results

After performing a query, you may wish to view the search hits in a variety of ways. The default
is to show you all records in the infobase. This allows you to view the search hits in context. You
may also view only those records that have hits or an entire partition that has hits. Or, using the
HitList pane, you may view the most relevant hits (if a ranked query is performed).
To view records or partitions with hits:

1.   Perform a query. See Searching the Infobase, Searching a Subset of the Infobase, or
     Performing a Relevancy Ranked Search for more information.
2.   Choose **Records With Hits** or **Partitions With Hits** from the **View** menu. All of the
     records which contain search hits are gathered into a single view (extraneous records
     disappear from the view).
3.   Choose **All Records** from the **View** menu again to restore the view.

To use the HitList:

1.   Perform a ranked query. See Performing a Relevancy Ranked Search or Simple Ranked
     Query for more information.
2.   Click the **All** tab at the bottom of the infobase view to display the hit list. The most
     relevant hits are displayed first in the hit list.
3.   Double-click an item in the HitList to go directly to it in the infobase. Click a column
     header in the hit list to change how the items are sorted (ascending or descending
     alphanumeric order).

Table 3.A-1 Advanced Query options

Operator or Scope	Example
And	one two one & two one and two
Or	me | you me or you
Not	^him not him her ^ him
Exclusive or (Xor)	apples ~ oranges apples xor oranges
Phrase	"to be or not" "fourscore and seven"
Single character wildcard	wom?n g??b?r
Multiple character wildcard	work* h*t*
Ordered proximity	"united states of america"/10
Unordered proximity	"uncle sams army"@7
Record proximity	"smith jones theft deny"#5
Sentence proximity	"search query"/s "search operators"@s
Paragraph proximity	"create build infobase"/p "index stop words"@p
Stem (word form)	run% great%
Thesaurus (synonym)	flying$ alterations$
Contents	[Contents Old Testament,Genesis] noah and ark
Partition	[Partition Chapter] advanced query
Rank	[Rank 10] dogs chase cats
Fields	[Field judge: scalia]
Range	[Field weapons: > .357 < .45]
Highlighters	[Highlighter humor: marx | stooge]
Pop-ups and notes	[Note words to find] or [Popup my favorite feature]
Groups	[Group animals] warthog lion rat
Headings	[Heading <level name>,<heading path>: query] [Heading Chapter: import files] [Heading Chapter, Open: import files]
Levels	[Level <level name>: <query>] [Level Chapter: reconcile shadow files]

4

CHAPTER 4 – BRAIN TEASERS:

Using FARS to Untangle the Mystery

Brain Teaser 1: Dissents Portending Future?

Always Read the Dissent

Buddy: I remember my undergraduate professor's suggestion that whenever we read a financial accounting standard, we should carefully read through the dissents, if any are reported.

Jeannie: It would seem with the reasonably small size of the Financial Accounting Standards Board, that the members could reach total consensus. Given the Statements of Financial Accounting Standards set generally accepted accounting principles for the entire country, why not require that at least all the board members be convinced before moving forward?

Buddy: Well, as a matter of fact, my understanding is that it was proposed to change the voting rules, not to total consensus, but to a different mix of required votes for approval, and it caused a real political debate. It seems many thought that the shift toward more approving votes being required was perceived to be a strategy that was intended to cause a stalemate, which would slow down the standard-setting process.

Jeannie: Oh, how could it get any slower? The stock options project began in the early 1980s and took well over a decade before the SFAS No. 123 was issued. I believe the pension projects spanned over a decade as well!

Buddy: You do have a point. Perhaps that is why timeliness is one of the virtues of accounting that could not withstand a total consensus requirement by the Board.

Jeannie: Well, I can tell you that sometimes the dissents seem more logical, or at least they accurately portend what will need additional attention in the future.

Buddy: Do you have something particular in mind?

Jeannie: As a matter of fact, I do. I vaguely remember hearing about a dissent that specifically warned that the way the statement had been written implied that a new materiality standard was being set. Well, that warning was ignored, and sure enough, a later statement had to be issued by the FASB to address that very point.... I am pretty sure it was associated with materiality.

Buddy: I, for one, would like to see that. Could you find the dissent, as well as the superseding SFAS, so we could look it over?

Jeannie: Thank goodness for technology: with the Boolean logic in FARS, I'm sure this should not be too difficult.... Let's go to the program and try.

Required:

Use the Financial Accounting Research System (FARS) to find the dissent to which Jeannie is referring, as well as the subsequent Statement of Financial Accounting Standards (SFAS) issued to correct the problem highlighted in the original pronouncement's dissent. If you had been a member of the original board, do you believe you would have joined the majority position or the dissent? Why or why not?

Brain Teaser 2: Hybrid Historical Cost and Market Value - Why the Mix?

What's A Hybrid?

Ken: I keep seeing in the financial press references to *hybrid* accounting. What's a hybrid?

Pat: The term I've seen just as often is *multiattribute* accounting. The point of the articles I've read seems to be that we accountants have not decided whether historical cost or market value is the "right" valuation basis, so now we have a hybrid throughout the balance sheet.

Ken: If the issue is between historical cost and market value, why is the term *multiattribute* popular? Doesn't the term *multi* mean more than just two choices?

Pat: Actually, far more than two values do appear on the balance sheet. Think about the lower of cost or market concept applied to inventory – that is neither a historical cost nor a market value, but a bit of a blend of the two. Then we have some estimates, such as net realizable receivables, that likewise blend historical cost transactions with a concurrent estimate of which of those amounts may prove to be uncollectible.

Ken: Now that you mention it, I do not even think that our historical cost and market value definitions are all of similar ilk. For example, we write down an historical cost of a fixed asset through depreciation and report book value thereafter. It would seem that book value is neither historical cost nor market value.

Pat: I have concern that when we say market value, many think of the New York Stock Exchange as the source of value, whereas many entities hold securities that are not traded on well-developed markets. The question becomes, what is the essence of market value that we do report in such cases?

Ken: I think the problem of hybrids is worsening. The concept of impairment accounting moves away from either a clear market value or a historical cost concept. It seems to often rely on an estimated cash flow projection based on tailored intended use of the asset in question. Without an arm's-length transaction and potentially no secondary market to speak of for specialized assets, it would seem that the basis of accounts in the balance sheet would have a plethora of definitions.

Pat: Multiattributes indeed! You know, I've been asked to speak on the topic of account valuation to a group of analysts. I think a great "take-away" would be examples of the basis of accounting presently in generally accepted accounting principles, especially how market value is defined in relation to various pronouncements.

Ken: I wonder if it would be possible to analyze the pros and cons of historical cost, market value, or some selected alternative basis of accounting.

Pat: That's a great idea! I certainly hope the standards would imply why the diversity of definitions has evolved. If not, just posing the question of 'why the difference' would be food for thought.

Ken: I'll give you a hand. Let's access FARS. You know, one angle to consider is that historical cost and market value equal one another at the date of acquisition. You could point that fact out and then pose the question, "So why and how do they differ?"

Required:

Use the Financial Accounting Research System (FARS) and prepare a table on all definitions you are able to identify as to the specific basis of accounting used in valuation. As you prepare the table, keep track of how you went about finding each definition and be prepared to brainstorm with colleagues about other effective means of identifying definitions of this type. In the table itself, be certain to include full citations and the succinct definitions found. Read the materials surrounding the excerpts to see if they can help you develop an explanation as to why the particular definition was included in the guidance. In other words, what are its comparative advantages relative to alternatives? In addition to preparing a table of citations and definitions as to basis of valuation, prepare a list of the pros and cons of historical cost relative to market value. Keep in mind that the table and the list are intended to be self-contained hand-outs for distribution to a group of professionals involved in financial statement analysis. By focusing on a particular audience, you may find it easier to develop a hand-out that effectively communicates.

Brain Teaser 3: Cash Basis or Accrual Basis?

Is Accrual Accounting Superior to Cash Basis?

Alicia: In the finance literature, there seems to be an emphasis on cash. Stock prices are discussed as the present value of future cash flows. Most of the capital budgeting applications in which investment decisions are made appear to focus on the cash required at acquisition and the cash flows expected during the life of that investment. If cash is so important, why is accrual accounting the focus in generally accepted accounting principles?

John: A problem with just following the cash is that you can collect cash or pay cash and really have little economic activity underlying those cash exchanges. Indeed, I can structure terms of payment almost any way I choose in a contract, including so-called balloon payments, where almost all the cash changes hands at the end of a contract. If all accounting statements did was track the cash, little information would be provided as to how the cash had actually been generated, invested, or lost.

Alicia: Last night on the news, there was a story about a college student who had managed to run up almost $20,000 in debt on his credit card, while still an undergraduate student. On a cash basis, if someone thought he had received that $20,000 for some actual economic service, that would clearly be way off the mark. I mean, cash acquired through debt has to be different from cash that one receives because he or she has performed some service or sold some asset. In fact, receiving cash from selling something is not at all the same as receiving cash as an employee for providing services. After all, you can only sell an asset once, whereas services can continue to be provided, generating recurring cash flows.

John: I remember someone once asserting that cash flow was all that was important, and accountants just "mess things up" by imposing the accrual accounting framework on the analysis of cash flows. It made no sense when I heard it, and the more I learn about economic activity, the less sense that assertion makes. Besides, we accountants, after all, do prepare statements of cash flow as well. However, we respect the differences in operating, financing, and investing activities.

Alicia: Of course, I've never quite understood why we call interest an operating item and not a financing item. Nonetheless, I agree that the Statement of Cash Flows alone or the publication of an entity's bank statement would in no way reflect performance effectively. Yet, it is obvious that many investors are at least confused as to the nature of accrual accounting and its importance relative to cash flow analysis.

John: I wonder whether generally accepted accounting principles explain the importance of accrual accounting relative to a cash basis?

Alicia: Let's find out.

Required:

Use the Financial Accounting Research System (FARS) to identify what standard setters have said as to the superiority of accrual accounting relative to a cash basis. Do you agree with the justification offered for accrual accounting? Explain.

Brain Teaser 4: Where Are Charitable Donations on Corporate Income Statements?

Why Is There No Line Item for Charitable Donations?

Christine: I believe in giving to charities, and I know that corporate America does as well. Yet, every time that I read a financial statement, even those from my socially responsible mutual fund companies, I notice that the income statement has no separate line item reporting charitable donations. My question is, why?

Christina: That's a good question. I would think companies would want credit for their charitable gifts.

Charlie: You no doubt have noticed, though, that very few line items appear on the income statement. I mean, it's not easy to discern what was spent on employees' salaries, or even whether research and development expenses were incurred, in some cases.

Christine: You're right about the simplicity of the usual income statement. I mean, a handful of line items are typical. The press releases tend to have even fewer line items. Yet, I know the Securities and Exchange Commission is a proponent of full disclosure.

Christina: Sometimes I have been able to find additional detail in the notes to the financial statements, even though it is not provided as a line item. Yet, I do not recall seeing details on charitable donations in the notes, so your question remains unanswered.

Charlie: Well, given generally accepted accounting principles are supposed to provide guidance on reporting, there must be some explanation for the line items we see reported and those that appear to be missing.

Christine: You're right, let's see if we can solve the puzzle.

Sophia: Can I help?

Required:

Use the Financial Accounting Research System (FARS) to find an explanation for why certain line items dominate the income statements of public companies. Does the absence of a line item mean that expense was not incurred? Specifically, is the apparent absence of charitable donations as a line item indicative of corporate companies not making contributions? Explain. Choose a major company in which you have an interest and access its Web page. See if that company home Web page references community activities and charitable donations. Note the scope and types of disclosures provided. Does what you find correspond to the income statement presentations by that company? Is what you find reconcilable to the guidance you located in FARS? Explain.

Brain Teaser 5: Deferred Debits and Deferred Credits

What Is the Nature of a Deferred Debit and How Does It Differ from a Deferred Credit?

Cynthia: I thought that accounts within information systems were supposed to be clearly labeled to communicate with financial statement users. Yet, I have seen references to deferred debits and to deferred credits, and I find those titles unclear. I mean, what is a deferred debit? Is it a balance sheet item? How should it be classified and why? How is it different from a deferred credit? What is the effect on cash flows of such items?

John Jr.: You always have fifty questions. The basic question to which you really want an answer is from where do they come: what generates a deferred debit or a deferred credit?

Cynthia: You're right. That is the basic question, and I suppose if we understand the answer of how they originate, we could deduce the answer to some of my other questions.

John Jr.: I remember a professor recounting how deferred taxes were being referred to as 'UGOs' or 'Unidentified Growing Objects' because their size relative to total assets was anything but trivial.

Cynthia: I also recall some discussion of *dangling debits* when the standard-setting community was debating the issue of how derivatives and hedges should be recorded. I don't remember any details, but I do think more than taxes are involved in the area of these deferred debits and credits.

John Jr.: There is one way to find out. Let's search FARS and see if we can find some explanations for when deferred debits and credits arise.

Required:

Use the Financial Accounting Research System (FARS) to answer each of the questions posed by both Cynthia and John Jr.

Brain Teaser 6: Time Value of Money: Gone Today but Here Tomorrow?

Why the Inconsistent Attention to Time Value of Money in Evaluating Impairments?

Nancy: I'm more than a little perplexed.

Kenny: What about?

Nancy: I've been reading the guidance on fixed assets and the treatment of impairments.

Kenny: Did you have insomnia last night, or what?

Nancy: Seriously, I have a client with a large book value for fixed assets, and I have to determine whether our team needs to accord attention to the area of impairment. And the problem I have is that it seems to me that present value is not used at all in considering whether current book values exceed future cash flows. However, if the future cash flows in nominal, undiscounted dollars are expected to fall below the recorded book value, then it's a whole new ballgame.

Kenny: I see your point. We had an impairment situation at a client last year, and you are right that when an impairment trigger occurs, the impairment guidance requires that future cash flows be discounted to evaluate the amount that should be recorded as the basis.

Nancy: I find it more than a little curious that time value of money is used for cash flows when you value impaired assets, while they are not used to determine impairment. Why is this the case?

Kenny: Well, it would certainly make a difference if the trigger involved discounting, wouldn't it? Now you have me perplexed.

Nancy: Let's take a careful look at the present value literature and the impairment guidance and see if we can figure out the reason for the inconsistency.

Elizabeth: Can I help?

Required:

Use the Financial Accounting Research System (FARS) to find out the logic of time value of money concepts being used in a manner that appears to be inconsistent. Explain how you believe fixed assets would be affected if the present value of money were consistently used both in assessing triggers for impairment analysis and in valuing assets deemed to be impaired. Provide a numeric example to illustrate the effects described. Be certain to clearly state your assumptions and show the related calculations to demonstrate your perspective and related conclusions.

Brain Teaser 7: What Do We Record When Interest Rates Diverge?

Stated, Implicit, Imputed, and Effective Interest Rates: What If They Diverge?

Bill: We have to record some interest for the financing element of the transaction.

Steve: The question is, what amount? There is no stated rate on the instrument itself.

Bill: Even if there were a stated rate, since the instrument's transaction value was different from the face of the instrument, an effective interest would have to be recorded, and that would differ from whatever stated rate was reported. Of course, that does not even apply here.

Steve: One approach would be to determine an implicit rate, whereby we back into the rate by looking at the cash flows.

Bill: That means we have to know the cash flows on both sides of the transaction, right? Do we have that detail?

Steve: I'm not sure if we do or not.

Bill: The other alternative is an imputed rate. That entails looking at the borrowing rate on other instruments. I think we need to do some research before we make a decision.

Steve: I read you. I'll access FARS and prepare a table of definitions of stated, effective, implicit, and imputed rate. Alongside the definitions, I will see if the standards provide a clear example of where each approach is to be used.

Bill: If it is not clear which definition and context fits our transaction, what should we do if the approaches diverge? While you're doing the research, be on the lookout for whether these are mutually exclusive definitions, or whether there is some basis for choosing from among varying approaches.

Steve: I'll see what I can do.

Required:

Use the Financial Accounting Research System (FARS) to prepare the table described. In your judgment, are the definitions and examples you have identified mutually exclusive, or is there an overlap that requires judgment? If you were to apply these definitions to a single transaction and found there to be a divergence, how would you proceed? Why might the approaches generate different interest rates for a single transaction? Could a single company apply different definitions to multiple transactions? Choose a company and access its 10-K filing from http://www.sec.gov. Read through the financial statements and accompanying notes, and list every interest rate identified, alongside the type of transaction to which it relates. Why might a single company record disparate interest rates on different transactions?

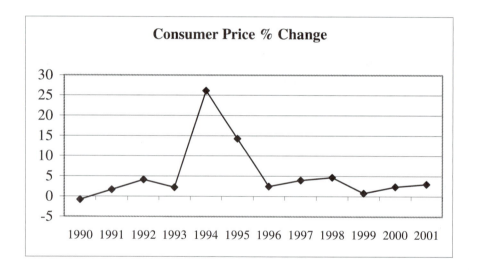

Figure 4.7-1 Given economic rates vary over time, is it surprising reported rates of any given company likewise vary?

Brain Teaser 8: Inventoriable Costs?

What's All the Fuss about _Dot-Coms_?

Cheryl: It seems as though I can't pick up a newspaper or business journal without seeing some commentary on the accounting practices of _dot-coms_.

Jim: I don't see what the fuss is about.

Cheryl: Well, I read an article that reminded me of an old case I had when I was in cost accounting called "The Clever President,"…only in reverse.

Jim: Oh, I think we had that case, too. I'm foggy on recollection, but wasn't it about some CEO who negotiated to be compensated on reported income when he took the helm at a troubled company, proceeded to report big profits, and then resigned, leaving with a huge bonus?

Cheryl: Yes, and the so-called cleverness had to do with shoveling costs into inventory, building a stockpile of two years' worth of sales, and thereby enhancing gross profit and, in turn, net income.

Jim: Remind me of why that worked.

Cheryl: Well, the idea has to do with fixed cost allocation. Since fixed costs don't change as production increases, by stockpiling inventory through doubling or even tripling production, the fixed costs were spread over two to three times as many units, cutting the per-unit allocation to only a half or a third of its previous level.

Jim: In other words, the inventoriable costs in total grew as inventory grew, but the per-unit cost shrunk because of the per-unit fixed cost assignment. Now I remember.

Cheryl: As I understand the _dot.com_ debates, a good deal has to do with whether things should have been inventoried rather than treated as period costs. You might look at the problem as the reverse of "The Clever President" case.

Jim: I'm confused. If "The Clever President" case is supposed to illustrate an abuse of accounting, then how is it that the opposite is also an abuse?

Cheryl: Well, two wrongs never make a right.

Jim: I hear you, but I still don't agree.

Cheryl: Okay, here's an example of the problem. The *dot.coms* have a line item they call "fulfillment costs." These costs are described as including costs attributable to receiving, inspecting, and warehousing inventories, as well as picking, packaging, and preparing customers' orders for shipment. The line item of fulfillment costs is being included in marketing expenses as a period cost. In other words, they are not being treated as a product cost at all. The question raised is whether they should be inventoriable costs.

Jim: What's the harm if everything hits net income anyway? It sounds conservative to me.

Cheryl: Remember, conservatism for its own sake is not laudable. Accounting is intended to be neutral. Moreover, *where* something hits the income statement matters. By taking inventoriable costs and placing them as a period expense, the gross profit looks a great deal better than it ought to look to investors and others supplying capital. I've seen estimates that argue this maneuver can effectively quadruple the gross profit on sales.

Jim: Why have the *dot.coms* presumed they have the choice of not placing at least some of these fulfillment costs into cost of goods sold? Isn't generally accepted accounting clear on this matter?

Cheryl: Well, we certainly have to figure the situation out, because we have a new client that is a *dot.com*, and I'm certain we'll be asked for our view on the classification of costs. Let's see what we can find in the authoritative literature.

Required:

Use the Financial Accounting Research System (FARS) to provide a basis from which Jim and Cheryl can formulate a position as to the appropriate classification of the fulfillment cost components described in this case. Provide citations and key excerpts, and prioritize the guidance identified, based on the generally accepted accounting principles (GAAP) hierarchy. Given your research, what is your view regarding the appropriate accounting practice?

Brain Teaser 9: Valuation of Inventory and Purchase Commitments

How Many Ways Are There to Value Inventory? What About Purchase Commitments?

Glen: I read somewhere that an enormous number of choices are available for valuing inventory. I thought the main approach was historical cost. In other words, what you pay for it is the value of the inventory.

Jerry: What about retailers? I know there's a retail method of accounting, and there's an approach that records mark-ups and mark-downs.

Glen: I wonder at how the retail method can work, given profits are not supposed to be recorded until sales are made.

Jerry: Oh, I think it is similar to removing transfer pricing profits from the financial statements for third parties. In other words, the profit embedded in the retail valuation is adjusted out of the numbers to ensure against premature profit recognition.

Glen: What about purchase commitments? These days, sole-source suppliers are popular. If a purchase commitment is made to that supplier, is that purchase commitment valued in the financial statements? If no valuation appears in the balance sheet, is there disclosure required in the notes?

Jerry: That's an interesting question. We know that executory contracts such as compensation packages are commitments to purchase services of an employee, and yet I don't believe we record those commitments.

Glen: I wonder what the reasoning is regarding whether purchase commitments are recorded and, as you say, whether they are recorded for goods but not for services.

Jerry: We can find out the answer. Let's explore the FARS database and see if it can help sort this out.

Required:

Use the Financial Accounting Research System (FARS) to provide a listing of all of the approaches cited regarding the valuation of inventory. Likewise, describe the accounting treatment prescribed for purchase commitments. Be specific as to whether valuations appear on the financial statements and/or in the notes to the financial statements. Determine if there is a different treatment for executory contracts such as executives' compensation, relative to purchase commitments. What do you believe is the reasoning for the accounting treatments you identify. Specifically, why is there such a variety of inventory valuations permitted? Why is the treatment distinctive for inventory relative to purchase commitments? Explain the approach prescribed for executory contracts.

Brain Teaser 10: Are Capital Expenditure Numbers Comparable?

Why Might Capital Expenditures of One Company Differ from Those of Another?

Shareena: I have been asked to analyze the relative capital expenditures by a set of competitors in three industries. I'm to include a comparison of property, plant, and equipment investments by each entity. I have set up a prototype spreadsheet for collecting information from the financial statements, and I am wondering what other details I should record. It will be much easier if I can identify what I need so that I don't have to "go to the well" twice.

Alan: Describe what you have so far.

Shareena: I thought I would track the last ten years. I will record the beginning and ending balances of property, plant, and equipment – including the accumulated depreciation numbers. In addition, from the cash flow statement I will collect all purchases and sales, as well as retirements of fixed assets. I thought I should record whatever details there are on useful life and salvage values. What do you think?

Alan: You're on the right track. However, what about self-constructed assets? What are the industries you are analyzing? Is it likely that self-constructed assets would be a prominent part of their operations?

Shareena: I hadn't even thought about that dimension. Indeed, one of the industries in particular is likely to self-construct assets.

Alan: That means you will want to consider the element of capitalized interest. Consider the hypothetical that two of the companies you are analyzing both self-construct assets, but one has high leverage, while the second one has virtually no leverage.

Shareena: I'm not that acquainted with interest capitalization. Where should I look to gain a background on that issue, so I can decide what information I ought to track?

Alan: I suggest you begin with FARS. Why not prepare an executive summary as to how interest capitalization can influence the companies you are analyzing as to their investment in property, plant, and equipment? Be specific as to what attributes of the company can influence what actually is recorded on the balance sheet, as well as both the cash flow statement and the income statement. Then integrate the implications from your summary into your data collection spreadsheet. I'll be happy to review your next draft.

Shareena: Thanks. As usual, your assistance is invaluable.

Required:

Use the Financial Accounting Research System (FARS) to draft the executive summary and to propose a worksheet format for data collection. Be specific as to the information fields you need to collect and why. Be certain in the executive summary to include specific cites to the key determinants of self-constructed asset valuations according to generally accepted accounting principles (GAAP). Your executive summary should completely address Alan's hypothetical. From a managerial accounting perspective, would you suggest that other information be considered beyond the GAAP framework? Why or why not?

Brain Teaser 11: Why the Proposed Staff Accounting Bulletin (SAB)?

What GAAP Does Not Require

Aamer: I make a point to browse the EDGAR site of the SEC periodically, just to review current proposals and to determine which ones have been finalized and what they have to say.

Denise: So do I. That Web site is such a resource, and so easy to access.

Aamer: I noticed a proposal that relates to estimates of useful life and salvage value of property, plant, and equipment. The interesting aspect of the proposed Staff Accounting Bulletin was its recognition that generally accepted accounting principles do not require certain disclosures.

Denise: I've been thinking about the proposal in light of industry practices. I was preparing a presentation on diversity within industries and noted that some companies disclose useful lives for buildings of three to twenty-five years, with others in the same industry reporting twenty to fifty years. Ranges are reported by some entities, while other companies give a single figure, like thirty years or forty years.

Aamer: It's not just in regard to buildings. I noted that machinery and equipment disclosures often have ranges, such as four years to twenty years.

Denise: I recall the proposed SAB's interest in disclosure requirements pertaining to adjustments in useful life and salvage value.

Aamer: There is an irony historically. I remember when I was an undergraduate student, the 10-K SEC filings had some detailed exhibits for Property, Plant, and Equipment that provided some added insights regarding accumulated depreciation, but those were eliminated from the requirements. I think it was part of a simplification movement.

Denise: What goes around comes around. I wonder if any changes in GAAP have occurred in the interim that might explain why the SAB has been proposed at this point in time.

Aamer: Why don't we prepare a joint analysis? It might be a basis for writing a commentary to the SEC proposal and could also lead to an article comparing industry practices.

Denise: Good idea. Let's begin with a catalogue of current GAAP, including the citations, date of requirement, and specific guidance in the areas of useful life, salvage value, and changes therein.

Aamer: Then we can expand to an actual practices analysis, using LEXIS/NEXIS.

Required:

Use the Financial Accounting Research System (FARS) to prepare the catalogue of current GAAP associated with useful life, salvage value, and changes in either of these estimates. Focus on disclosure requirements associated with any of these three dimensions. Based on your work, explain why you believe the SEC might have decided to propose additional disclosures in this area. Would you support such increased disclosures? Why or why not? Select three companies in the same industry and collect information as to what they disclose regarding the three dimensions of interest – useful life, salvage value, and changes in either. Explain why you believe these estimates are sufficiently informative or ought to be revised. If the latter, what specific changes would you propose?

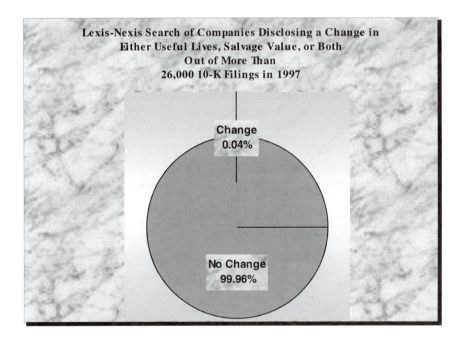

Figure 4.11-1 An example of the relative rarity of disclosure of changes in useful life and salvage value

Brain Teaser 12: Is Goodwill Indefinite or Indeterminate?

If Indeterminate Duration, Why Capitalize Goodwill but Not Research and Development?

Reneé: The politics and theory of accounting sometimes are hard to separate. I was reading that in order to gain support for the elimination of pooling of interests accounting, the FASB had decided not to require amortization of goodwill. What is it that justifies a presumed indefinite life for goodwill?

Raj: You don't find compromise to be sufficient justification?

Reneé: Not at all. For the standards to guide professionals in reaching judgments, I think we need to retain the elegance of theoretical justification.

Raj: I suppose the theoretical explanation for no amortization is that the asset will have to be evaluated for impairment.

Reneé: Well, that may be true, but consider the fact that impairment tests are now called for with plant and equipment, but depreciation is still recorded. It would seem that in parallel fashion, we could do impairment tests on goodwill and nonetheless amortize the balance.

Raj: It must be some sort of analogy between land and goodwill, contending that both are indefinite in life, since land is not depreciated.

Reneé: I can buy the idea that as long as land is not being depleted, it should hold its value, but I have difficulty seeing the analogy between tangible land and intangible goodwill.

Raj: What about works of art? They have intangible value: Picasso is certainly not valued based on the cost of the canvass and oils.

Reneé: It's not the valuation of the intangible initially that is the issue, it's the concept that the value persists indefinitely. After all, the premium paid on a company that is merged into another would not seem to rival a Picasso or Monet in durability of intrinsic value.

Raj: I seem to remember that many years back, a common approach was to capitalize goodwill and then not to amortize it at all. A debate ensued regarding how one should compare companies with goodwill on their balance sheets to other entities that never made acquisitions and hence had no such goodwill on their balance sheets.

Reneé: Some analysts reportedly set goodwill aside in their evaluations, which in itself raises questions as to its perceived value, let alone its indefinite value status!

Raj: I have to admit that I find it ironic that an ill-specified asset category such as goodwill is capitalized and potentially unamortized, while research and development expenses – by and large – are expensed.

Reneé: The benefits are deemed indeterminate for R&D since so many projects are initiated in order to achieve the single commercially successful product or process. Of course, many a failed merger fills the history of business. One thing for certain, the argument of no amortization of goodwill because the life is indeterminate would seem to argue more for expensing than indefinite capitalization.

Raj: Isn't it somewhat incredulous that goodwill is deemed indeterminate or indefinite in life when 10-K filings have repeatedly presented estimated amortization periods, often ranging from five to forty years?

Reneé: I'm enough of a history buff that I'm very curious about the historical development, as well as the contrasts drawn among intangibles such as goodwill relative to research and development.

Raj: I have a minor in history, and I firmly believe that those who do not have an understanding of the past are destined to repeat its mistakes.

Required:

Use the Financial Accounting Research System (FARS) to provide an historical account, with appropriate citations as to how goodwill has been accounted for at various points in time, as well as research and development (R&D). Check the FASB web site http://www.fasb.org for related details and proposals that may not yet be reflected in FARS. Can you find an elegant theoretical framework to explain the accounting treatment of each, as well as the possibility of no amortization of goodwill – remembering the presumption that impairment analysis will be required in the presence of certain triggers? Prepare a brief presentation of your framework or an explanation of why you believe the treatments are irreconcilable without reference to the political context of standard-setting activities.

Brain Teaser 13: Expected to Be Refinanced?

Is Anticipating Refinancing Analogous to a Gain Contingency?

Hector: I don't understand why you are making me reclassify my long-term debt as current. You and I both know that I will be refinancing before the maturity date hits, and then I will rollover the existing debt into a new instrument, and never have a real short-term payout in the current fiscal year.

Ira: I know you are unhappy about the reclassification, but generally accepted accounting principles are very clear on this issue.

Hector: I thought substance was supposed to dominate form. Your balance sheet portrayal certainly seems to emphasize form and ignore the substance of the way we do business.

Ira: The substance of the situation is that you have not as yet renegotiated or refinanced that debt. If you were to anticipate refinancing, in substance, you would be including a sort of gain contingency attitude in your accounting treatment. We conservative accountants do not anticipate gains.

Hector: How did gain enter the picture? I'm talking about the balance sheet, not the income statement!

Ira: I know. I was just making an analogy. I mean, you cannot be certain that the refinancing will occur until it happens.

Hector: Actually, you've made not refinancing more of a possibility. Lenders want healthy current ratios, and thanks to your classification of that debt, the economic picture for my business has really been tarnished.

Ira: You made my point. If a possibility exists that refinancing will not occur, then the last thing you should do is call the debt with maturity nine months from now a long-term commitment. Your credibility with your financial statement users would really 'go south.'

Hector: Is there any action I can take to change this short-term liability to a long-term liability?

Required:

Use the Financial Accounting Research System (FARS) to provide an answer to Hector. Be specific as to what generally accepted accounting principles require with respect to the classification of debt to be refinanced. Do you believe that Ira made a good analogy when he mentioned the issue of gain contingency? Explain your point of view and include citations from FARS to support your perspective.

Brain Teaser 14: Extinguishing Debt Is Extraordinary?

How Can This Be, Unless It's Troubled Debt Forgiven?

Kristin: I was reading over the financial statements of a number of public companies for some research I've been doing. I have been paying particular attention to the nature of extraordinary items. I cannot get over the fact that the extinguishment of debt is reported as an extraordinary item. I mean, what is extraordinary about paying off one's debt?

Ali: Good question. Are you certain it was just paid off in the normal course of business? I mean, could it be that the company had some hard times and negotiated some type of troubled debt arrangement with its creditors? I could see where that might be something out of the ordinary.

Kristin: Interesting that you should mention troubled debt restructuring. Another thing that struck me in reading through this set of financial statements was the incidence of gains from troubled debt by the very companies in trouble. I mean, it just does not make sense to me that one can generate gains from borrowing, let alone from getting into an economic hardship situation.

Ali: It does sound ironic. It seems to me we need to find out the whole story. I mean, what is the definition of an extraordinary item? What is the appropriate accounting treatment when debt is extinguished in the normal course of business, and why? When troubled debt restructuring occurs, why might a gain result?

Kristin: And for completeness, how is the gain from troubled debt restructuring to be recorded? Is it an extraordinary item, and if it is not, why is that – given the treatment of the extinguishment of debt?

Ali: I've read where such troubled debt restructuring might involve off-balance- sheet financing. I'm a bit uncertain as to what is meant by that term and how it could influence the accounting results. For example, could a troubled debt agreement bring something that was off the balance sheet onto that financial statement?

Required:

Use the Financial Accounting Research System (FARS) to find out the whole story on the questions posed by Kristin and Ali. In all cases, provide the citations that support your answer.

Brain Teaser 15: What Happens When You Barter with Stock?

Does It Matter Whether It's Treasury Stock or Newly Issued Stock?

Clyde: I acquired this land for my business by issuing stock. I did not pay a penny. Since it's my stock, and I decided how much to give up for the land, does that mean I get to determine the value of the land on my balance sheet?

Fredrika: You could have issued the stock to somebody else, taken the cash received, and paid for the land, right?

Clyde: I suppose I could have, but I did not.

Fredrika: The fact that you could have does imply there is some value for the stock and that it can be determined by referring to the market for that stock.

Clyde: I also bartered for some equipment. I exchanged some treasury stock for those assets. I suppose you are going to suggest that I could have reissued that treasury stock to somebody else, taken the proceeds, and purchased the equipment instead. While I could have, I did not.

Fredrika: What exactly did you expect the advantage to be of bartering with treasury stock? For that matter, why did you issue stock for the land rather than merely pay cash?

Clyde: Frankly, I thought that would allow me to set the value of both the land and the equipment. I mean, when you pay cash, that is the amount paid – open and shut. Whereas, when you barter with goods, services, or in my case stock, don't I have some discretion then?

Fredrika: Do you believe you paid a fair price in stock?

Clyde: Certainly. I mean, I would not have given up the stock unless I thought I received fair value in exchange.

Fredrika: You just explained why an "arm's-length exchange" between two parties is expected to arrive at a fair value that is recorded as the historical cost of the assets acquired.

Clyde: Are you telling me that the identical value would be recorded in my barter exchanges as if I had given up cash instead of stock or treasury stock?

Required:

Use the Financial Accounting Research System (FARS) to find out whether Clyde has more discretion in the recording of his bartering exchanges than he would have had by paying cash. Provide specific citations to support your conclusion. Is your answer affected by whether the barter arrangement involved newly issued stock or treasury stock?

Brain Teaser 16: What Is the Substance of an Appropriation of Retained Earnings?

What Does a Dated Retained Earnings Imply?

Norvald: I have been studying retained earnings-related disclosures in financial statements. Appropriations of retained earnings are frequently reported. I recall in the past, hearing about retained earnings as though it represented a surplus, and I also remember the term 'reserve for plant expansion' somewhere along the line. Now, what I am trying to recall is the exact distinction between those characterizations and appropriations.

Aase: I remember that retained earnings are the accumulation of all prior years' net profit, less net loss, and less dividends declared. I remember appropriations being a sort of earmarking of those retained earnings for special purposes.

Norvald: Yes, but when an earmarking occurs, does that also mean cash is set aside for some purpose, or does it merely represent a sort of claim against the retained earnings?

Aase: My recollection is that retained earnings have nothing to do with cash. In fact, I'm reasonably certain that if you examine the Statement of Cash Flows for one of those companies with an appropriation, you will see nothing related to appropriations as either a cash source or use. I agree with your claim idea, but certainly it's not a liability. I mean, retained earnings are the shareholders' interests, not a creditor's claim.

Norvald: You're right there. I was thinking more in line of a restriction of some sort. In other words, there has to be some purpose for an appropriation, and if it is not cash and does not involve a third-party claim, then it must be something else.

Aase: You mentioned earlier the notion of reserves and surplus. I am reasonably certain that the standard-setters discourage use of those terms. Too many people think of reserves as something tangible or put aside, while surplus almost sounds like you don't need it. Neither term would seem to fit retained earnings very well, or for that matter, restrictions on retained earnings.

Norvald: There is something else I have noticed in my research. Every so often, I noticed that a date appeared beside retained earnings.

Aase: I do remember that there is some type of transaction that leads to a requirement of retained earnings being dated, and not just in one year, but for a time period.

Norvald: We are indeed rusty on some of the details we once knew. I'm going to access FARS and see if I can get some answers.

Required:

Use the Financial Accounting Research System (FARS) to find out the precise circumstances under which appropriations of retained earnings arise and what they represent. Confirm the recollections of Norvald and Aase concerning: the discouragement of the terms surplus and reserve, the noninclusion of appropriations on the Statement of Cash Flows, and the nature of the restriction that is represented by appropriations. When are dates associated with retained earnings, and for how long must they be disclosed? Describe the type of transactions that lead to such dating of the retained earnings balance and the rationale for requiring that particular type of disclosure.

Brain Teaser 17: Stock Option Compensation Dilutes Earnings Per Share?

Yet Such Dilution Fails to Be Reflected?

Charles: I remember many of my MBA colleagues contemplating job offers that were loaded with stock options. The market was hot, and it seemed a far better potential than cash compensation. Of course, that story changed dramatically when the market went south.

Andrea: Some of my friends are with companies who have repriced the stock options that are "under water," just to ensure the employees receive some portion of what they were expecting. Yet, I remember that the whole point of options was to create incentives aligned with stockholders. In other words, if the stock price benefits, the employees benefit. Otherwise, no return results. This repricing seems to be a convoluted back door to changing options effectively to cash compensation. In other words, you win whether your price goes up or not, because we choose to lower the price you paid when the bottom drops out of the market.

Charles: I guess that part of the argument is that the employees are not responsible for the general market decline, and they only accepted the options in lieu of cash because they expected the total compensation would at least compare with other offers.

Andrea: Yet, do you really think the employees were responsible for the hot market run-up? I mean, I haven't heard of employees saying, no I do not want the benefits that accrued to my stock options, because I was not responsible for their increase in value: the market was responsible. It sounds a good deal like "heads I win, tails you lose."

Charles: Indeed, those who lose do seem to be the stockholders. The repricing and eventual exercise of options creates a dilutive effect on the already issued stock.

Andrea: I would say that as soon as the stock options are issued, a dilutive effect occurs. Consider the analogy that we split the pie of a corporation among 500,000 existing shares of common stock. The board of directors then turns around and issues stock options that can be exercised and become an additional 200,000 shares. It seems to me that the slice of the pie represented by one share has fallen from $1/500,000^{th}$ to $1/700,000^{th}$, and that is a smaller slice, no matter how you cut it. No pun intended.

Charles: You are assuming that all 200,000 shares become a reality, through exercise of the stock options.

Andrea: I believe that is more likely than zero shares, particularly with this repricing phenomenon we're observing.

Charles: That must be part of the reason that some corporate boards proposing changes in their stock option plans have been met with defeat by stockholders' voting power. I believe they understand dilutive effects, especially when the game of repricing has increased in popularity.

Andrea: What I am really curious about is whether the earnings per share that are reported quarterly, and annually for that matter, show this dilutive effect of stock compensation. Does it?

Required:

Use the Financial Accounting Research System (FARS) to answer Andrea's question. Is there a difference in your response as it regards quarterly and annual earnings per share (EPS)? Elaborate on what information stockholders receive as to the influence of stock compensation on their ownership share. Do you believe it is sufficient disclosure? Explain. Given repricing and current accounting treatment, do you believe options motivate employees to perform in line with stockholders' interests? Discuss the basis for your beliefs.

Brain Teaser 18: Why Do Transfers Among Portfolios of Investments Affect Accounting?

Isn't that Doing Business with Itself? Why Is Intent Rather Than Realization Determinative?

Milly: I read that regulators were sanctioning a large financial institution for its accounting treatment of investments.

Jean: What was the nature of the mishandling?

Milly: It seems that management has to express its intent as to whether an investment held is to be in a trading portfolio or is to be held to maturity. That intent determines which portfolio contains an instrument and, in turn, determines the accounting treatment.

Jean: I was under the impression that accounting dealt with what actually happened as opposed to what somebody intended to happen. I know that some areas of practice require estimations, but it would seem that for investments, one could just watch what was done and then record it when it happened.

Milly: Actually, the reality sounded even stranger. What I gathered from the media coverage is that the financial institution first assigned an investment to one portfolio and then later in that same day, due to some dramatic market fluctuations, it switched certain investments from one portfolio to another. The result was a differing accounting treatment that had a substantial difference from what would have occurred had the "original intent" of the management not been altered.

Jean: Now that sounds like the company is doing business with itself. I mean, if it can create different accounting treatments merely from shifting its own assets among its own portfolios, that does not sound like any type of arm's-length exchange!

Milly: It does sound a bit like you and I being able to make money by taking our change from the right pocket and placing it in the left pocket.

Jean: I agree. It just does not sound logical. Maybe the media left something out that was important to know.

Required:

Use the Financial Accounting Research System (FARS) to explain how management intent influences the accounting for investments if at all. Also describe how transfers among portfolios can affect the accounting result. Consider the dialogue between Milly and Jean relative to what you find out from your study of FARS. Specifically, is this an example of accounting reflecting transactions of a business with itself? Why or why not? Is the absence of a market exchange problematic? Do you concur with the current accounting treatment of investments in marketable securities? Explain.

Brain Teaser 19: When Does Channel Stuffing Transform Sales into Consignment Sales?

What Role Does Collectibility Play?

Dorn: A company with aggressive selling tactics to independent distributors seems to face many more challenges today. The Securities and Exchange Commission has that Staff Accounting Bulletin on revenue recognition where the "bottom line" seems to be a warning to take care and not to anticipate revenue.

Greg: Channel stuffing has always been an issue with independent distributorship networks. When a manufacturer's or wholesaler's sales topple, instinctively, the sales force begins to push its customers. The question becomes, just how many additional sales can any single distributor actually bring to fruition?

Dorn: I always wonder what type of side agreements might be necessary to get the distributor to go along. For example, does the sales representative promise to take back any unsold merchandise?

Greg: It seems that any such commitment transforms the sale into a consignment sale, resulting in no real revenue for the manufacturer or wholesaler.

Dorn: Assume that no commitment were made regarding returns, but the salesman is aware of a marginal financial situation of the distributor and its customers. Then it would seem collectibility becomes an issue, particularly in the wake of channel stuffing.

Greg: Then the question becomes, is this actually an installment sale, in which case, the revenue picture changes as well.

Dorn: I wonder what type of bright lines exist in the literature, if any, to help the chief financial officers, as well as the auditors, understand when sales get transformed into consignment sales and when even those might better be regarded as installment sales?

Greg: Let's find out; we can use FARS.

Required:

Use the Financial Accounting Research System (FARS) to identify any bright lines that distinguish when sales should be reported as consignment sales. Likewise, explore the guidance associated with determining when the installment sales approach should be applied. Is there special attention in the standards to channel stuffing? In what sense does channel stuffing relate to either the need for consignment sales accounting or installment sales? Explain.

Brain Teaser 20: Why Can the Same Company Have Both a Tax Asset and a Tax Liability?

How Do Tax Assets Differ from Recording Contingent Gains?

Peggy: I was looking at a balance sheet of a company that reported both a tax asset and a tax liability for the same year.

Tina: Why wouldn't you either owe the Internal Revenue Service or have it owe you?

Peggy: That's exactly my quandary.

Tina: With all the recent changes in tax law and legislation altering rates and deductions over time, how do companies determine their tax obligation or claim? Do they presume that even if something will not occur until several years in the future and could always be rescinded, that once legislation exists in any given year, that is the right rate to estimate the numbers in the financial statements? Is there a role for the probability of altering such legislation in any given four-year period?

Peggy: I remember that this issue came up in spades when the retroactive tax adjustments of the Clinton era occurred. I believe some guidance speaks directly to which rate is used under what circumstances.

Tina: I have always been a bit puzzled by the idea of a tax asset. Given the nature of tax law over time, I wonder why such numbers are not analogous to the entire area of litigation. My understanding is that gains from awards in litigation cannot be anticipated in any manner. Essentially, the award must be realized in order to reflect the results of that award in the accounting statements. Yet, for taxes, it is as though the future anticipated reward for some tax strategy is permitted to get into the books. We all understand that the entire legal framework on which the gain is based can change at any given point in time. Moreover, is it not the case that some of these tax assets can be a part of ongoing tax audits and disputes in Tax Courts? I must be missing something.

Peggy: As a matter of fact, one area that I believe dovetails with your thought process is the entire matter of net operating loss carryforwards. Legislation permits past losses to offset future gains, but after all, such losses are worth nothing if the entity continues to have net losses throughout the period that such an offset is permitted. Does that not seem like a gain contingency if an asset is created in anticipation of claiming that carryforward?

Tina: I remember discussing the matter of a likelihood aspect to tax assets that is phrased "more likely than not." A bit of a mystery exists in my mind. I recently read through an international standard IAS 37, titled "Provisions, Contingent Liabilities and Contingent Assets." Paragraph 2b of that standard stated, "…it is probable (i.e., more likely than not) that an outflow of resources embodying economic benefits will be required to settle the obligation." This parenthetical seems at total odds with the U.S. literature. I know that there is a sort of 'bright-line distinction' between *probable* and *more likely than not* that is being communicated by the FASB.

Required:

Use the Financial Accounting Research System (FARS) to find out how it is possible for a single company to present both a tax asset and a tax liability. Do you believe that a tax asset constitutes a gain contingency? Why or why not? Support your position with appropriate citations. Is the *more likely than not* threshold in the tax asset accounting treatment different from the usual meaning of *probable* within the standards? Justify your position, providing related citations.

Brain Teaser 21: Isn't the Corridor Approach for Pensions and Postretirement Benefits Smoothing?

Do Expected Relative to Actual Returns Matter if a Defined Contribution Plan Replaces a Defined Benefit Plan?

Andy: The corridor approach that is applied to pensions and postretirement benefits is a conundrum. It seems to be merely a smoothing device endorsed by the Financial Accounting Standards Board. Is smoothing a worthy objective for reporting?

Alice: I believe one of the most common complaints among lobby letters written to the FASB concerns the volatility of earnings. The claim is that a smoother depiction of operations facilitates forecasts and is thereby a desirable outcome.

Andy: I would think that accountants ought to report results no matter how volatile and then let the forecasters do the smoothing of the data set. I mean, macroeconomic statistics can be accessed as seasonally adjusted or in raw form. Why not provide the economic results, however disparate over time, and let the users of those numbers grapple with the question of how they can be used looking forward?

Alice: Intellectually, I think a "fly in the ointment" is the periodicity principle. Any entity has numerous multiperiod asset and liability balances that inevitably involve long-term estimates. That makes it no simple matter to derive the single figure for reporting purposes as of any given date. I think pensions and postretirement benefits are great examples of long-term obligations that are a challenge to determine in one year. Those related commitments will not actually be met for twenty to fifty years!

Andy: Nonetheless, if you have asset investments to meet that liability twenty years later, you have to admit that you do know what return you actually earned on those assets as of a point in time, right?

Alice: Even then, it would seem you're asking whether market value can be effectively derived at a single point in time, even if some investments are subject to a buy-and-hold strategy that arguably fails to earn the current market return because they are not traded at propitious points in time.

Andy: I suppose that those are the types of concerns, in part, that lead companies to change from defined benefit to defined contribution plans. Then all the company does is contribute a given amount today, and the rest of the picture is the employee's responsibility. If the employee pursues buy-and-hold strategies, or trades actively, that individual accrues the benefits or losses and the company has met the specified obligation of original contribution. I suppose you could also say the shift to a defined contribution plan is itself a smoothing device, since the contributions should be far smoother in quantity than any defined benefit plan accounting effects would be!

Alice: Maybe the corridor approach is a means to encourage companies not to shift to defined contribution plans for such reasons, by providing an alternative means of having relative stability.

Andy: Yes, perhaps, but the substance of a defined benefit plan seems very different to me from the defined contribution plan. For example, presume that I expect a 10 percent return and only earn a two percent return on a defined benefit plan's assets. I will have to meet the same commitment regardless of my return, which means in effect that I have to make up an 8 percent shortfall. Whereas, for defined contribution plans, an expected return does not even enter the picture.

Alice: It does from the employees' point of view, most assuredly. They have to decide whether to go to work for a company offering a defined contribution plan or a defined benefit plan. If the former, the employee has investment responsibility, which means expected return can be critical in his or her financial planning.

Andy: You're right, I should not have said that expected return does not even enter the picture. It has to be an ingredient to a company's analysis of what type of pensions and benefits to offer.

Alice: Getting back to the corridor approach, how does that work? Is it symmetrical, and if so, is there not a type of anticipated gain that results? How do we reconcile that with conservatism? Do we make a distinction between the accounting for unexpected and expected gains and losses?

Andy: You bring up an interesting point. I've thought about the issue of discounting as well. It seems that the discounting of pension and postemployment retirement benefits is well accepted, and yet discounting is not applied to a number of other accounting areas, even though they involve long-term estimates. Why is that the case? One could say the result is a conservative reflection of the obligation, relative to the undiscounted number in any case.

Alice: I agree about the lack of consistency among standards being an issue, but I would think present value is virtually always a preferred means of reflecting current claims.

Andy: We choose not to discount the short-term obligations for time value of money, yet a year's interest is far from trivial. Besides, it is not easy to set the appropriate rates for either expected return or discounting. Perhaps it would be a wash, and the entire accounting approach could be simplified.

Alice: Whenever I hear the phrase "it's a wash," I always have a concern as to what exactly is being *washed out*. You're suggesting that the expected return would offset the effect of discounting, right? I can appreciate the fact that some things need aggregation, and in so doing, certain offsets do become embedded in the assessment. Yet, aren't return and discount distinctive concepts?

Andy: You have a legitimate point.

Alice: I think one of the interesting aspects of pensions involves the requirement that accumulated benefit obligations be compared with the fair value of plan assets as a basis for a minimum liability accrual. I wonder how symmetry fits into the picture, if at all? If the fair value of plan assets impounds unexpected gains and losses, not realized due to a buy-and-hold strategy, is the accounting treatment any different?

Andy: I started with a few questions, and now we have a set of them. I'm going to roll up my sleeves and see whether FARS can help to solve some of our queries.

Required:

Use the Financial Accounting Research System (FARS) to formulate a brief position paper regarding the pros and cons of the corridor approach as it relates to smoothing. Also assume that your company is contemplating a change from a defined benefit to a defined contribution plan. Prepare a short information sheet for fellow employees as to the differences between the two types of plans, from the point of view of the individual employee's responsibilities relative to those of the company. Finally, prepare an executive summary for top management as to the anticipated differences in accounting effects of a defined contribution plan relative to the former defined benefit plan. Explain specifically what accounting-associated estimates will no longer have to be made, and provide cites to support your key findings. Comment on the role of discounting and the expected rate of return in the accounting for either pensions or postretirement benefits. Could a wash type of approach simplify the picture, or would it merely muddy the picture? Explain your reasoning, using FARS citations in support.

Brain Teaser 22: Lease Accounting – Why Is It Asymmetrical?

A Bargain Purchase from Whose Perspective?

Miklos: A single lease transaction can spawn one type of lease accounting for the lessor and another for the lessee. It always puzzles me that symmetry is not an inherent part of a transaction. Indeed, some of the recent media sensations have involved contracts between two parties in which one side recognizes the revenue but the other side does not book the transaction until a later period in time. I understand that internal decision making affects the recording of transactions, but in a way, a transaction would seem to have two sides of the same coin. I would expect the factual coin would drive both sides of the recording process. Yet, I know that does not result under lease accounting.

Salvatore: Perhaps that is why the Financial Accounting Standards Board itself has stated that lease accounting is broken and needs attention.

Miklos: A number of groups have recommended that all lease transactions be capitalized, alongside all executory contracts.

Salvatore: You remind me of the interesting irony that the minimum lease payment under current lease accounting guidance is to exclude executory costs. Not that executory costs and executory contracts are synonyms....

Miklos: There are a number of intricacies to current guidance. The volume of related guidance alone is mind boggling.

Salvatore: One concept I have difficulty with in practice is determining when a bargain purchase exists. It seems to me that what one party may deem a bargain may not be similarly viewed by another.

Miklos: I have seen transactions which claimed at the point of initial negotiation that a bargain purchase option existed, yet at the end of the lease, no such purchase occurred. If it had really been a bargain, you would expect that the purchase would be automatic.

Salvatore: I just think a real challenge exists in recording what could be a 99-year lease, anticipating what happens almost a century from today. Talk about forward-looking information!

Miklos: The reason all of this is on my mind is that I am about to dive into the accounting treatment for a set of proposed lease arrangements. The decision maker wants to understand the accounting consequences if they decide to proceed with the leases as currently written.

Required:

Use the Financial Accounting Research System (FARS) to prepare a list of all guidance within the system that deals with the accounting for leases, as a resource for Miklos. In addition, determine whether any requirement of symmetry exists and explain for a given type of lease why the lessor's accounting can differ from that of a lessee's. Since the issue of bargain purchase will need attention by Miklos, define what that term means and its effects on the accounting for leases. The dialogue suggests that part of the decision on whether to move forward with a proposed lease will be the accounting treatment for that lease. Do you believe it is appropriate for the sequence of the events in decision making to include the accounting ramifications of a transaction? Why or why not? If the entity were to adjust the lease transaction to ensure that a particular accounting approach would apply, would that be acceptable? Do your consider it prudence and/or earnings management to consider accounting implications of business transactions during their negotiation? Are such actions normal, advisable, acceptable, and or objectionable? Explain.

Brain Teaser 23: How Are Changes in Warranties to Be Recorded?

What if We Make the Change in the Third Quarter?

Daniel: The company has changed from one warranty arrangement to another. Competition has made that a necessity. I have been asked to analyze the accounting implications of that change.

Mary Anne: I suggest you access FARS and prepare an analysis of which accounts will be affected by the change, in what direction, and then the implications for both reported income and the balance sheet accounts.

Daniel: There has been some discussion about whether our existing customers should be provided with some improved warranty status, particularly if they have made purchases recently. We want to keep rapport with our current customers, rather than merely attracting new customers. If we do increase the benefits of products sold in the past, does that mean we made an error? Or is this merely a change in estimate? Do I record it retroactively, currently, or prospectively?

Mary Anne: FARS will help with those questions as well.

Daniel: We have some choices as to when we make the final decision and the timing of the accounting treatment, right? If we decide in the third quarter instead of the fourth quarter, does that mean the consequence of our accounting will differ for the year?

Mary Anne: Do you think it should? I suggest that you prepare two draft documents. The first should be an analysis of the change and its effects on the accounts. The second should be an outline of the relevant accounting citations, including regarding your interim reporting issue. I'll review those when they are completed.

Daniel: I'll do my best.

Katie: I'll help.

Required:

Use the Financial Accounting Research System (FARS) to prepare both reports for Mary Anne's review. Be certain to distinguish between accounting changes and accounting errors and their implications for accounting treatment.

Brain Teaser 24: Does the Statement of Cash Flows Give the Full Picture?

What about Noncash Transactions?

Chee: For years, the expression *off-balance-sheet financing* has been in vogue. I think we ought to introduce the phrase *off-cash-flow-statement* transactions.

Shyam: I can understand why a company might want a liability off their balance sheet, but what do you have in mind with the cash flow statement?

Chee: In similar vein, why not avoid showing a large outflow of cash by merely negotiating some sort of noncash transaction? Couldn't that really distort the picture?

Shyam: Now you are arguing substance versus form, assuming the users of cash flow statements care about more than cash.

Chee: Assume a company owes $40 million to a creditor and when it comes due, simply exchanges preferred stock for that debt instead of paying cash. That constitutes a noncash exchange and would not appear on the statement of cash flows.

Shyam: Granted, but it will appear somewhere in a report of noncash transactions.

Chee: That's my point. How is it any different from saying you can go to the notes to the financial statements to learn more about off-balance-sheet items?

Shyam: I agree that you have a point. Then there is the quagmire of how stock options interact with reporting earnings and cash flows, especially tax-related cash flows.

Chee: What about transactions like stock dividends or stock splits?

Shyam: Would the user of a cash flow statement have an interest in appropriations of retained earnings, and if so, should there be some type of linkage as to where they ought to look for such "signs of future outflows?"

Chee: Our financial statement analysis course ought to be extremely clear as to what the differences are among operating, investing, and financing categories in the

Statement of Cash Flows, what the problems are that arise in gathering the details, and what might be elsewhere, yet relevant.

Shyam: I agree. We need a roadmap. Barter arrangements were one of the issues that received attention in regulating revenue recognition issues for advertising among 'dot.coms.' We ought to tie that in as an example of the problem at hand.

Required:

Use the Financial Accounting Research System (FARS) to prepare the roadmap. Specifically define the difference in operating, investing, and financing cash flows. Explain the nature of noncash transactions and be comprehensive in listing the sorts of transactions that might appear in such a presentation. What latitude does a company have in terms of where to report such disclosures. Use the http://www.sec.gov EDGAR (electronic data gathering and retrieval) resource to identify a company with noncash transactions reported and indicate the company name, the type of transaction, and where it is reported in the 10-K filing. Explain whether stock dividends, stock splits, and appropriations of retained earnings are relevant, in your judgment, to the evaluation of the cash flow statement. Where can information on any of these transactions be found, under generally accepted accounting principles? Provide cites from FARS in support of each aspect of your roadmap and related explanations. In your judgment, does the Statement of Cash Flows give the full picture? Why or why not?

Brain Teaser 25: Why Are Segment Disclosures Non-GAAP?

What Information Is Provided at Interim?

Erik: I have been interested in segment-level disclosures as a means of exploring capital allocation within a company. In other words, in which segments is corporate office investing and how? My problem is that I wanted to do some time-series comparisons. However, I understand that the entire approach to defining segments has changed in the 1990s. Does that mean that I should not include any data earlier than the point of the change in the accounting for segmental disclosures?

Corine: You are right about the definition of segments changing. The focus is now on how managers operate their business. If a certain segmental approach is demonstrated in the internal reporting framework of a business, the managers are thereby contending that this is the relevant approach to analyzing the operations of the business. Hence, it is that management strategy that guides the definition of segments. They need have little relationship to the segments disclosed prior to the change by FASB.

Judy: Another wrinkle relates to what is reported. The segment disclosures can be non-GAAP if that happens to be what is used in the internal report. The argument is similar to the initial definition of segments: If management does not find it useful in its internal reports to allocate costs or to use GAAP accounting, then whatever basis is used in the internal report can be the essence of these segment disclosures. Of course, a *plug* is required to show the difference in those numbers and what would have been GAAP, but the plug I believe may be an amalgamation of differences in revenue recognition, cost tracking, allocations, and other things.

Erik: That sounds as though it may be such a hodge podge as to be uninformative.

Corine: I know that many expressed a concern about the lack of comparability, not merely among companies but even over time for a given company. If management changes its internal reporting framework, the segmental disclosures are expected to likewise fluctuate.

Judy: We all know that restructuring is far from a rare event.

Erik: Consider acquisitions, divestitures, spin-offs, downsizing, rightsizing, and the rest of the possibilities.

Corine:	Another problem is that if you are interested in any information on interim dates, I don't believe you will find segmental disclosures in the interim reports. Hence, it is only once a year that you can look inside and investigate the parts or segments of the entity.
Judy:	There is one exception. I think when you dispose of a segment, some sort of interim disclosure is required.
Erik:	Another aspect of interest to my work is the identification of major customers. Has that changed as well?
Corine:	To actually figure out which common costs and what types of disclosures are expected, you ought to access FARS. It should answer those questions, the current requirements associated with major customers, and the extent to which annual and interim reporting apply to anything having to do with segments.
Erik:	I need an understanding of this non-GAAP dimension, because it certainly sounds as though I won't even be able to compare revenue figures. What if a single entity uses different revenue recognition for different lines of business? Does that mean the revenues among segments within a single entity even fail the comparability test?
Judy:	Good questions, and I believe conceptually that could occur. You need to check to see if the FASB considered such a possibility and included any safeguards at all.
Corine:	What if management's internal reports choose not to break an operation into segments? Is it not possible for management to state that its strategy is to manage the company as a single holistic unit? Would that mean no details for segments? Or is that a circumstance that FASB precluded?
Erik:	I better get to work and find some answers.

Required:

Use the Financial Accounting Research System (FARS) to answer the questions raised concerning segment reporting. Be certain to define the criteria used to define segments, any minimum number of segments that must appear, the annual relative to interim requirements, the non-GAAP latitude permitted, and the issue of major customers. In your opinion, are these segmental disclosures preferable to the previous standards on segmental disclosures? Why or why not?

CHAPTER 5 – CASES TO ACCOMPANY FARS

5

OUTLINE

CASE 1

New Financing: Do Credit Agreements Pose Unique Accounting and Disclosure Challenges? Gunther International

CASE TOPICS OUTLINE

1. Terms of New Credit Arrangement
   A. Restructuring
   B. Guarantors
2. Collateral
3. Subordination

4. Warrants
   A. Valuation
   B. Disclosure
   C. Context
5. Rights Offering

Gunther International has had a rocky road, financially. You joined the company upon graduation and recall having heard about it being significantly restructured in September of 1992. It was then that two shareholders assumed control of the corporation and infused additional capital. Your department has been rocked by recent discoveries of accounting issues that have caused a delay in reported numbers. You assisted in crafting the language that appeared in the 8-K filing:

> "Item 5. Other Events.
>
> On June 23, 1998, the registrant issued a press release announcing that it does not expect to release its final results for the fourth quarter and the full fiscal year ended March 31, 1998 until later in July 1998. A copy of the press release is attached hereto as an exhibit. During the course of the year-end audit, the Company's auditors, Arthur Andersen LLP, identified errors in the accumulation of contract costs and certain items of expense that were not properly accounted for. The Company, with the assistance of its auditors, is continuing to review the nature and extent of these matters, as well as the effect these matters may have on the Company's financial results. Based on the information that is available at this time, the Company currently expects to report a net loss for the fiscal year ended March 31, 1998 of approximately $2.4

to $3.0 million. The Company also expects to restate its results for each of the first three quarters of fiscal 1998. Previously issued financial statements for the interim periods of fiscal 1998 should not be relied upon.

The net losses referred to above are expected to result in a violation of certain financial covenants contained in the Company's senior credit facility. The Company has informed representatives of its senior lender about these matters and intends to meet with them to discuss a satisfactory resolution of the situation. If a satisfactory resolution is not reached, the Company may suffer an event of default under its senior credit facility and the Company's ability to continue to borrow thereunder may be impaired.

The Company is moving forward at an aggressive pace to definitively announce its financial results as quickly as possible. The Company continues to maintain a large installed base of customers using its products and believes that its products continue to be well received in the market place. The Company expects to have a record backlog of sales under contract in excess of $5 million as of June 30, 1998.

The Company's expectations are preliminary and are subject to the completion of its year-end audit. The estimated amount of loss, anticipated release of final results and the potential consequences of these matters, including without limitation the resolution of expected violations under the Company's senior credit facility discussed in this report constitute forward-looking statements, and the Company's actual results could differ from those discussed above...." *Source: 8-K filed June 23, 1998*

As the 8-K suggests, a good deal of uncertainty surrounds the financing arrangements of the company going forward. The treasurer's department has been working long hours to explore the options. They requested financial numbers under the existing, though somewhat tenuous financing arrangement. While in preliminary form, assume you have access to something similar to what eventually appeared as the restated financial disclosures in Tables 5.1-1 and 5.1-2.

Table 5.1-1 Summary Financial Data – Income Statement Related*

	Year Ended March 31, 1998 (As Restated)	Year Ended March 31, 1997 (As Restated)	Year Ended March 31, 1996
Sales:			
Systems	$ 8,630,103	$ 8,716,473	$ 8,458,700
Maintenance	6,454,716	4,911,794	4,022,562
Total Sales	15,084,819	13,628,267	12,481,262
Cost of Sales:			
Systems	7,030,092	5,573,323	5,821,526
Maintenance	4,771,692	4,088,858	2,826,853
Total Cost of Sales	11,801,784	9,662,181	8,648,379
Gross Profit	3,283,035	3,966,086	3,832,883

Operating Expenses:			
Selling and Administrative	5,050,863	4,680,946	4,213,832
Research and Development	618,735	435,404	255,243
Total Operating Expenses	5,669,598	5,116,350	4,469,075
Operating Loss	(2,386,563)	(1,150,264)	(636,192)
Other Expenses:			
Interest Expense, Net	(245,552)	(184,426)	(243,363)
Net Loss	$ (2,632,115)	$ (1,334,690)	$ (879,555)
Net Loss Per Share	$ (0.61)	$ (0.32)	$ (0.23)

*The summary financial data presented should be read in conjunction with the information set forth in the financial statements and notes thereto. *Source:* January 14, 1999 10-KSB/A filing by Gunther International.

Table 5.1-2 Summary Financial Data – Balance Sheet Related*

	1998 (As Restated)	1997 (As Restated)
Current Assets	$ 3,118,386	$ 3,616,493
Total Assets	8,036,929	8,663,040
Current Liabilities	7,981,871	5,661,800
Long-Term Debt, less current maturities	1,884,551	2,213,618
Stockholders' Equity (Deficit)	(1,829,493)	787,622

*The summary financial data presented should be read in conjunction with the information set forth in the financial statements and notes thereto. *Source:* January 14, 1999 10-KSB/A filing by Gunther International.

The reason for the tenuous situation with the creditors is the reported error that resulted in the debt covenant violations on the line of credit held by Bank of Boston. Credit agreements, often the lifeblood of a company, can take a variety of forms, with diverse covenants and commitments. Gunther's solution to this covenant violation has been to find new financing and pay off the line of credit with the Bank of Boston. You have worked with colleagues in both the Controller's Office and the Treasurer's Department to craft the following language for inclusion in yet another 8-K filing:

"GUNTHER ANNOUNCES COMPLETION OF COMPREHENSIVE FINANCING TRANSACTION
NORWICH, CT, (October 2, 1998) Gunther International, Ltd. (NASDAQ: SORT) today announced it has successfully completed a comprehensive $5.7 million financing transaction, the proceeds of which have been utilized to completely restructure and replace the Company's pre-existing senior line of credit, fund a full settlement with the Company's third party service provider, and provide additional working capital to fund the Company's ongoing business operations.

Under the terms of the transaction, a newly formed limited Liability company organized by the Tisch Family Interests and Mr. Robert Spiegel (the "New Lender") loaned an aggregate of $4 million to the Company. At the same time, the Company's senior lender reached an agreement with the guarantor of a portion of the Company's senior line of credit (the "Guarantor") whereby the Guarantor consented to the liquidation of approximately $1.7 million of collateral and the application of the proceeds of such collateral to satisfy and repay in full a like amount of indebtedness outstanding under the senior credit facility. The balance of the indebtedness outstanding under the senior credit facility, approximating $350,000, was repaid in full from the proceeds of the new financing. The Company executed a new promissory note in favor of the Guarantor evidencing the Company's obligation to repay the amount of the collateral that was liquidated by the senior lender. The Company's obligations to the Guarantor are completely subordinated to the Company's obligations to the New Lender. In addition, approximately $1.4 million of the new financing was utilized to pay the Company's third party service provider all amounts that were due and owing to the service provider for performing maintenance on Company systems.

To induce the New Lender to enter into the financing transaction, the Company, the New Lender, Park Investment Partners, Gerald H. Newman, the estate of Harold S. Geneen (the "Estate"), Four Partners, and Robert Spiegel Entered into a separate voting agreement, pursuant to which they each agreed to vote all shares of Gunther stock held by them in favor of (i) that number of persons nominated by the New Lender constituting a majority of the Board of Directors, (ii) one person nominated by the Estate and (iii) one person nominated by Park Investment Partners. In addition, the Company granted the New Lender a stock purchase warrant entitling the New Lender, any time during the period commencing on January 1, 1999 and ending on the fifth anniversary of the transaction, to purchase up to 35% of the pro forma, fully diluted number of shares of the Common Stock of the Company, determined as of the date of exercise. The exercise price of the warrant is $1.50 per share.

Contemporaneously with the consummation of the transaction, Frederick W. Kolling III and James H. Whitney resigned from the Board of Directors, and Thomas Steinberg and Robert Spiegel were elected to fill the vacancies created by the resignations. Another inside director, Alan W. Morton, resigned from the Board prior to the consummation of the transactions.

The Company is continuing to review the previously announced issues regarding the accumulation of contract costs and the recognition of revenues and expenses relating to the Company's systems business. The Company expects to be in a position to release information concerning the results of the review by the end of October.

Gunther International, Ltd. is a leading manufacturer of intelligent document finishing systems and ink jet printing solutions." *(Source: 8-K, Filed as of October 7, 1998)*

Requirement A.1: Disclosure

As soon as the 8-K is released, the company's attention is directed toward the anticipated filing of a 10-K, which will need to provide full disclosure concerning this new financing arrangement in accordance with generally accepted accounting principles. You have been asked to outline all associated accounting and disclosure issues that arise as a result of this transaction. The intent is that your outline will become a basis for a joint presentation with the controller to the board of directors.

1. List all relevant FARS references in the order of relevance to the transaction.
2. Clearly set forth permissible alternatives.
3. Draft your recommendation, as to both accounting for and disclosing of the transaction.

Hints Regarding Solution

a. Develop a comprehensive list of search words associated with the transaction.
b. Consider how the former arrangement might have been recorded in comparison to the current transaction, including potential balance sheet, income statement, and cash flow implications.
c. Consider broader disclosure requirements' association with particular transactions.
d. Context matters to accounting and disclosure decisions. Carefully consider the inter-relationship of the two press releases, giving particular attention to the various stakeholders affected by your recommendations.

Requirement A.2: Interdisciplinary Considerations

The board of directors is expected to be very interested in details concerning the transaction, making it imperative that interdisciplinary considerations be discussed as a part of your presentation.

1. Why is corporate governance so interrelated with credit arrangements?
2. Why are warrants frequently integrated into lending contracts?
3. Do contracts in economic settings generally slip into default when problems with past representations in financial statements arise? Be specific.
4. What are the consequences of delaying financial statement information for four months or longer?
5. Describe and justify a management strategy for Gunther International, in light of these past events.

Requirement B: Subsequent Filings

On January 14, 1999, Gunther International filed a 10-KSB/A (accessible at http://www.sec.gov) that contained the following disclosures:

> "The undersigned registrant hereby amends its Annual Report on
> Form 10-KSB for the fiscal year ended March 31, 1998 to amend Items 6 and 7 of Part II
> and Item 13 of Part III, as set forth in this amendment.
> ITEM 6. MANAGEMENT'S DISCUSSION AND ANALYSIS OR PLAN OF
> OPERATIONS.
>   SUMMARY OF RECENT EVENTS
> … The Audit Committee's review has since been completed and it has been determined
> that accounts receivable were overstated and accounts payable and deferred service
> revenues were understated at March 31, 1997 and costs and estimated earnings in excess
> of billings on uncompleted contracts were overstated at March 31, 1998. As a result, the
> accompanying financial statements and management's discussion and analysis of financial
> condition and results of operations include restated results as of and for the years ended
> March 31, 1997 and 1998. Also, certain amounts were reclassified between selling and

administrative expenses, cost of sales, and research and development expenses to more appropriately reflect the results of operations. The effect of the restatement for the year ended March 31, 1997 was to reduce operating results to a net loss of $(1,334,690), or $(0.32) per share, from net income of $258,889, or $0.06 per share. The effect of the restatement for the year ended March 31, 1998 was to decrease the net loss to $(2,632,115), or $(0.61) per share, from a net loss of $(2,701,819), or $(0.63) per share.

On October 2, 1998, the Company entered into a $5.7 million comprehensive financing transaction with the Bank of Boston, Connecticut, N.A. (the "Bank"), the Estate of Harold S. Geneen (the "Estate") and Gunther Partners LLC (the "New Lender"), the proceeds of which have been utilized to restructure and replace the Company's pre-existing senior line of credit, fund a full settlement with the Company's third party service provider and provide additional working capital to fund the Company's ongoing business operations. Under the terms of the transaction, the New Lender loaned an aggregate of $4.0 million to the Company. At the same time, the Bank reached an agreement with the Estate, which had guaranteed a portion of the Company's senior line of credit, whereby the Estate consented to the liquidation of approximately $1.7 million of collateral and the application of the proceeds of such collateral to satisfy and repay in full a like amount of indebtedness outstanding under the senior credit facility. The balance of the indebtedness outstanding under the senior credit facility, approximately $350,000, was repaid in full from the proceeds of the new financing. The Company executed a new promissory note in favor of the Estate evidencing the Company's obligation to repay the amount of the collateral that was liquidated by the Bank. The Company's obligations to the Estate are subordinated to the Company's obligations to the New Lender. The principal balance of the $4.0 million debt is to be repaid in monthly installments of $100,000 from November 1, 1998 and continuing to and including September 1, 1999, $400,000 on October 1, 1999 and the balance shall be due on October 1, 2003. Interest shall be paid quarterly, at the rate of 8% per annum, beginning January 1, 1999 and continuing until the principal and interest due is paid in full. The debt is secured by a first priority interest in all tangible and intangible property and a secondary interest in patents and trademarks....

The promissory note in favor of the Estate for approximately $1.7 million is to be repaid at the earlier of one year after the Company's obligations to the New Lender are paid in full or on October 2, 2004. Interest, at 5.44% per annum, shall accrue on principal and unpaid interest, which is added to the outstanding balance and is due at the time of principal payments. The indebtedness is secured by all tangible and intangible personal property of the Company but is subordinated to all rights of the New Lender." (*Source:* January 14, 1999, 10-KSB/A filing by Gunther International.)

1. Given these subsequent disclosures, would you propose any adjustments to the accounting or disclosure suggestions you presented prior to the resolution of the restatement? Explain the basis for your response.
2. Would you expect the new lender to make any adjustments to the current contractual arrangement when the credit arrangement is reconsidered at renewal?
3. What would be the accounting or disclosure implications of your expectations? Explain how the following subsequent development might influence your expectations, if you were requested to update your evaluation as of July 1999.

On June 29, 1999, a 10-KSB filing states within the Management's Discussion and Analysis (Item 6, Subhead Liquidity and Capital Resources):

"The company did not make its required payments on their respective due dates and
certain other information required by the loan agreement was not provided to the New
Lender. The New Lender waived these deficiencies. As of March 31, 1999, all
amounts due on the debt had been paid."…

"In the event the Company is unable to meet its payment obligations through April 1,
2000, in accordance with the Note Loan and Security Agreement, the new Lender will
be willing to renegotiate the payment terms based upon available cash flow such that
the payment terms would be acceptable to both the Company and the Lender."

Requirement C: The Aftermath

At fiscal year ended March 31, 2001, in its 10KSB/A fiiling as of July 3, 2001, events associated
with the past financing arrangements are detailed, alongside the following disclosure:

"Through June 30, 1999, the Company had made principal payments to Gunther
Partners LLC aggregating $800,000, plus interest. In September 1999, the Company
experienced a deficiency in operating cash flow and Gunther Partners LLC agreed
to lend the Company an additional $800,000 and to otherwise restructure the
payment terms of the note. As amended, the outstanding balance due Gunther
Partners LLC is due in principal installments of $200,000 commencing on October
1, 2001 through April 1, 2002; $100,000 on May 1, 2002; and $2,500,000 on
October 1, 2003. If, at any time prior to October 1, 2001, the accumulated
deficit of the Company improves by $1.0 million or more compared to the amount
at June 30, 1999 of $14.4 million (a "Triggering Event"), then the principal
payments otherwise due from October 1, 2001 through May 1, 2002 shall be become
due in consecutive monthly installments beginning on the first day of the second
month following the Triggering Event. On April 4, 2000, the Company borrowed an
additional $500,000 from Gunther Partners LLC.

In June 2001, the Company entered into a recapitalization agreement (the
"Recapitalization Agreement") with the Estate, Gunther Partners LLC and certain
other stockholders. The Recapitalization Agreement provides that the Company
will effectuate a registered public offering ("Rights Offering") of up to
16,000,000 shares of its Common Stock (the "Offered Shares") to its existing
stockholders by subscription right on a pro-rata basis at a subscription price
of $0.50 per share. The rights to subscribe to the Offered Shares will be
granted at a ratio to be determined by the Board of Directors of the Company
(the "Basic Subscription Right"). In addition, the Company's stockholders will
be granted the right to "oversubscribe" for additional shares not purchased by
other stockholders, up to the total amount of the Offered Shares (the
"Oversubscription Right"). In the event that the Company's stockholders, other
than Gunther Partners LLC, do not subscribe for and purchase all 16,000,000 of
the Offered Shares, Gunther Partners LLC will subscribe for and purchase from
the Company in the Rights Offering a number of shares equal to 16,000,000 less
the number of shares subscribed for stockholders other than Gunther Partners
LLC, up to a maximum of 14,000,000 shares. The net proceeds of the Rights
Offering (a minimum of $7 million less offering expenses), will be used to repay
in full the notes payable to Gunther Partners LLC ($4.5 million) and a
stockholder and director ($500,000), to purchase all notes payable to the Estate
for a total of $500,000 and to purchase 919,568 shares of the Company's Common
Stock held by the Estate for $137,935 (or $0.15 per share). The balance of the

net proceeds from the Rights Offering will be used for general working capital purposes." *(Source: Gunther International Ltd 10KSB/A 7/30/2001)*

1.   How much of the net proceeds from the rights offering will likely be available for general working capital purposes?
2.   Compare the terms of the rights offering to the warrants embedded in the earlier financing arrangement. Why do you believe a rights offering approach is being pursued rather than a shelf registration targeting new shareholders?
3.   What disclosures would you recommend be made by the company related to its financing, liquidity, and capital resources?

Key Terms and Glossary

balloon payment a large final payment on a loan that is repaid in installments.

collateral assets that agreement gives the creditor the right to repossess and/or to convert into cash if the borrower defaults on the lending arrangement; also referred to as security for a loan, leading to the terminology of secured debt

compound interest distinguished from simple interest by reinvesting each interest payment in order to earn more interest

continuous compounding assumes continuous compounding of interest rather than compounding at fixed intervals

cum rights with rights or rights on, distinguished from *ex rights*

deficit arises in retained earnings when the cumulation of all prior years' net income or losses, less dividends declared, is negative.

ex rights purchase of shares not entitled to the rights to buy shares in the company's rights issue

exercise price the price at which the holder of a warrant or similar instrument is permitted to buy the stock or other instrument to which it is convertible or is transferable

funded debt matures after more than one year

guarantor that individual or entity promising to pay should the borrower default

line of credit a credit arrangement that permits a borrow to obtain funds up to a certain amount with prespecified terms, and an associated cost for the unused line of credit

maturity that date at which an agreement comes to an end, such as a bond, reaching that date on which repayment is demanded in the absence of a renewal

promissory note a written agreement specifying the terms of the debt

restatement adjustment of past reported financial statements

restructuring when applied to debt, refers to the renegotiation of terms that could include extension of the due date of principal and interest payments, reduction in the rate of interest on existing debt, and/or forgiveness by creditors of a portion of principal or accrued interest; also applied to changes in strategy and operations of a company (e.g., downsizing)

rights offering the issue of securities to current stockholders that is sometimes referred to as a privileged subscription issue

secured debt refers to obligations that if defaulted upon, lead to a first claim on specified assets

subordination refers to the rights of a party being legally set behind another's, such as subordination of debt meaning that claims would not be fulfilled until unsubordinated debt commitments were met; subordinated debt is often called junior debt, receiving payment only after senior debt has been paid in full

warrant instrument permitting the purchase of a specified number of shares at a specified dollar amount

working capital current assets less current liabilities (i.e., net working capital)

Further Readings

Beneish, Messod D., and Eric Press. 1993. "Costs of technical violation of accounting-based covenants." *The Accounting Review* 68, no. 2 (April), pp. 233-257.

Berger, A., and G. Udell. 1995. "Relationship lending and lines of credit in small firm finance." *Journal of Business* 68 (July), pp. 351-381.

Leftwich, R. 1983. "Accounting information in private markets: Evidence from private lending agreements." *Accounting Review* (January), pp. 23-42.

Opler, Tim C. 1993. "Controlling financial distress costs in leveraged buyouts with financial innovations." *Financial Management* (Financial Distress Special

Berle, A., and G. Means. 1932. *The Modern Corporation and Private Property*. New York: McMillian.

Bitler, M., A. Robb, and J. Wolken. 2001. "Financial services used by small businesses: Evidence from the 1998 survey of small business finances." *Federal Reserve Bulletin* (April), pp. 183-205.

Black, B. 1992. "Institutional investors and corporate governance: The case for institutional voice." *Journal of Applied Corporate Finance* 5, pp. 19-32.

Cravens, Karen S., and Wanda A. Wallace. 2001. "A frame-work for determining the influence of the corporate board of directors in accounting studies*."* *Corporate Governance: An International Review* 9, No. 1 (January), pp. 2-24 (Blackwell Publishers in Oxford, United Kingdom).

Cravens, K.S., and W.A. Wallace. 1999. "Blue ribbon plan requires more disclosure to work." *Accounting Today* (July 26-August 8), pp. 14, 17, 40, 41.

Diamond, D. 1991. "Monitoring the reputation: The choice between bank loans and directly placed debt." *Journal of Political Economy* 99 (4), pp. 689-721.

Guenther, D., and M. Willenborg. 1999. "Capital gains tax rates and the cost of capital for small business: Evidence from the IPO market." *Journal of Financial Economics* 53, pp. 385-408.

Issue, September), pp. 79-93.

Petersen, M., and R. Rajan. 1994. "The benefits of lending relationships: Evidence from small business data." *Journal of Finance* 49 (March), pp. 3-37.

Press, E., and J. Weintrop. 1991. "Financial statement disclosure of accounting-based debt covenants." *Accounting Horizons* (March), p. 70.

Shleifer, A., and R.W. Vishny. 1997. "A survey of corporate governance." *Journal of Finance* 52 (2), pp. 737-783.

Scott, Jr., J.H. 1979. "Bankruptcy, secured debt, and optimal capital structure: reply." *Journal of Finance* (March), pp. 254-260.

Smith, Jr., C.W., and J.B. Warner. 1979. "On financial contracting: An analysis of bond covenants." *Journal of Financial Economics* (June), pp. 117-161.

Smith, Jr., C.W., and J.B. Warner. 1979. "Bankruptcy, secured debt, and optimal capital structure: Comment." *Journal of Finance* (March), pp. 247-251.

Williamson, O.E. 1985. *The Economic Institution of Capitalism: Firms, Markets and Relational Contracting*. New York: Free Press.

Williamson, O.E. 1984. "Corporate governance." *Yale Law Journal* (93), pp. 1197-1230.

Williamson, O. E. 1979. "Transaction-cost economics. The governance of contractual relations." *The Journal of Law and Economics*, pp. 233-261.

"The creditors are a superstitious sect, great observers of set days and times. Blessed is he that expects nothing for he shall never be disappointed."

Benjamin Franklin, Poor Richard's Almanac

CASE 2

Microsoft: Does Income Statement Classification Matter?

CASE TOPICS OUTLINE
1. Microsoft Disclosure
   A. Primary Business Alignment
   B. Direct Cost Recording
2. Consistency of Presentation

Microsoft filed its 10-K on September 28, 1999, and disclosed the following:

> "Reclassifications. The Company changed the way it reports revenue and costs associated with product support, consulting, MSN Internet access, and certification and training of system integrators. Amounts received from customers for these activities have been classified as revenue in a manner more consistent with Microsoft's primary businesses. Direct costs of these activities are classified as cost of revenue. Prior financial statements have been reclassified for consistent presentation. Certain other reclassifications have also been made for consistent presentation." *Source: 10-K filed September 28, 1999*

The financial statements for 1999 and 1998, as originally reported and as reclassified, are reported in Table 5.2-1.

Table 5.2-1 Reclassified Historical Income Statements By Year*

Microsoft Corporation Reclassified Income Statements (In millions; Unaudited)	Reported 1999	Reclassified 1999	Reported 1998	Reclassified 1998
Revenue	$13,222	$13,983	$14,484	$15,262
Operating expenses:				
Cost of revenue	1,090	2,145	1,197	2,460
Research and development	1,889	2,030	2,502	2,601
Acquired in-process technology	0	0	296	296

Microsoft Corporation Reclassified Income Statements (In millions; Unaudited)	Reported 1999	Reclassified 1999	Reported 1998	Reclassified 1998
Sales and marketing	2,766	2,331	3,412	2,828
General and administrative	392	392	433	433
Other expenses	60	60	230	230
Total operating expenses	6,197	6,958	8,070	8,848
Operating income	7,025	7,025	6,414	6,414
Investment income	1,318	1,318	703	703
Gain on sale	160	160	0	0
Income before income taxes	8,503	8,503	7,117	7,117
Provision for income taxes	2,920	2,920	2,627	2,627
Net income	$5,583	$5,583	$4,490	$4,490
Earnings per share:				
Basic	$ 1.11	$ 1.11	$ 0.92	$ 0.92
Diluted	$ 1.02	$ 1.02	$ 0.84	$ 0.84

[*]1997 Fiscal Year Reclassifications are likewise presented as reported and reclassified in the Microsoft filing.

Requirement: Disclosure and Strategy-Related Considerations

You are a personal financial advisor to a number of clients, one of whom is a sophisticated investor in Microsoft. The client, who just received the September 1999 10-K filing is perplexed as to the meaning of the reclassifications, reflected in Table 5.2-1. Moreover, given the earnings per share effects are zero, the client does not understand why the disclosure was made at all.

1.   Explain why Microsoft has provided the detail evidenced in Table 5.2-1. Support your explanation with appropriate citations from the Financial Accounting Research System (FARS).

2.   Do you believe that the type of disclosure provided by Microsoft was essential in order for the corporation to comply with generally accepted accounting principles? Why or why not?

3.   Should business strategy influence the classification of revenue and associated costs in an information system? Give an example of how classification of revenue and associated costs might differ between two companies that provide services associated with system design, software development, Internet sites, and other products analogous to those of Microsoft.

Key Terms and Glossary

consistency comparability across time of generally accepted accounting principles' application

direct costs those costs that fluctuate directly with the product, such as raw materials and direct labor used to create physical products

reclassifications changes in the account used to record or present a transaction, event, or estimate

Further Readings

Alexander, David. 1999. "A benchmark for the adequacy of published financial statements." *Accounting and Business Research* 29, no. 3, pp. 239-253.

Bell, Timothy, Frank Marrs, Ira Solomon, and Howard, Thomas. 1997. *Auditing Organizations Through a Strategic-Systems Lens.* KPMG Peat Marwick LLP.

Cato, Sid. 1988. "Manager's Journal: When preparing annual reports, less is definitely not more." *The Wall Street Journal* (August 22), 1988 WL-WSJ 454421.

Doyle, Robert K., and F. Gordon Spoor. 1999. "How to start an investment advisory practice." *Journal of Accountancy* 187, no. 1 (January).

Golub, Steven J., and Robert J. Kueppers. 1983. *Summary Reporting of Financial Information: Moving Toward More Readable Annual Reports* (A Research Study Prepared for Financial Executives Research Foundation).

Jacobs, Sanford L. 1988. "Annual reports in short form fail to catch on." *The Wall Street Journal* (April 14, 1988-WL-WSJ 468976).

Littleton, A.C. 1953. *Structure of Accounting Theory.* American Accounting Association Monograph No. 5 (Sarasota, Florida: American Accounting Association), pp. 39-40, and 44.

Price, Reneé, and Wanda A. Wallace. 1996-1997. "Too many shades of materiality only serve to confuse." Audit & Accounting Forum, *Accounting Today* (December 16- January 5), p. 61.

Price, Reneé, and Wanda A. Wallace. 2001. *Shades of Materiality* (The Canadian Certified General Accountants' Research Foundation, Research Monograph 24 published on CD-ROM): ISBN 1-55219-328-4.

Securities and Exchange Commission (SEC). 1995. WL 385858 (SEC Release No.) 59 SEC Docket 1556, Release No. 33-7183, Release No. 34-35893, Release No. IC-21, 166. "Use of Abbreviated Financial Statements in Documents Delivered to Investors Pursuant to the Securities Act of 1933 and Securities Exchange Act of 1934," File No. S7-13-95, RIN 3235-AG49, June 27.

"Make the scheme of accounts conform with the operating organization of the enterprise, because accounting data can thus be made to reveal the results of management's use of its opportunities."   – A.C. Littleton

[Source: Structure of Accounting Theory, American Accounting Association Monograph No. 5 (Sarasota, Florida: American Accounting Association, 1966), p. 191]

CASE 3

Charitable Contributions and Debt: A Comparison of St. Jude Children's Research Hospital/ALSAC and Universal Health Services

CASE TOPICS OUTLINE

1. St. Jude Children's Research Hospital/ALSAC
   A. Primary Objective
   B. Sources of Capital
   C. Reporting Practices
2. Universal Health Services
   A. Investor-Owned Hospital
   B. Debt Including Leases
3. Comparison

Hospitals are an industry in which both not-for-profits and investor-owned facilities operate. The sources of capital available to the not-for-profits include charitable contributions and debt offerings – unless they are governmental, in which case, higher taxes are also an alternative. Debt availability is always, in part, a function of performance, and just as failures have arisen in both sectors, about one-third of the investor-owned hospitals have been described as losing money. Of interest is how can one effectively evaluate such an industry, with this type of diversity in organizational forms and capital availability? A necessary prerequisite to such an evaluation is to have a firm understanding of how charitable contributions are presented.

St. Jude Children's Research Hospital/ALSAC has the mission of finding cures for children with catastrophic diseases through research and treatment. For the fiscal year 1999, this entity reported total assets of $221,664,232 and income of $177,071,890. A Web site at http://www.stjude.org, as well as Guidestar's listing, references a Form 990 (Return of Organization Exempt From Income Tax) filing, availability of audited financial statements upon request, and information that the hospital has 2,100 employees and 350 volunteers. Founded in 1962, the organization seeks funds from contributions and grants for unrestricted operating expenses, specific projects, buildings, and endowments. More than 4,000 patients are seen annually, with a hospital maintaining 56 beds. The Form 990, Part III states that the hospital provided 15,231 inpatient days of care during the fiscal year and patients made 40,982 clinic visits. ALSAC is the American Lebanese Syrian Associated Charities, Inc., the fund-raising arm of St. Jude Children's Research Hospital. It reported 1999 total assets of $1,007,699,320 and income of $274,123,399. This organization reports the number of employees as 565 and the number of volunteers as 800,000. With its sole focus on the hospital, ALSAC's self-description explains that no child has ever been turned away due to an inability to pay for treatment and explains key accomplishments in the research area achieved by St. Jude's research and treatment of children with catastrophic diseases. What is borne out by the example of St. Jude is the fact that a review of the Form 990 filed for the fiscal year ending 6/30/99 indicates in Part VI the names of related organizations: ALSAC and St. Jude Hospital Foundation, both of which are exempt. To gain a sense of capital availability to a not-for-profit entity, affiliated entities must be considered.   In addition, the role of volunteers is a source of human capital not effectively captured within the framework of financial statements for not-for-profits, as reflected in the Form 990 for the fiscal year ending 6/30/99 for ALSAC, which states in Part VI:

> "Unpaid volunteers have made significant contributions of their time, principally in fund-raising activities. The value of these services is not recognized in the financial statements since it is not susceptible to an objective measurement or valuation and because the activities of these volunteers are not subject to the operating supervision and control present in an employer/employee relationship."

Hence, as one evaluates capital sources and uses by not-for-profits, care is needed to consider affiliated organizations' role, total contributions, and the effect of volunteerism on the comparability between not-for-profit and investor-owned operations.

Universal Health Services, Inc. filed its 10-K on March 28, 2001, for the calendar year 2000, which includes comparative information for 1999. Analysts have described the company as the most aggressive company in the industry over the 1999 to 2001 time frame in making acquisitions, particularly of not-for-profit operations and investor-owned operations experiencing losses. The company is praised for it high operating leverage, the relatively small number of shareholders relative to the magnitude of total revenue, and stock price as a multiple of earnings. The company operates 59 hospitals and, as of 1999, had an average number of licensed beds of 4,806 at acute care hospitals and 1,976 at behavioral health centers, with patient days of 963,842 and 444,632, respectively. Of interest is a commentary on the competition found in the company's filing:

> "Competition
>
> In all geographical areas in which the Company operates, there are other hospitals which provide services comparable to those offered by the Company's hospitals, some of which are owned by governmental agencies and supported by tax revenues, and others of which are owned by nonprofit corporations and may be supported to a large extent by endowments and charitable contributions. Such support is not available to the Company's hospitals. Certain of the Company's competitors have greater financial resources, are better equipped and offer a broader range of services than the Company. Outpatient treatment and diagnostic facilities, outpatient surgical centers and freestanding ambulatory surgical centers also impact the healthcare marketplace. In recent years, competition among healthcare providers for patients has intensified as hospital occupancy rates in the United States have declined due to, among other things, regulatory and technological changes, increasing use of managed care payment systems, cost containment pressures, a shift toward outpatient treatment and an increasing supply of physicians. The Company's strategies are

designed, and management believes that its facilities are positioned, to be competitive under these changing circumstances." *(Source: 10-K filed 3/28/ 2001)*

Financial information is provided in Tables 5.3-1 and 5.3-2 for both the not-for-profit and the investor-owned hospitals.

Table 5.3-1 Financial Comparisons of the Not-for-Profit Entities

Fiscal Year Ended 1999	*St. Jude Children's Research Hospital Form 990**	*American Lebanese Syrian Associated Charities, Inc. (ALSAC) Form 990**
Contributions, gifts, grants and similar amounts received: Direct public support	$91,978,426	$231,793,748
Indirect public support		2,906,934
Government contributions (grants)	31,469,447	
Program service revenue, including government fees and contracts (i.e., health insurance revenue)	46,034,710	
Accounts receivable	24,217,029	4,230,764
Pledges receivable		23,604,748
Allowance for doubtful accounts	9,363,328	
Program service expenses		99,282,906
Program service expenses: Research	87,225,830	
Program service expenses: Education and training	5,471,186	
Program service expenses: Medical Services	93,735,602	
Reconciliation of revenue, gains, and other support to audited numbers: net unrealized gains on investments	-4,023,815	65,891,269
Deferred grant revenue	1,857,628 (Statement 5)	
Support from American Lebanese Syrian Associated Charities, Inc.	91,978,426 (Statement 7)	91,978,426 (paid per Statements 4, 6)
Excluded contributions		2,746,295 (Statement 1)
Excess or (deficit) for the year	-10,933,191	120,521,982
Net assets or fund balances at end of year	199,707,440	994,501,910
Temporarily restricted		15,715,890
Permanently restricted	14,000,000	247,147,826
Total liabilities	21,956,792	7,017,192
Schedule of deferred debits & credits by contract (FAS 116 adjustment noted to result in this deferred revenue)	157,628	

*The Guidestar.org web site provides access to Forms 990 in pdf format.

Table 5.3-2 Universal Health Services, Inc.'s Financial Excerpts*

Income Statements (In thousands)	Reported 1999 Calendar Year
Net revenues	$2,042,380
Operating charges	1,913,346
Components:	
Salaries, wages and benefits	793,529
Provision for doubtful accounts	166,139
Lease and rental expense	49,029
Interest expense, net	26,872
Net income	77,775
Total assets	1,497,973
Total liabilities	856,362
Total retained earnings	482,960
Capital stock	306
Paid-in capital in excess of par	158,345

*The 10-K filing as of 3/28/2001 at EDGAR provides financial statement information for 2000 and 1999.

Requirement A: Recording Revenue

1. What is meant by the reference in Table 5.3-1 to a FAS 116 adjustment?
2. How are contributions recorded? Is there a distinction between pledges receivable and accounts receivable?
3. Are there circumstances when financial statements can quantify volunteers' services?
4. Can financial statement users of not-for-profit hospitals' financial statements expect to be fully informed regarding affiliated parties, such as the linkages between St. Jude's Hospital, ALSAC, and the foundation cited? Explain.

Requirement B: Revenue Mix (Strategy-Related Considerations)

The 10-K filing of Universal Health Services, Inc. describes the mix of revenue sources, as depicted in Table 5.3-3.

Table 5.3-3 Patient Revenue Mix

	"PERCENTAGE OF NET PATIENT REVENUES				
	2000	1999	1998	1997	1996
Third Party Payors					
Medicare......................…........	32.3%	33.5%	34.3%	35.6%	35.6%
Medicaid......................…........	11.5%	12.6%	11.3%	14.5%	15.3%
Managed Care (HMOs and PPOs)...	34.5%	31.5%	27.2%	19.1%	N/A
Other Sources................................	21.7%	22.4%	27.2%	30.8%	49.1%
Total..........................…...........	100%	100%	100%	100%	100%

N/A-Not available" *(Source: 10-K filed 3/28/ 2001)*

1. How does this revenue mix compare with the revenue blend of the not-for-profit entity, St. Jude Children's Research Hospital (ALSAC)?
2. What does that imply as to the strategies of investor-owned hospitals in managing risk and ensuring adequate capital relative to not-for-profit entities? An opportunity exists to explore the greater social and political questions that are frequently debated about the compatibility of profit-oriented entities and quality of health care, relative to not-for-profit entities.

Key Terms and Glossary

fund balance "refers…to a common group of assets and related liabilities within a not-for-profit organization and to the net amount of those assets and liabilities. …While some not-for-profit organizations may choose to classify assets and liabilities into fund groups, information about those groupings is not a necessary part of general purpose external financial reporting." (CON6, Footnote 45); fund balances may refer to such fund groups as operating, plant, endowment, and other funds (FAS 117, Par. 98)

permanent restriction "A donor-imposed restriction that stipulates that resources be maintained permanently but permits the organization to use up or expend part or all of the income (or other economic benefits) derived from the donated assets." (FAS 117, Par. 168) Information about permanent restrictions is useful in determining the extent to which an organization's net assets are not a source of cash for payments to present or prospective lenders, suppliers, or employees and thus are not expected to be directly available for providing services or paying creditors (FAS 117, Par. 98)

pledges receipts of promises to give

temporary restriction "A donor-imposed restriction that permits the donee organization to use up or expend the donated assets as specified and is satisfied either by the passage of time or by actions of the organization." (FAS 117, Par. 168) Separate line items may be reported within temporarily restricted net assets or in notes to financial statements to distinguish between temporary restrictions for (a) support of particular operating activities, (b) investment for a specified term, (c) use in a specified future period, or (d) acquisition of long-lived assets. Donors' temporary restrictions may require that resources be used in a later period or after a specified date (time restrictions), or that resources be used for a specified purpose (purpose restrictions), or both. For example, gifts of cash and other assets with stipulations that they be invested to provide a source of income for a specified term and that the income be used for a specified purpose are both time and purpose restricted. Those gifts often are called *term endowments*. (FAS 117, Par. 15)

Further Readings

Council of Better Business Bureaus (CBBB). 2001. Web site for the Philanthropic Advisory Service reports: www.bbb.org/pas/reports.

Guidestar. 2001. Web site that reports Form 990, Return of Organization Exempt From Income Tax, information for charities: www.guidestar.org.

Peebles, Laura. 2001. "The right philanthropic vehicle." *Journal of Accountancy* (July), pp. 22-27.

Ripperger, Matt. 2001. "Analyst [A director with Warburg Dillon Read's Healthcare Research Group] interview: Hospital management services." *Wall Street Journal Transcript* (February 7), Document # LAQ901.

Wallace, Wanda A. 2001. "How accountable are charities for their performance?" *Accounting Today* (June 18-July 1), pp. 18, 20.

"Accounting deals with a system which is a human creation, designed to satisfy human needs, and which must therefore, above all, be useful. The accounting environment is prone to many influences of a nondeterministic nature, influences related not only to long-term legal, cultural and political traditions, but also to short-term movements of mass psychology…The subject matter is of such diversity

and changing complexity that attempts to make predictions in accounting are akin to the difficulties of predicting the conditions of turbulence inside a tornado or the problem of "forecasting" next month's weather.

In principle it is possible for meteorologists to predict the weather at noon in Chicago on January 1st 1981, just as it is possible in principle to predict an eclipse of the sun a thousand years hence. In practice, weather predictions (unlike astronomical predictions) are unreliable over the space of a month let alone a millennium. Accountants, like meteorologists, are also faced with a complex world of many interacting bodies. Nevertheless, they might be able to adopt the pure scientific method, and perhaps enjoy as much success with it as meteorologists, if – like – meteorologists – they only had to deal with the behavior of inhuman molecules. But in contrast, the accountant's "molecules" think and feel, they have traditions and cultures, they are governed by laws, act sometimes rationally and often irrationally, and are susceptible to an enormous variety of psychological, social, economic, cultural, and political influences….Accountancy…deals with problems involving equity and balance and the resolution of conflict between different groups of human beings with widely varying interest and objectives."

- Edward Stamp

[Source: "Why Can Accounting Not Become a Science Like Physics?" <u>ABACUS</u> (Vol. 17, No. 1, 1981), p. 21]

CASE 4

Clarus Corporation: Recurring Revenue Recognition

CASE TOPICS OUTLINE

1. Clarus Corporation
   A. Press Release
   B. Analysts' Observations

2. The New Economy Meets Tradition

Clarus Corporation announced a change in its business strategy to support a broader range of software licensing arrangements. This meant definitionally that the company would move from the up-front license fee revenue model that had been used toward a subscription-based licensing arrangement that would require a ratable revenue recognition approach. The company understood that as a result of this change in policy, historical and future financial statement figures might not be comparable. Clarus Corporation issued a press release on December 15, 2000, excerpts from which follow:

> "Clarus Expands Business Strategy and Model; Clarus Announces Initiatives To Serve the Growing Large to Mid-Sized Enterprise Market
> Clarus (NASDAQ:CLRS), a leading business-to-business (B2B) e-commerce solution provider, today announced its strategy to meet the growing demand in the large to mid-size enterprise (LME) market. This expansion of its market strategy is designed to accelerate adoption and results in a business model with a greater emphasis on recurring revenue.
>
> Clarus has focused on the LME market and has established itself as a leader in B2B e-commerce solutions... Industry experts... report the LME market is entering a period of accelerated adoption. The Clarus solutions are designed to meet the needs of this target market by offering lower cost of ownership and speed of deployment advantages. As Clarus intensifies its focus on the needs of the LME market it will leverage key strategic partners... to deliver "turnkey" packages and fixed-fee offerings.
>
> "Global market adoption of electronic procurement solutions is less than one percent and even lower in the LME space," said Steve Jeffery, president and CEO of Clarus. "Clarus is positioned to meet this market opportunity with the right mix of products, services, partnerships and pricing."

Key to meeting the demand in this market will be breaking down the barriers to widespread adoption by reducing the risks and costs associated with traditional licensing and implementation of software. Clarus will move to a business model that will provide its customers greater flexibility to choose the way in which they procure their e-commerce solutions. Under this model, Clarus will recognize revenue from the sale of its products over a fixed period of time, reducing the upfront revenue recorded as compared with its traditional model, while generating an increase in the amount of sales backlog.

"This business model and strategy is an evolution of Clarus' longtime focus on the LME market," stated Jeffery. "We believe this shift will not only allow us to drive rapid customer adoption through directly addressing the needs of this target market, but will also provide a more stable and predictable financial model."

In order to meet the unique needs of the LME market, the majority of future Clarus contracts with customers will not meet the criteria for immediate revenue recognition. Instead, a recurring, predictable revenue stream will be recognized over an estimated 12 to 24 month period. Clarus anticipates that approximately 90 percent of its license business will be contracted under agreements requiring ratable revenue recognition.

Clarus also provided guidance for fourth quarter 2000 and for its fiscal year 2001 and 2002. Under the ratable revenue recognition model, the company expects fourth quarter 2000 revenue to be in the range of $4 million to $4.5 million, with an operating loss per share, excluding non-cash charges, of approximately $1.40. For fiscal year 2001, the company expects revenue to be in the range of $45 million to $50 million, and EPS, excluding non-cash charges, of ($2.14). Fiscal year 2002 projections are for revenues in the range of $115 million to $120 million, and EPS, excluding non-cash charges, of $1.08. The company plans to reach breakeven on a cash basis in the first quarter 2002, with profitability on a cash basis projected for the second quarter 2002....

Clarus will host an investor conference call to discuss this announcement today...

About Clarus Corp.

Atlanta-based Clarus Corporation (www.claruscorp.com; NASDAQ: CLRS), a leader in business-to-business (B2B) e-commerce, provides B2B procurement software and trading services that exploit the global marketplace of the Internet to manage corporate purchasing and enable digital marketplaces. ... provides a comprehensive range of critical trading services such as payment settlement, supplier enablement, auctions, integration, and analytics. Designed to provide unprecedented interoperability...

THIS PRESS RELEASE CONTAINS FORWARD-LOOKING STATEMENTS WITHIN THE MEANING OF SECTION 27A OF THE SECURITIES ACT OF 1933 AND SECTION 21E OF THE EXCHANGE ACT. ACTUAL RESULTS COULD DIFFER MATERIALLY FROM THOSE PROJECTED IN THE FORWARD-LOOKING STATEMENTS AS A RESULT OF CERTAIN RISKS INCLUDING THAT THE BENEFITS EXPECTED BY THE COMPANY AS A RESULT OF THIS ANNOUNCEMENT MAY NOT OCCUR..."

Analysts describe Clarus as a company providing e-business solutions that enable procurement, supply-chain management, customer-and-supplier relationship management, and demand management processes of various enterprises – citing such competitors as Global Sources, Commerce One, FreeMarkets, and Ariba. In evaluating Clarus, the analysts compare a trading price in mid-2001 around $6 as low relative to a so-called cash per share value estimate from $7 to $10. The analysts point out that revenue growth is not evidenced in the financial statements because of a change in revenue recognition from what they refer to as a traditional license model and an up-front license model, toward a recurring revenue recognition model. As a result, quarter-to-quarter revenue comparisons witness a large decline from September to December. An interesting point is that the increased backlogs are essentially sources of future revenues.

In its annual filing with the Securities and Exchange Commission, Clarus Corporation described its revenue stream and relevant accounting principles as follows:

"Sources of Revenue

The Company's revenue consists of license fees and services fees. License fees are generated from the licensing of the Company's suite of products. Services fees are generated from consulting, implementation, training, content aggregation and maintenance support services.

Revenue Recognition

The Company recognizes revenue from two primary sources, software licenses and services. Revenue from software licensing and services fees is recognized in accordance with Statement of Position ("SOP") 97-2, "Software Revenue Recognition", and SOP 98-9, "Software Revenue Recognition with Respect to Certain Transactions". Accordingly, the Company recognizes software license revenue when: (1) persuasive evidence of an arrangement exists; (2) delivery has occurred; (3) the fee is fixed or determinable; and (4) collectibility is probable.

SOP No. 97-2 generally requires revenue earned on software arrangements involving multiple elements to be allocated to each element based on the relative fair values of the elements. The fair value of an element must be based on evidence that is specific to the vendor. License fee revenue allocated to software products generally is recognized upon delivery of the products or deferred and recognized in future periods to the extent that an arrangement includes one or more elements to be delivered at a future date and for which fair values have not been established. Revenue allocated to maintenance is recognized ratably over the maintenance term, which is typically 12 months and revenue allocated to training and other service elements is recognized as the services are performed.

Under SOP No. 98-9, if evidence of fair value does not exist for all elements of a license agreement and post-contract customer support is the only undelivered element, then all revenue for the license arrangement is recognized ratably over the term of the agreement as license revenue. If evidence of fair value of all undelivered elements exists but evidence does not exist for one or more delivered elements, then revenue is recognized using the residual method. Under the residual method, the fair value of the undelivered elements is deferred and the remaining portion of the arrangement fee is recognized as revenue. Revenue from hosted software agreements are recognized ratably over the term of the hosting arrangements." *(Source: 10/K filing on 3/21/2001)*

Requirement A: Comparing Revenue Recognition Approaches

Clarus Corporation's 1999 and 2000 data divided between its previous human resources and financial software business (ERP) and the current e-commerce business, along with a few other pieces of financial information are reported in Table 5.4-1.

Table 5.4-1 Financial Information

Clarus Corporation Results of Operations* (In thousands)	Year Ended December 31, 2000	Year Ended December 31, 1999
Revenues: e-commerce		
License fees	$24,686	$9,969
Services fees	9,361	1,515
Total revenues development	34,047	11,484
Revenues: ERP		
License fees	0	5,132
Services fees	0	21,526
Total revenues	0	26,658
Cost of revenues: e-commerce		
License fees	154	400
Services fees	12,776	3,130
Total cost of revenues	12,930	3,530
Cost of revenues: ERP		
License fees	0	951
Services fees	0	11,387
Total cost of revenues	0	12,338
Total operating expenses	98,455	37,429
Operating loss	(77,338)	(15,155)

*Source: 10-K filing on 3/21/2001.

1. How does the described revenue recognition approach compare to other industry settings?
2. The analysts' reference to traditional license models in B2B (business-to-business) relate to up-front models in the "new economy," yet some would argue that tradition in accounting defers revenue to match the earnings process over time. In what sense has the new economy met tradition in the Clarus Company example? Explain, with support from the Financial Accounting Research System (FARS).
3. Do you concur that the recurring revenue recognition will enhance both visibility and predictability of financial results? Why or why not?
   (*Hint:* Access the Staff Accounting Bulletin (SAB) 101 on Revenue Recognition at http://www.sec.gov/interps/account/sab101.htm.)

Requirement B: Strategy-Related Considerations

Clarus Corporation accords attention to the fact that in October 1999, the Company sold its ERP business. Are there added complications of such an event for the evaluator of the company's financial performance? Explain.

Key Terms and Glossary

revenue recognition when revenue is recorded: revenue must be earned and realized or realizable before being recognized – two key criteria for recognition: (1) what constitutes substantive performance by a vendor (i.e., when is the earnings process substantially complete – SFAC No. 5, par. 83(b))? and (2) how much assurance of collectibility is needed to justify recognition of revenue (i.e., when is revenue realized or realizable)?

subscription revenue an example might be revenues for a newspaper, which tend to be recorded as earned, pro rata, on a monthly basis, over the life of the subscriptions

"turnkey" packages reference to off-the-shelf product as distinguished from tailor-made software; the idea is to just "turn the key" to start the ready-made, standardized software

Further Readings

Berenson, Alex. 2001. "A software company runs out of tricks." *The New York Times Company* (April 29).

Berenson, Alex. 2001. "Computer Associates officials defend accounting methods." *The New York Times Company* (May 1).

Bonner, S.E., Z. Palmrose, and S.M. Young. 1998. "Fraud type and auditor litigation: An analysis of SEC accounting and auditing enforcement releases." *The Accounting Review*, 73, no. 4, pp. 503-532.

Davis, A.K. 2001. "The information content of earnings and revenue announcements for Internet firms: Does reporting grossed-up or barter revenue make a difference?" *Journal of Accounting Research*, forthcoming.

Feroz, E.H., K. Park, and V.S. Pastena. 1991. "The financial and market effects of the SEC's accounting and auditing enforcement releases." *Journal of Accounting Research* 29 (Supplement), pp. 107-142.

Guidera, Jerry. 2001. "Computer Associates posts quarterly loss of $410 million." *The Wall Street Journal* (May 23), p. B6.

Henry, David. 2001. "The numbers game." *Business Week* (May 14), pp. 100-110.

Hudack, Lawrence R. and John P. McAllister. 1994. "An investigation of the FASB's application of its decision usefulness criteria." *Accounting Horizons* 8, no. 3, pp. 1-18.

McNamee, David and Sally Chan. 2001. "Understanding e-commerce risk." *Internal Auditor* (April), pp. 60-61.

Ness, Joseph A., Michael J. Schroeck, Rick A. Letendre, and Willmar J. Doublas. 2001. "The role of ABM in measuring customer value, Part one," *Strategic Finance* (March), pp. 32-37.

"News report: Financial reporting – Online financial reports show problems and promise." 2000. *Journal of Accountancy* (February), 1,021 words.

OECD Convention on Combating Bribery of Foreign Public Officials. 2000. "Financial transparency and accountability initiative: Overall observations" (April 17): access at http://www.transparency-usa.org.

Philipich, Kirk L., Michael L. Costigan, and Linda M. Lovata. 1994. "The corroborative relation between earnings and cash flow information." *Advances in Accounting* 12, pp. 31-50.

Phillips, Jr., Thomas J., Michael S. Luehlfing, Cynthia M. Daily. "Financial Reporting/Auditing – The right way to recognize revenue." *Journal of Accountancy* (June), 4,430 words.

Price, Jimmy. 2001. "Auditing e-business applications." *Internal Auditor* (August), pp. 21-23.

Securities and Exchange Commission. 1999. "SEC Staff Accounting Bulletin (SAB): No. 101 – Revenue Recognition in Financial Statements 17 CFR Part 211.

Shridharani, Kaushik. 2001. "E-business applications." Analyst interview (Managing Director in equity research with Bear, Stearns & Co., New York is a CFA), *WSJ Transcript* (May 21).

"Special report, professional issues – COSO's new fraud study: What it means for CPAs." 1999. *Journal of Accountancy* (May), 1,230 words. [The Institute's Web site (www.aicpa.org) has an executive summary of the study.]

Thurm, Scott and Jonathan Weil. 2001. "Money & investing: Tech companies charge now, may profit later." *The Wall Street Journal* (April 27).

Tie, Robert. 2001. "E-commerce: Get ready for the world of B2B." *Journal of Accountancy* (June), 3,029 words.

Wallace, Wanda A. 2001. "EBITDA: Freedom of speech or freedom to confuse?" *Accounting Today* 15, no. 7 (April 16-May 6), pp. 34, 35, 45.

Zarowin, Stanley. 2001. "Facing the future." *Journal of Accountancy* (April), pp. 26-31.

"As we all know, profit figures are not reached by a formula. "Proper and appropriate" provisions may be necessary and in thus providing, prudent judgment is needed. It is when judgment is involved with a desire to reach a particular figure that "profit" becomes meaningless, and we are reminded of a company chairman

who, in the days when accounts were not as clear as they are now, advised shareholders not to rely too much on the figures before them. Other figures, he said, could have been produced which would equally well have earned a clear [clean] certificate!" *[Source: The Accountant (November 8, 1956), p. 571]*

"Indeed, this point was made before a senate subcommittee when one CPA reported an agency had made a profit of $5,226,000 when another reported a loss of $6,448,000. The dispute concerned the recognition of interest revenue."

[Source: "Two Accountants Disagree on RFC 'Profits,'" The Journal of Accountancy (June 1950), p. 467]

CASE 5

When Would Market to Book Be Less Than One? Does Acquisition by Stock Explain JDS Uniphase Corp.?

CASE TOPICS OUTLINE

1. JDS Uniphase Corp. 10-Q Filing
   A. Press Release and Media Commentary
   B. SEC Advice Sought and Results Noted

2. Revaluation

Market to book is a term applied to the ratio of a company's market value of equity (capitalization) to the book value of the equity of the company, and descriptive statistics in the literature for empirical samples of thousands of public companies over the past decades report medians (i.e., midway points within the sample, with half of the companies lying above and half lying below) of approximately 2. The 10-Q for March 31, 2001, filed on May 11, 2001, by JDS Uniphase Corp. included the following disclosures:

> "The Company is currently evaluating the carrying value of certain long-lived assets and acquired equity method investments, consisting primarily of $56.2 billion of goodwill and the Company's $757 million equity method investment in ADVA (see Note 10) recorded on its balance sheet at March 31, 2001. Pursuant to accounting rules, the majority of the goodwill was recorded based on stock prices at the time merger agreements were executed and announced. The Company's policy is to assess enterprise level goodwill if the market capitalization of the Company is less than its net assets. Goodwill will be reduced to the extent that net assets are greater than market capitalization. At March 31, 2001, the value of the Company's net assets, including unamortized goodwill exceeded the Company's market capitalization by approximately $39.5 billion. The Company also examines the carrying value of equity method investments for recoverability on a regular basis, based on a number of factors including financial condition and business prospects of the investee and the market value of the investee's common stock. Downturns in telecommunications equipment and financial markets have created unique circumstances with regard to the assessment of goodwill and

equity method investments for recoverability, and the Company has sought the counsel of the Staff of the SEC on the interpretation of generally accepted accounting principles with regard to these matters. The Company anticipates recording additional charges to reduce the carrying value of the unamortized goodwill and acquired equity method investments and such adjustments could represent a substantial portion of their carrying value. Some of these charges may be recorded as an adjustment to the Company's financial statements at March 31, 2001 and should they be the Company would restate its March 31, 2001 financial statements in subsequent SEC filings."

… "Note 10. Equity Method of Accounting

As of March 31, 2001, the Company had a 29 percent ownership stake in ADVA, a publicly traded German company that develops and manufactures fiber optic components and products and a 40 percent ownership stake in the Photonics Fund ("Photonics Fund"), LLP, a California limited liability partnership (the "Partnership"), which emphasizes privately negotiated venture capital equity investments. The Company accounts for its investments in ADVA and the Photonics Fund under the equity method. Due to the limited availability of timely data, the Company records the adjustments to its equity method investments in the subsequent quarter.

For the three and nine months ended March 31, 2001, the Company recorded $44.5 million and $133.7 million, respectively, in amortization expense related to the difference between the cost of the investment and the underlying equity in the net assets of ADVA. At June 30, 2000, the Company's cost and estimated fair value of its investment in ADVA was $701.1 million. In the process of completing the E-TEK purchase accounting, the Company increased the cost and estimated fair value of its investment in ADVA to $931.5 million during the first fiscal quarter. The difference between the cost of the investment and the underlying equity in the net assets of ADVA is being amortized over a 5 year period. For the three and nine months ended March 31, 2001, the Company recorded a $0.6 million and $5.7 million net loss in ADVA relating to their three and six months ended December 30, 2000 financial results, respectfully. As of May 7, 2001, ADVA had not announced their financial results for the three months ended March 31, 2000. The Company will record its share of the income or loss of ADVA in the three months ended June 30, 2001.

In the three and nine months ended March 31, 2001, the Company recorded a loss of $0.3 million and a gain of $0.6 million, which represented the Company's share of the earnings of the Photonics Fund Partnership for the three and six months ended December 30, 2000. The Company's share of the gain of the Partnership for the three months ended March 31, 2001 was approximately $0.8 million, which will be recorded by the Company during the three months ended June 30, 2001." *(SOURCE: 10-Q May 11, 2001)*

The company later issued an 8-K that includes a press release containing the following related discussion:

"Goodwill discussion

As we announced in April and reported in our 10-Q, the Company has evaluated the carrying value of certain long-lived assets and acquired equity investments, consisting primarily of goodwill and … our investment in ADVA. Pursuant to accounting rules, the majority of the goodwill was recorded based on stock prices at the time merger agreements were executed and announced. The Company's policy is to assess enterprise level goodwill if the market capitalization of the Company is less than its net assets with goodwill being reduced to the extent net assets are greater than market capitalization.

Downturns in telecommunications equipment and financial markets have created unique circumstances with regard to the assessment of long-lived assets, and we sought the counsel of the Staff of the Securities and Exchange Commission on the interpretation of generally accepted accounting principles with regard to this matter. We have had communications with the Staff of the SEC, and we will amend our Quarterly Report on Form 10-Q for the quarter ended March 31, 2001 to reduce the carrying value of goodwill by $38.7 billion for that quarter. In addition, we recorded a $6.1 billion reduction for goodwill in the quarter ended June 30 following further declines in our market capitalization. Finally, approximately $300 million in certain amounts paid to SDL executives in connection with the acquisition which were previously recorded as acquisition costs in the quarter ended March 31, 2001 have been reclassified as a one-time charge for that period and we also recorded a $715 million charge for that period to write down the value of our equity investment in ADVA. Because of the significant industry downturn we are in the process of performing a review of our long-lived assets in accordance with GAAP, and this may result in further charges being recorded for the fourth quarter of fiscal 2001 based on the value of such assets.

The largest portion of the Company's goodwill arose from the merger of JDS FITEL and Uniphase and the subsequent acquisition of SDL, E-TEK, and OCLI. The businesses associated with these business combinations remain significant operations within JDS Uniphase notwithstanding the current business downturn and change in market valuations.

This significant reduction in our goodwill and other assets no doubt will result in press reports or articles about a sizeable loss, so let me explain what it really means. This goodwill resulted from our acquiring good companies when valuations were high. But keep in mind that while we purchased highly valued shares, we were also in effect selling highly valued shares at the same time as none of the transactions resulting in large goodwill amounts were done for cash. Had these transactions been done at different times when valuations were lower with exactly the same share exchange ratios, the goodwill amounts would have been considerably smaller. Of course, these good companies likely would have become parts of other companies and we would not have had the opportunity to acquire them. So by avoiding goodwill we would have foregone many opportunities to strengthen JDS Uniphase. And when you assess these charges, please keep in mind that they were recorded at a time when our cash increased sharply, so these charges in no way impaired our financial health or strength.

We are reporting a pro forma loss of $477 million or $0.36 per share for the fourth quarter and net income of $67 million or $0.06 per share for the year ended June 30, 2001. These results reflect the costs of the Global Realignment Program and charges for the write-down of excess inventory and exclude the costs we have historically excluded, primarily those related to merger and acquisition charges." *(SOURCE: 8-K July 26, 2001)*

The media discussed how the pro forma figure of $67.4 million for the fiscal year ended June 30, 2001, contrasted with the $50.6 billion full-year net loss for that period. It was observed that the pro forma numbers excluded 98 percent of the company's $52 billion operating expenses, suggesting these were mainly write-offs of assets that had been purchased for inflated prices during the tech bubble. These charges are asserted by JDS to have not impaired either its financial health or strength because the company had purchased them with stock instead of cash. The analysts on Wall Street appear to have embraced the pro forma perspective of the company from the media coverage. Excerpts from the note in the quarterly filing that describes acquisitions completed during the first nine months of fiscal 2001, using the purchase method of accounting, are reported in Table 5.5-1.

Table 5.5-1 ACQUISITIONS OF JDS UNIPHASE CORPORATION

Note 9	Date	Purchase Price (In millions) (Unaudited)	Purchased Intangibles	Net Tangible Assets	In Process Research & Development	Goodwill
SDL	February 2001	$41,514.8	$967.0	$617.4	$380.7	$39,549.7
OPA	January 2001	168.5	$5.6	$ (4.6)	$3.0	$124.5
Iridian	October 2000	40.3	$ -	$2.3	$ -	$38.0
Epion*	September 2000	184.5	$14.6	$11.0	$8.9	$150.0
Other		10.2	$ -	$(0.3)	$ -	$10.5

*The purchase price includes the issuance of contingent consideration based on milestones reached during the nine months ended March 31, 2001, subsequent to the acquisition date. *(SOURCE: JDS Uniphase Corporation 10-Q For the quarterly period ended March 31, 2001, filed May 11, 2001)*

Requirement A: Market-to-Book Ratio

1. Why is the ratio of market to book an important consideration in evaluating a company's recorded values? Is it necessarily the case that market to book never drop below a value of 1.0? Why or why not?
2. How important is the fact that the acquisitions were by stock instead of cash?
   Support your position with appropriate citations from the Financial Accounting Research System (FARS). Do you believe that the reported adjustments are sufficient to achieve a reasonable market to book?
3. Is the equity method being applied acceptable? What seems distinctive about JDS Uniphase Corporation's practice?

Requirement B: Strategy-Related Considerations

Company management determines press-release content, and it is not restricted in the same manner as in 10-Q or 10-K filings, as long as nothing fraudulent is included.

1. Do you believe JDS Uniphase was wise to emphasize a pro forma figure in the press release? Why or why not?
2. Do you believe that actions should be taken by regulators to proscribe disclosures that fail to conform with generally accepted accounting principles in their press releases? Why or why not?
3. As an investor, how would you evaluate the company in light of the materials in this case, as well as subsequent evidence on the performance of JDS Uniphase?

Key Terms and Glossary

ebitda earnings before interest, taxes, depreciation and amortization is the general definition, but since this is not defined by generally accepted accounting principles, its application in practice has been observed to vary substantially, excluding a wide variety of costs – as examples, some companies exclude start-up costs, in-process research and development, merger-related costs, stock option compensation, and financing costs, among others

fair value "the amount at which an asset (or liability) could be bought (or incurred) or sold (or settled) in a current transaction between willing parties, that is, other than in a forced or liquidation sale" (Appendix F Glossary, FAS 142)

goodwill "the excess of the cost of an acquired entity over the net of the amounts assigned to assets acquired and liabilities assumed" (Appendix F Glossary, FAS 142)

pro forma historically referred to "as if" presentations, associated with two merging companies, to display comparative historical numbers as if the companies had been operating together for years; more recently, the term refers to disclosures in press releases that do not conform with a definition under generally accepted accounting principles (GAAP) but tend to be characterized as earnings without special or one-time charges, as well as charges management contends are unusual or unimportant, in order to communicate core earnings indicative of future operating earnings

Further Readings

Aboody, David and Ron Kasznik. 2000. "CEO stock option awards and the timing of corporate voluntary disclosures." *Journal of Accounting & Economics* (29, February), pp. 73-100.

Brown, Stephen, Kim Lo, and Thomas Lys. 1999. "Use of R^2 in accounting research: Measuring changes in value relevance over the last four decades." *Journal of Accounting & Economics* 28 (December), pp. 83-115.

Elstein, Aaron. 2001. "Firms fatten up profit outlooks on FASB rule," Heard On The Street, *The Wall Street Journal* (August 21), pp. C1-C2.

Erickson, Merle and Shiing-wu Wang. 1999. "Earnings management by acquiring firms in stock for stock mergers." *Journal of Accounting & Economics* (27), pp. 149-176.

Financial Accounting Standards Board. 2001. "Financial Accounting Series, Statement of Financial Accounting Standards No. 142, Goodwill and Other Intangible Assets" (Norwalk, Connecticut: FASB, June).

Financial Executives International and National Investor Relations. 2001. "Best practice" guidelines for earnings releases (April): see http://www.fei.org.

Miller, Gregory S. and Douglas J. Skinner. 1998. "Determinants of the valuation allowance for deferred tax assets under SFAS No. 109." *The Accounting Review* 73, no. 2 (April), pp. 213-233.

Price, Reneé and Wanda A. Wallace. 2001. "Probability and materiality." *The CPA Journal* LXXI, no. 6 (June 2001), pp. 18-24.

Scherreik, Susan. 2001. "What the earnings reports don't tell you." *Business Week* (October 16), pp. 201-204.

Teoh, Siew Hong and T.J. Wong. 1993. "Perceived auditor quality and the earnings response coefficient." *The Accounting Review* 68, no. 2 (April), pp. 346-366.

Wallace, Wanda A. 2001. "Wording of earnings releases is a story in itself." *Accounting Today* (September 24-October 7), p. 69.

Wallace, Wanda A. 2001. "EBITDA: Freedom of speech or freedom to confuse?" *Accounting Today* 15, no. 7 (April 16-May 6), pp. 34, 35, 45.

Weil, Jonathan. 2001. "Moving target: What's the P/E ratio? Well, depends on what is meant by earnings." *The Wall Street Journal* (August 21), pp. A1, A8.

"Accounting measurement which measures the economic performance of an entity is, therefore, not only a passive representative of real world phenomena, but is also an active agent affecting the real world through its influence upon the decision maker. Thus, we have a situation where two worlds, the real world and the informational world, mutually interact. One is not merely a shadow of the other. The importance of accounting in business should be analyzed within this dual framework." - Yuji Ijiri *[Source: Theory of Accounting Measurement, Studies in Accounting Research no. 10 (Sarasota, Fla.: American Accounting Association, 1975), p. 188]*

CASE 6

UPS: The Tax Environment and Disclosure of Contingencies

CASE TOPICS OUTLINE

A Tax Court case involves disputes between the Commissioner of Revenue and various taxpayers, including corporate entities. United Parcel Service was involved in such a case, the decision for which was filed on August 9, 1999. As shown in the following excerpts, deficiencies are first summarized, then findings of fact are detailed, and finally an opinion is expressed.

The actual Tax Court case is 60 pages long; these excerpts provide a reasonably succinct depiction of the nature of the dispute and basis for the Tax Court's findings. As you read, references to n followed by a number represent footnote numbers that are interspersed within the excerpts.

It is useful to become acquainted with the manner in which tax disputes are evaluated and reported; as you review these excerpts, consider the nature of the business, the allegations being analyzed, the defense of the taxpayer, and the position of the court.

"UNITED PARCEL SERVICE OF AMERICA, INC. ON BEHALF OF ITSELF
AND ITS CONSOLIDATED SUBSIDIARIES, Petitioner v. COMMISSIONER OF
INTERNAL REVENUE, Respondent" No. 15993-95
UNITED STATES TAX COURT T.C. Memo 1999-268; 1999 Tax Ct. Memo
LEXIS 304; 78 T.C.M. (CCH) 262; T.C.M. (RIA) 99268
August 9, 1999, Filed
… OPINION: MEMORANDUM FINDINGS OF FACT AND OPINION

RUWE, JUDGE: Respondent determined deficiencies in petitioner's Federal income
taxes and additions to tax as follows:

Additions to Tax

Year	Deficiency	Sec. 6653(a)(1)	Sec. 6653(a)(2)	Sec. 6661
1983	$ 2,330,687	--	--	--
1984	64,870,674	$ 3,243,534	50% of the interest due on $ 45,122,925	$ 11,280,731

[*4]

Respondent also determined that petitioner is liable for increased interest pursuant to section 6621(c) n1 on the portion of the 1984 deficiency attributable to respondent's determination that excess value charges are includable in petitioner's income.

- - - - - - - - - - - - - - - - -Footnotes- - - - - - - - - - - - - - - - - -

n1 Unless otherwise indicated, all section references are to the Internal Revenue Code in effect for the years in issue, and all Rule references are to the Tax Court Rules of Practice and Procedure.

- - - - - - - - - - - - - - -End Footnotes- - - - - - - - - - - - - - - - -

After concessions, n2 the issues for decision are:

(1) Whether amounts collected by petitioner as "excess value charges" (EVC's) n3 from its customers must be included in gross income in 1984 pursuant to section 61. We hold that EVC's must be included in petitioner's income. n4

(2) Whether petitioner is entitled to deductions under section 162 for any amounts paid to National Union Fire Insurance Co. of Pittsburgh, Pennsylvania (NUF). We hold that petitioner is not entitled to those deductions.

(3) Whether respondent properly disallowed petitioner's deduction of $11,151,675 paid to Liberty Mutual Insurance Group (Liberty Mutual) as California workers' compensation premiums. We hold that the deduction is [*5] allowable.

(4) Whether petitioner is liable for an addition to tax pursuant to section 6653(a)(1) and (2) for negligence or intentional disregard of rules or regulations for the tax year 1984. We hold that it is.

(5) Whether petitioner is liable for an addition to tax under section 6661 for a substantial understatement of tax for 1984. We hold that it is.

(6) Whether petitioner is liable for increased interest on substantial underpayments attributable to tax-motivated transactions under section 6621 for 1984. We hold that it is.

- - - - - - - - - - - - - - - - -Footnotes- - - - - - - - - - - - - - - - - -

n2 Respondent concedes that $8,855,121 of income earned on funds invested by Overseas Partners, Ltd. (OPL), is not income to petitioner pursuant to sec. 481. Respondent determined that if petitioner must include excess value charges in gross income, petitioner is entitled to a corresponding deduction of $32,543,889 for shippers' claims.

Respondent concedes that $325,740 of the $1.2 million paid Liberty Mutual Insurance Group (Liberty Mutual) for claims adjustment services is deductible. Respondent further concedes the deductibility of $50,000 paid by petitioner to Liberty Mutual for the retained layer of liability for losses above $250,000. These concessions reduce the amount of the deduction at issue with respect to the Liberty Mutual policy to $11,151,675.

In the notice of deficiency, respondent disallowed sec. 38 investment tax credits of $1.6 million and $19,006,175 reported by petitioner in 1983 and 1984, respectively. On Sept. 15, 1997, the parties filed a Joint Motion to Sever, requesting that the Court sever the investment tax credit issue. On Sept. 15, 1997, the motion to sever the sec. 38 investment tax credit was granted. The parties subsequently engaged in mediation and settled this issue.

n3 Throughout the opinion, "EVC" represents "excess value charge" and "EVC's" represents "excess value charges".

n4 As a result of our holding, we need not consider respondent's alternative arguments under secs. 482 and 845(a).

- - - - - - - - - - - - - - -End Footnotes- - - - - - - - - - - - - - - - -

Some of the facts have been stipulated and are so found. The stipulations of facts are incorporated herein by this reference. At the time the petition was filed, petitioner was a Delaware corporation with its principal office in Atlanta, Georgia.

FINDINGS OF FACT

I. General

A. United Parcel Service

Petitioner is the largest motor carrier in the United States with a principal business consisting of the pickup and delivery of small packages and parcels. During 1983 and 1984, petitioner conducted its business through wholly owned subsidiaries in the United States, Canada, and West Germany. Petitioner, United Parcel Service of America, Inc. (UPS), had several [*6] wholly owned subsidiaries, including United Parcel Service, Inc. -- New York (UPS- New York), United Parcel Service, Inc. -- Ohio (UPS-Ohio), and United Parcel Service General Services Co. (UPS-General Services). UPS- General Services provides management services to affiliates of UPS. UPS-New York provides ground delivery services in the eastern region of the United States. UPS-Ohio provides ground delivery services in the central and western region of the United States. Within the United States, petitioner generally provided statewide intrastate service n5 and interstate service between all points in the States and the District of Columbia. n6 Another subsidiary, UPS-Air, provided air delivery service for packages traveling partially by air.

- - - - - - - - - - - - - - - - -Footnotes- - - - - - - - - - - - - - - - -

n5 Petitioner did not provide intrastate service within Texas.

n6 There were limited exceptions pertaining to Texas, Hawaii, and Alaska in which petitioners did not provide full services.

- - - - - - - - - - - - - - -End Footnotes- - - - - - - - - - - - - - - - -

Petitioner had 62 operating districts in the United States. Each district had an operational and administrative staff and a manager who was responsible for all district operations. The district manager reported to 1 of 11 regional managers, who, in turn, reported to the corporate headquarters.

Generally, each package picked up by a UPS driver is delivered to a package operating center. At each center, packages are unloaded from package cars and [*7] loaded onto trailers, which haul the packages either directly to another center for delivery or to a UPS sorting hub. At the hub, packages are sorted by destination, loaded back onto trailers, and hauled to the appropriate center, where they are loaded onto package cars for delivery. Packages traveling by air are sorted at an air hub and transported to the center for delivery.

B. Shipping Rates and Tariffs

As a domestic motor common carrier, petitioner was regulated by the Interstate Commerce Commission (ICC). Petitioner's intrastate service was regulated by State transportation agencies and public utility commissions. As an air carrier, petitioner was regulated by the Civil Aeronautics Board. ...

1. Pre-1984

a. Excess Value Charges

Petitioner refers to its customers as shippers. Petitioner charged its shippers a fee for the shipment of each package based on the weight of the package, the distance that the package would travel, the value of the package, and various accessorial services offered by petitioner. Petitioner's [*9] rates were governed by the tariffs, which it submitted to the ICC and the various States.

... Petitioner provided its shippers with a rate card that enabled shippers to determine what petitioner would charge for a particular shipment. The distance a package was to travel determined the number of zones from the point of origin that the package would cross. A package shipped to zone 2, for example, would travel approximately 150 miles. A package shipped to zone 3 would travel up to 300 miles. Zone 8 was [*10] the furthest zone and distance a package would travel within the United States. Zones 2 through 8 were represented as column headings at the top of the rate card.

Weight categories also determined how much petitioner charged shippers for transporting a particular package. The rate card listed weights down the left side of the table in 1-pound increments from 1 pound to 50 pounds. By cross-referencing the zone and the weight, a shipper could determine the exact shipping charge for a particular package whose released value did not exceed $100. There was an additional charge under the tariff when a shipper declared the value of the package to be in excess of $100.

Under the tariff, shippers could also elect to purchase accessorial services that had additional charges. Accessorial services included, among other things, collection on delivery (COD) and acknowledgment of delivery (AOD). ...

DAMAGED AND UNCLAIMED PROPERTY ...

Under the provisions of the tariff, petitioner received from its shippers 25 cents for each additional $100 of declared value of a package shipped, and petitioner referred to the additional amount as an "excess value charge" (EVC). If a shipper paid the EVC of 25 cents per [*13] $100 of value, part or all of the declared value of the package would be paid to the shipper in the event that the package was damaged, lost, or destroyed. In the event that a shipper did not declare the value of the package to be in excess of $100, petitioner was liable to the shipper for the value of the package up to $100.

In June 1983, petitioner filed supplements to its ICC tariffs amending the provision related to the method of determining rates for shippers under the original tariff. The supplements provided an additional clause with respect to the method of determining rates:

Unless otherwise directed by the shipper, the carrier may remit excess valuation charges to an insurance company as a premium for excess valuation cargo insurance for the shipper's account and on its behalf. If the carrier does so, claims for loss of or damage

to the shipper's property will be filed with and settled by the
carrier on behalf of the insurance company. In the event that the
insurance company fails to pay any claim for loss of or damage to
the shipper's property under the terms of its policy, the carrier
will remain liable for loss or damage [*14] within the limits declared
and paid for. n11

- - - - - - - - - - - - - - - - -Footnotes- - - - - - - - - - - - - - - - -

n11 Identical changes were made to petitioner's State tariffs.

- - - - - - - - - - - - - -End Footnotes- - - - - - - - - - - - - - - -

Although the supplements were filed June 1983 and became effective July 1983,
petitioner did not remit EVC's to an insurance company before 1984.

The declared value in excess of $100 is indicated on petitioner's package
pickup record. n12 The package pickup record was used to enter billing
information into petitioner's billing system. Billing information for regular
customers and shippers who shipped parcels from petitioner's customer counters
was entered into petitioner's computer system regularly by each district, and
petitioner billed its regular customers weekly. The bills sent to petitioner's
regular shippers reflected all amounts to be collected from those shippers.
Included, and itemized separately, on those bills were the EVC's and other
miscellaneous charges. All amounts collected from shippers by petitioner,
including amounts for EVC's, were deposited into petitioner's bank accounts.

- - - - - - - - - - - - - - - - -Footnotes- - - - - - - - - - - - - - - - -

n12 Petitioner's pickup record states:

Unless a greater value is declared in writing on this receipt, the shipper
hereby declares and agrees that the released value of each package or article
not enclosed in a package covered by this receipt is $100, which is a
reasonable value under the circumstances surrounding the transportation. The
entry of a C.O.D. amount is not a declaration of value. In addition, the maximum
value for an air service package is $5,000 and the maximum carrier liability is
$5,000. Claims not made to carrier within 9 months of shipment date are waived. ...

- - - - - - - - - - - - - - - -End Footnotes- - - - - - - - - - - - - - - -

For the taxable year ended December 31, 1983, EVC's billed and/or collected from
shippers were included in petitioner's reported income for tax, financial
accounting, ICC, State regulatory, and Securities and Exchange Commission (SEC)
reporting [*15] purposes. ...

(2) AIG/NUF

American International Group, Inc. (AIG), was a holding company and the parent
of over 500 subsidiary operating insurance and subsidiary companies. AIG Risk
Management, Inc. (AIGRM), was a subsidiary of AIG. Mr. Joseph Smetana served as
president and CEO of AIGRM and senior vice president of NUF. NUF was [*26] a
wholly owned subsidiary of AIG and operated as a domestic insurance company...

(4) UPSINCO, Ltd./OPL

On June 9, 1983, pursuant to petitioner's plan, Hall, through Parker &
Co.-Interocean, Ltd. (Parker & Co.), n17 prepared a summary of a proposal to
organize an insurance subsidiary domiciled in Bermuda under the name UPSINCO,
Ltd. (UPSINCO). ...

On August 1, 1983, UPSINCO was certified as an insurer in Bermuda by the Minister of Finance. ...By resolution dated October 31, 1983, the executive committee of the board of directors of petitioner authorized a capital contribution in the amount of $41,017,575 in cash to UPSINCO. In addition, the executive committee of the board of directors of petitioner resolved to take all actions necessary to effect a change of the name UPSINCO to Overseas Partners, Ltd. (OPL). ...

b. Accounting

For the taxable years ended December 31, 1983 and 1984, UPS-New York and UPS-Ohio were required to file annual reports with the ICC and were required to follow the rules of accounting and use the accounts established by the ICC in connection with ICC accounting and reporting requirements. Petitioner was also required to follow Generally Accepted Accounting Principles. For financial accounting and managerial reporting purposes, petitioner used a system of accounts that was generally the same as the ICC system of account numbers. However, petitioner's expense accounts are much more detailed than ICC expense accounts used [*46] for ICC accounting purposes.

With respect to a shipment made by a regular customer, there was no change in the method in which journal entries were made in 1983 and 1984. Petitioner generally debited accounts receivable and credited an intercompany account. When petitioner received the EVC amounts from its shippers, the amounts were deposited in petitioner's bank accounts. Petitioner paid shippers' claims out of corporate bank accounts.

Petitioner did make changes to its internal accounting worksheets at its district level in 1984. The worksheets detailed the EVC's differently in 1984 than in 1983. However, petitioner's accounting journal entries were the same in 1984 as they were in 1983 at the district level. ...

OPINION

I. Excess Value Charges

Respondent determined that EVC's in the amount of $99,794,790 must be included in petitioner's 1984 income pursuant to section 61. Section 61(a) provides in part that "gross income means all income from whatever source derived". It is fundamental to our system of taxation that income must be taxed to the [*61] one who earns it. See *Commissioner v. Culbertson*, 337 U.S. 733, 739-740 (1949). The incidents of taxation cannot be avoided through an anticipatory assignment of income. See *United States v. Basye*, 410 U.S. 441, 447, 449-450 (1973); *Lucas v. Earl*, 281 U.S. 111, 114, 115 (1930). This has been described as "the first principle of taxation". *Commissioner v. Culbertson*, supra at 739. The question of who should be taxed depends on which person or entity in fact controls the earning of the income rather than who ultimately receives the income.... A taxpayer realizes income if he controls the [*62] disposition of that which he could have received himself but diverts to another as a means of procuring the satisfaction of his goals. The receipt of income by the other party under such circumstances is merely the fruition of the taxpayer's economic gain. See *Commissioner v. Sunnen*, supra at 605-606; *Helvering v. Horst*, 311 U.S. 112, 116-117 (1940).

Respondent does not, and need not, challenge OPL's separate existence as a valid corporate entity. The classic assignment of income cases involve persons and entities whose separate existence was unquestioned. See *United States v. Basye*, supra; *Lucas v. Earl*, supra; *Leavell v. Commissioner*, 104 T.C. 140 (1995). The Supreme Court's articulation of the assignment of income doctrine requires no challenge to the separate existence of the persons or entities to which the doctrine applies. As the Court stated:

> The entity earning the income -- whether a partnership or an individual taxpayer -- cannot avoid taxation by entering into a contractual arrangement whereby that income is diverted to [*63] some other person or entity. Such arrangements, known to the tax law as "anticipatory assignments of income," have frequently been held ineffective as means of avoiding tax liability. * * *

[*United States v. Basye*, supra at 449-450.]

Therefore, the issue we must decide is whether petitioner, rather than NUF and OPL, earned the EVC's.

During the years prior to 1984, petitioner properly reported revenues from EVC's as income for Federal income tax purposes. During those years petitioner performed the following EVC functions and activities:

1. Maintained and advertised the shipping activity, which provided a customer base for petitioner's excess value activity.
2. Printed shipping forms with an excess value election.
3. Published excess value rates in tariffs.
4. Incurred liability for damage or loss to packages in excess of $100 when the shipper declared such excess value and paid an EVC. n26

- - - - - - - - - - - - - - - - -Footnotes- - - - - - - - - - - - - - - - -

n26 Petitioner accepted liability for damage or loss to packages up to $100 and made payment for such loss or damages.

- - - - - - - - - - - - - - -End Footnotes- - - - - - - - - - - - - - - -

5. Billed shippers for EVC's.
6. Collected EVC's.
7. Deposited EVC's into petitioner's bank accounts.
8. Retained interest paid on EVC income held in [*64] petitioner's accounts.
9. Processed excess value claims.
10. Investigated excess value claims.
11. Traced lost parcels.
12. Inspected damaged parcels.
13. Paid excess value claims.
14. Maintained a "loss prevention" manual and personnel to audit and implement it.
15. Defended against lawsuits brought by shippers whose excess value claims had been denied.
16. Incurred all costs associated with the administration of its excess value activity.
17. Obtained and paid for catastrophic insurance to cover its liability for lost or damaged shipments.

After January 1, 1984, petitioner continued to perform all these functions and activities. This continuity in petitioner's EVC activity after January 1, 1984, was consistent with a plan petitioner had formulated during 1983.

During 1983 petitioner asked AIG to submit a proposal for restructuring petitioner's excess value program. AIG's proposal contemplated that NUF would perform in a "fronting" capacity; a capacity in which NUF would receive excess value income under the Shippers Interest contract and reinsure its liability under the Shippers [*65] Interest contract with OPL. In his letter dated April 27, 1983, Mr. Corde, of Hall, stated that NUF would exist "in a fronting capacity with essentially no risk or exposure to loss under the program." NUF retained an even $1 million in 1984 as a fronting service fee for agreeing to reinsure the Shippers Interest contract with OPL. n27

- - - - - - - - - - - - - - - - -Footnotes- - - - - - - - - - - - - - - - -

n27 A front has been generally described as an arrangement whereby an insurance company allows another company to use its name for a fee....

- - - - - - - - - - - - - - -End Footnotes- - - - - - - - - - - - - - - -

Mr. Smetana of AIG proposed that petitioner would continue to collect EVC's from shippers, administer and pay all valid claims, and remit excess value amounts to NUF net of claims. Mr. Smetana also proposed that petitioner be responsible for uncollectible EVC's. Mr. Smetana reasoned that "since * * * [AIG/NUF] would have no control over the payment of premium by shippers, * * * [AIG/NUF] would not take on the responsibility for any bad debt or uncollectables under the program." These proposals all became part of petitioner's method of operation on January 1, 1984.

Under the Facultative Reinsurance Agreement between NUF and OPL, article I, item B lists the Shippers Interest contract as the policy to be reinsured. Under article XVIII, subparagraph (A), neither NUF nor OPL could terminate the reinsurance agreement while the Shippers Interest policy remained [*66] in force. Article XVIII further requires that only in the event that the Shippers Interest contract is in fact terminated will the reinsurance agreement between NUF and OPL be terminated simultaneously therewith. Either petitioner or the "Named Insured" could cancel the Shipper's Interest contract under the terms of that agreement. n28

- - - - - - - - - - - - - - - - -Footnotes- - - - - - - - - - - - - - - - -

n28 We note that it is unrealistic to conceive of a situation in which a single shipper could cancel the whole Shipper's Interest contract or that all the unrelated shippers in unison could cancel the contract.

- - - - - - - - - - - - - - -End Footnotes- - - - - - - - - - - - - - - -

Beginning in January 1984, petitioner transferred excess value amounts billed to its regular shippers and collected from other shippers, net of claims paid in excess of $100, to NUF on a monthly basis. Petitioner did not reduce the amounts transferred to NUF in order to compensate itself for sales and marketing expenses that it incurred regarding the EVC's. Petitioner did not charge either NUF or OPL for providing the point of contact with shippers who declared excess value and paid EVC's. No interest on excess value amounts that had been collected before the excess value amounts were transferred to NUF was paid to NUF. During 1984, if a shipper did not pay a bill that included excess value amounts, petitioner attempted to collect the entire amount due from the shipper, including any EVC's included in the bill. Petitioner did not reduce the amount [*67] transferred to NUF by any amount uncollected or any cost it incurred in collecting delinquent EVC's. Petitioner also adjusted and paid all claims with respect to lost or damaged shipments. Petitioner also defended against shippers' claims that had been denied. Petitioner did not reduce the amounts it transferred to NUF in order to compensate itself for performing these activities and did not otherwise charge NUF or OPL for performing any of these activities.

Petitioner also continued to provide other services related to EVC's. Petitioner provided "controlled parcel handling" procedures, which were expensive and time consuming. Those procedures included bagging, tagging, and tracking high value packages that had declared values in excess of $100. Petitioner maintained a loss prevention department in which it employed personnel to audit controlled parcel handling procedures. Such audits took place at petitioner's hub and delivery center operations. Petitioner's special controlled parcel handling procedure with respect to high-value packages constituted extra services for shipments whose declared value exceeded $100. Petitioner did not reduce the amount transferred to NUF in return [*68] for performing the controlled parcel handling procedures and did not otherwise charge NUF or OPL for performing these activities.

Before January 1, 1984, petitioner performed all the functions and activities related to the EVC's and was liable for the damage or loss of packages up to their declared value. After January 1, 1984, petitioner continued to perform all the functions and activities related to EVC's, including billing for and receiving EVC's, and remained liable to shippers whose shipments were damaged or lost while in petitioner's possession. Petitioner continued to receive shippers' claims for lost or damaged goods, investigate and adjust such claims, and pay such claims out of the EVC revenue that it had collected from shippers. The difference between petitioner's EVC activity before and after January 1, 1984, was that after that date it remitted the excess of EVC revenues over claims paid, i.e., gross profit, to NUF, which, after subtracting relatively small fronting fees and expenses, paid the remainder to OPL, which was essentially owned by petitioner's shareholders.

The only potentially relevant change that occurred on January 1, 1984, was the introduction of the Shippers [*69] Interest contract between petitioner and NUF and the Facultative Reinsurance Agreement between NUF and OPL. Petitioner attempts to justify this arrangement on the ground that it was based on bona fide business considerations and that the arrangement had economic substance. If on the other hand the arrangement with NUF and OPL had neither business purpose nor economic substance, other than tax avoidance, the entire arrangement has all the earmarks of a classic assignment of income wherein petitioner was attempting to assign EVC income that had been earned through its own services and activities to OPL for the benefit of petitioner's and OPL's common shareholders.

On brief, petitioner relies on *Moline Properties, Inc. v. Commissioner*, 319 U.S. 436 (1943), for the proposition that it may rearrange, change, and divide business activities among business entities. We agree that, normally, a choice to transact business in corporate form will be recognized for tax purposes as long as there is a business purpose or the corporation engages in business activity. ...As previously noted, OPL's separate corporate existence is not being questioned. The issue then is whether the restructuring of petitioner's EVC activity in 1984 by inserting NUF and OPL as part of the EVC transactions had substance. If these transactions lack substance, then petitioner engaged in an anticipatory assignment of income and cannot avoid taxation "no matter how clever or subtle" the arrangement. *United States v. Basye*, 410 U.S. at 450. While a taxpayer may structure a transaction to minimize tax liability, that transaction must have economic substance if it is to be respected for tax purposes. *See Kirchman v. Commissioner*, 862 F.2d 1486 (11th Cir. 1989), affg. *Glass v. Commissioner*, 87 T.C. 1087 (1986).

The inquiry into whether transactions have sufficient substance to be respected for tax purposes turns on both the objective economic substance of the transactions and the subjective business motivation behind them.... The objective and subjective prongs of the inquiry are related factors both of which form the analysis of whether the transaction had sufficient substance apart from its tax consequences. ...

- - - - - - - - - - - - - - - -Footnotes- - - - - - - - - - - - - - - - -

n29 In *Kirchman v. Commissioner*, 862 F.2d 1486, 1492 (11th Cir. 1989), affg. *Glass v. Commissioner*, 87 T.C. 1087 (1986), the court observed:

Courts have recognized two basic types of sham transactions. Shams in fact are transactions that never occur. In such shams, taxpayers claim deductions for transactions that have been created on paper but which never took place. Shams in substance are transactions that actually occurred but which lack the substance their form represents. * * *

Because all the transactions at issue in this case actually occurred, we limit our inquiry to the question of whether their substance corresponds to their form.

- - - - - - - - - - - - - -End Footnotes- - - - - - - - - - - - - - -

In making our determination as to whether a transaction has substance, we will first look to whether the taxpayer had a business purpose for engaging in the transaction other than tax avoidance. ...The determination of whether the taxpayer had a legitimate business purpose in entering into the transaction involves a subjective analysis of the taxpayer's intent. See *Kirchman v. Commissioner*, supra at 1492.

Petitioner argues that it had legitimate business purposes for entering into the arrangement with NUF and OPL, other than tax avoidance. Petitioner specifically alleges that during 1983 it was seriously concerned that its continued receipt of the excess value income was potentially illegal under various State insurance laws and that it was this concern that motivated it to rearrange its method of handling its EVC activity. Therefore, petitioner argues, the EVC income cannot properly be considered to belong to petitioner. ...

Mr. Johnson's conversation with Mr. Corde in 1982 appears to be his and petitioner's last inquiry regarding problems with State insurance regulation. Neither Mr. Johnson nor petitioner sought legal advice regarding these alleged concerns. In addition, neither Mr. Johnson nor anyone else on petitioner's staff appears [*76] to have made an inquiry as to whether the EVC program, as proposed to be restructured, might violate State insurance regulations. No contemporaneously prepared documentary evidence was presented to indicate that petitioner had such concerns or to indicate that petitioner analyzed the alleged problem and considered the steps necessary to deal with its alleged concerns. ...

- - - - - - - - - - - - - - - - - -Footnotes- - - - - - - - - - - - - - - - - -

n30 During 1983, Mr. Corde of Frank B. Hall inquired about how other Hall clients handled cargo coverage in connection with analyzing the proposed UPS declared value program. Mr. Doug Brown of Hall prepared an internal memorandum to Mr. Corde dated Mar. 2, 1983, outlining the arrangements of other companies which were Hall clients. The concluding paragraph of Mr. Brown's memorandum states:

In my discussions with ...[F]rank B. Hall people and underwriters, the opinion with regard to the legality of selling shippers interest when in fact neither client is a licensed insurance agent was that provided the carrier is simply requesting an acceptance or declination from the shipper for the insurance does not put them in a brokerage or agency position. I find this questionable especially since both clients that I reviewed are doing very little domestic Shippers Interest coverage, consequently, the problem may not have arisen.

- - - - - - - - - - - - - - - -End Footnotes- - - - - - - - - - - - - - - - -

With nothing more than the sketchy testimony about vague concerns by Mr. Johnson, petitioner would have us conclude that it divested itself of a very profitable $100 million per year revenue source that was based on a decades-old system for setting shipping rates that had consistently received approval of the Federal and State Governments. [*81] We do not believe that petitioner would have restructured a significant portion of its business in order to avoid a potential State law problem without having thoroughly analyzed and considered the matter and the ramifications that any proposed change might have.... Petitioner treated liability for loss or damages associated with EVC's as arising from petitioner's tariffs in accordance with Federal law. Upon commencement of a relationship with its shippers, petitioner provided most shippers with a copy of petitioner's service explanation. While the service explanation referred to NUF and the Shippers Interest contract, petitioner did not generally provide a copy of the Shippers Interest contract to each of its shippers. As a result of tariff requirements 510 and 520, rather than filing claims with NUF under the Shippers Interest contract, shippers were required to file a claim only "against" petitioner within a specific time in order to be compensated for loss or damage. Even at the point when petitioner adjusted shippers' claims, petitioner does not appear to have informed the shippers that NUF was the insurer of the claim or that the shippers had any recourse against NUF. Thus, shippers' claims were presented to and resolved by petitioner in accordance with the provisions of the tariff. Petitioner represented to its customers in its quarterly publications that petitioner was liable for lost or damaged packages. In December 1983, petitioner's [*94] Roundups newsletter informed its customers that petitioner's drivers would leave packages without signatures at certain delivery locations. In the newsletter, petitioner assured its shippers that UPS would continue to assume liability for lost and damaged packages up to $100 or the declared value. On the basis of the foregoing facts, we find that after January 1, 1984, petitioner remained liable to shippers who had declared a value in excess of $100.

There still remains the question of whether the arrangement with NUF and OPL sufficiently reduced petitioner's financial exposure to be recognized as having economic substance. The Shippers Interest contract provided that NUF was not liable for the first $100 of value, and in no event did NUF's liability exceed the declared value of a shipper's package. The Shippers Interest contract also provided that if petitioner's liability for loss or damage to a shipper's package was covered by another insurance policy, then NUF would not be liable for the amount covered by petitioner's other insurance policy. Other insurance did exist.

Throughout 1984, petitioner maintained an insurance policy with Affiliated FM Insurance Co. (AFM policy) that [*95] covered petitioner's liability for loss or damage to shipper's packages. n42 Petitioner paid annual installment premiums of $356,945 of which $86,820 was allocated to property value related to parcels in transit. Under the policy, $86,820 of annual premium provided coverage for an average daily parcel value of $354,369,000. The AFM policy provided for a $25,000 deductible to all loss claims arising out of a loss occurrence.

- - - - - - - - - - - - - - - - -Footnotes- - - - - - - - - - - - - - - - -

n42 Petitioner's purchase of the AFM policy and its operation effect of covering "petitioner's liability" for packages shipped during 1984 is inconsistent with petitioner's argument that it had no such liability to shippers after Jan. 1, 1984.

- - - - - - - - - - - - - - -End Footnotes- - - - - - - - - - - - - - - -

To the extent that other insurance did not exist, the Shippers Interest contract generally did not limit claims to any maximum amount per loss occurrence. n43 The AFM policy covered petitioner's liability for package losses related to any single occurrence to the extent the liabilities were greater than $25,000 but did not exceed $10 million. Thus, there was a theoretical exposure for NUF and OPL, to the extent that one or more loss occurrences resulted in more than $10 million in loss per occurrence. For example, if petitioner incurred liability to shippers as a result of a single occurrence of three times the $10 million limit that petitioner was insured for under the AFM policy in 1984, NUF/OPL would have been liable for approximately $20 million. [*96] n44 (Twenty million dollars in additional claims would have reduced the gross profit percentage from EVC's in 1984 from 78 percent to 58 percent.) Even in this unlikely event, excess value revenue in 1984 would have exceeded over two times the amount of claims paid. Considering the extreme magnitude of a catastrophe that would have to occur before claims exceeded excess value revenue in a given year, we again find it unrealistic that petitioner or NUF/OPL would realize a loss in its excess value activity. n45

- - - - - - - - - - - - - - - - -Footnotes- - - - - - - - - - - - - - - - -

n43 With respect to packages send "UPS 2nd day Air" or "UPS next day air", the Shippers Interest contract limited NUF's liability to $25,000 per package.

n44 Disregarding the $25,000 deductible, petitioner would have coverage of $10 million under the AFM policy, and NUF/OPL would be liable for claims in excess of that.

n45 The only potential financial benefit that petitioner could realize from its arrangement with NUF and OPL was if liabilities for lost and damaged shipments were to exceed EVC revenue that it had given up.

- - - - - - - - - - - - - - -End Footnotes- - - - - - - - - - - - - - - -

Petitioner must have drawn the same conclusion. Through the AFM policy, petitioner was able to cover its liability for up to $10 million for any single occurrence in return for premiums of $86,820. n46 This amount of premium is less than one-tenth the amount petitioner agreed to pay NUF to be a "front" in the restructuring of the excess value activity. NUF and OPL were not liable for losses attributable to a single occurrence, to the extent such losses were between $25,000 and $10 million. Petitioner, in turn, was not dependent upon NUF and OPL for single-occurrence catastrophic losses above the deductible of $25,000 and under $10 million but would have been able to [*97] procure coverage for such liability in excess of $10 million for a relatively nominal premium.

- - - - - - - - - - - - - - - - -Footnotes- - - - - - - - - - - - - - - - -
n46 This AFM coverage excludes liabilities of up to $25,000 per occurrence.
- - - - - - - - - - - - - - -End Footnotes- - - - - - - - - - - - - - - -

Petitioner had a conservative, risk-averse insurance philosophy and sought to have sufficient coverage to protect its assets from a catastrophe...." ...
Finally, unlike petitioner's purported business reasons for its arrangement with NUF and OPL, there is contemporaneous documentation to establish that petitioner seriously considered and was motivated by the reduction of Federal income tax that would occur by transferring excess value income to OPL. In July 1982, petitioner's tax manager and another employee prepared a memorandum to Mr. Danielewski concerning tax and other implications of the insurance business. [*111] The memorandum was prompted by a meeting at which petitioner's EVC program was discussed. In September 1982, Hall prepared a memorandum regarding the feasibility of creating a United Parcel Service Insurance Subsidiary. Throughout the memorandum, Hall noted that there were a number of tax benefits if an offshore insurance company were to be created. The tax benefits were stated to be approximately $24 million.

In summary, the report states:
It has been the purpose of this brief preliminary report to
consider in some detail the immediate potential available to
[petitioner] in maximizing the profit potential in the declared
value protection which you are currently providing shippers and
also to acquaint you with some of the basic issues involved in a
captive operating in either a traditional role or within the
context of the declared value program as an insurance
subsidiary.
It appears obvious to us that the conversion of the declared
value program to an insured basis utilizing an offshore insurer
and F.I.R.S.T. will increase the profits generated by this
program by approximately $24,000,000. It is also obvious that
[*112]   there are many complex issues involved in this conversion which
should be considered by counsel.
The potential increase in after-tax profits appears to be totally dependent on projected savings in Federal income tax.

In March 1983, Hall prepared a memorandum that contained a description of the tax benefits if petitioner used the alternative structure for the excess value program. The memorandum indicated that the projected tax benefit to petitioner was $16,077,500 for the first year. Hall arrived at this amount by calculating the benefit to petitioner to be equal to the elimination of income tax on petitioner's expected EVC income, less the fronting fees, premium taxes, Federal excise taxes, and ceding commission. Thus, the documents generated by Hall portray the tax results of creating a Bermuda insurance company as the focus for improving the economic result of the transaction. The memorandum stated that the projection of tax savings prepared by Hall was to be submitted to petitioner's senior management by Mr. Danielewski.

Petitioner subsequently postponed its decision to go forward with the proposed EVC activity structure because of tax considerations. NUF had prepared [*113] a binder for the Shippers Interest contract to become effective as of August 8, 1983. On the same day the contract was to become effective, Mr. Corde sent a telex to Mr. Smetana indicating that petitioner postponed the finalization of the Shippers Interest program to allow for petitioner's review and evaluation of pending tax legislation. In April 1984, after restructuring its EVC activities, petitioner released a report to shareholders in which petitioner indicated that because OPL was organized as a Bermuda corporation doing no business in the United States, OPL's earnings were not expected to be subject to U.S. Federal or State taxes on income.

The contemporaneous documentation prepared by petitioner and Hall regarding the plan to restructure the excess value activity emphasized the resulting tax benefits to petitioner. Petitioner produced no documentation, such as corporate minutes, that was prepared during the period in which petitioner was considering or executing its EVC restructuring that indicates that petitioner had motives other than tax reduction.

Petitioner has failed to prove that the restructuring of its EVC activity was motivated by nontax business reasons or that the [*114] restructuring had economic substance. Rather, we find that the restructuring was done for the purpose of avoiding taxes and that the arrangement between petitioner, NUF, and OPL had no economic substance or business purpose. n58 Petitioner controlled and performed all activities and functions that resulted in EVC revenue. The EVC profits that were transferred to OPL for the benefit of petitioner's and OPL's shareholders were the fruition of petitioner's EVC activity. OPL provided nothing of value to petitioner. The purpose of the arrangement with NUF and OPL was to confer tax-free benefits on petitioner's and OPL's shareholders. Obviously, petitioner is not entitled to any deductions for profits transferred to OPL. As a result, petitioner must include EVC revenue in income for 1984 and is liable for tax on the resulting profits. n59

- - - - - - - - - - - - - - - - -Footnotes- - - - - - - - - - - - - - - - - -

n58 In arriving at our finding, we recognize that some of petitioner's witnesses testified that they considered State insurance regulation and other nontax considerations to be reasons for restructuring petitioner's EVC program. We have fully considered that testimony, the demeanor of the witnesses, and the statements they made before trial (in both contemporaneous documents and interviews) in addition to the aforementioned matters discussed in the text. In the final analysis, we do not believe that nontax business considerations were the reasons that motivated petitioner.

n59 Because we have held that petitioner's arrangement with NUF and OPL was an assignment of income and a sham, we do not reach the issue of whether an allocation must be made under sec. 482 or 845. Petitioner makes no argument that a sec. 482 analysis should be preferred over an assignment of income analysis. Nevertheless, we are aware that several court opinions appear to have expressed a general preference for application of a sec. 482 analysis over the assignment of income analysis. We believe those opinions are distinguishable because the facts in the instant case are both "more extreme" and "heavily freighted with tax motives". Cf. *Foglesong v. Commissioner*, 621 F.2d 865 (7th Cir. 1980), revg. and remanding T.C. Memo. 1976- 294; *Rubin v. Commissioner*, 429 F.2d 650 (2d Cir. 1970), revg. and remanding 51 T.C. 251 (1968).

- - - - - - - - - - - - - - -End Footnotes- - - - - - - - - - - - - - - -

[*115]

II. Section 162 Deductions

Having held that petitioner's restructuring of its excess value activity constituted a sham transaction that had no economic effect, we are presented with the question of whether petitioner is entitled to deduct the amounts retained by NUF. The amounts retained consisted of NUF's "commission" of $1 million plus allowances for various costs.

Section 162 allows as a deduction all ordinary and necessary expenses paid or incurred during the taxable year in carrying on any trade or business. See sec. 162(a). However, expenses incurred in furtherance of a sham transaction are not deductible. As stated by the Court of Appeals for the Eleventh Circuit in *Kirchman v. Commissioner*, 862 F.2d at 1490:

The sham transaction doctrine requires courts and the Commissioner to look beyond the form of a transaction and to determine whether its substance is of such a nature that expenses or losses incurred in connection with it are deductible under an applicable section of the Internal Revenue Code. If a transaction's form complies with the Code's requirements for deductibility, but the transaction lacks the [*116] factual or economic substance that form represents, then expenses or losses incurred in connection with the transaction are not deductible.

The Court of Appeals for the Second Circuit recently addressed a similar issue with respect to interest deductions under section 163. In *Lee v. Commissioner*, 155 F.3d 584 (2d Cir. 1998), affg. in part and remanding in part on another ground T.C. Memo. 1997-172, the taxpayers had entered into a sham investment transaction solely for the purpose of claiming tax deductions. See id. at 586. The taxpayers argued that interest arising from economically empty transactions may still be deducted so long as the debt itself has economic substance. The Court of Appeals for the Second Circuit declined to accept the taxpayers' argument and held that in order for an interest deduction to be valid under section 163, the underlying transaction must have economic substance. See id. at 587. In *Brown v. Commissioner*, 85 T.C. 968 (1985), affd. sub nom. *Sochin v. Commissioner*, 843 F.2d 351 (9th Cir. 1988), we held that deductions claimed by the taxpayers [*117] were not allowable because they were connected to sham transactions.

We have found that petitioner's restructuring of its EVC activity was a sham set up to reduce tax. Following the reasoning in cases such *as Kirchman v.*

Commissioner, supra; *Lee v. Commissioner*, supra; and *Brown v. Commissioner*, supra, we hold that the amounts retained by NUF are not deductible.

…With respect to the restructuring of the excess value income, we have found that petitioner engaged in ongoing sham transactions devoid of economic substance during the year at issue. Petitioner [*123] is a sophisticated taxpayer. The primary thrust of petitioner's argument was that it had valid business purposes for restructuring its EVC activities. We have not accepted this explanation. On the basis of the record as described above, we reject any contention that petitioner had a reasonable basis for the positions taken on the returns. We, therefore, sustain respondent's determination under section 6653(a)(1). We further sustain respondent's determination under section 6653(a)(2) with regard to that portion of the underpayment of tax that is attributable to the excess value charges.

…n62 The Tax Reform Act of 1986, Pub. L. 99-514, sec. 1535, 100 Stat. 2750, amended sec. 6621 to include sham or fraudulent transactions in the list of "tax motivated transactions" set forth in sec. 6621(c)(3). The amendment applies (1) to any underpayment with respect to which there was not a final court decision before the enactment of the act (i.e., Oct. 22, 1986), and (2) to interest accruing after Dec. 31, 1984. See *Price v. Commissioner*, 88 T.C. 860, 888 (1987).

- - - - - - - - - - - - - - - -End Footnotes- - - - - - - - - - - - - - - -

[*125]

Tax-motivated transactions include "any sham or fraudulent transaction." Sec. 6621(c)(3)(A)(v). n63 We have held that with respect to the restructuring of the excess value activity, petitioner engaged in sham transactions lacking in economic substance. On the basis of the findings set forth herein, and the fact that the underpayment of tax will exceed $1,000 in 1984, section 6621(c) is applicable to the underpayment attributable to those transactions that we have found to be shams. See *Price v. Commissioner*, 88 T.C. 860, 888-889 (1987).

- - - - - - - - - - - - - - - -Footnotes- - - - - - - - - - - - - - - - -

n63 See supra note 62.

- - - - - - - - - - - - - - - -End Footnotes- - - - - - - - - - - - - - - -

Decision will be entered under Rule 155."

NOTE TO FINANCIAL STATEMENTS

In its quarterly public filing, available from http://www.sec.gov, United Parcel Service described its experiences associated with a Tax Court dispute and possible ramifications of the decision. Excerpts from the filing in 1999 follow:

"UNITED PARCEL SERVICE OF AMERICA, INC., AND SUBSIDIARIES
NOTES TO UNAUDITED CONSOLIDATED FINANCIAL STATEMENTS …

4. On August 9, 1999 the U.S. Tax Court issued an opinion unfavorable to UPS regarding a previously announced Notice of Deficiency asserting that we are liable for additional tax for the 1983 and 1984 tax years. The Court held that we are liable for tax on income of Overseas Partners Ltd., a Bermuda company, which has reinsured excess value package insurance purchased by our customers beginning in 1984. The Court held that for the 1984 tax year we are liable for taxes of $31 million on income reported by OPL,

additions to tax of $93 million and interest for a total after-tax exposure we estimate at approximately $246 million. We are in the process of analyzing the Tax Court opinion and are evaluating our possible responses, including an appeal or negotiation of a settlement.

During the first quarter of 1999, the IRS issued two Notices of Deficiency asserting that we are liable for additional tax for the 1985 through 1987 tax years, and the 1988 through 1990 tax years. The primary assertions by the IRS relate to the reinsurance of excess value package insurance, the issue raised for the 1984 tax year. The additional tax sought by the IRS relating to package insurance for these periods ranges, based on alternative theories, from $115 million to $121 million for the 1985 through 1987 tax years, and from $131 million to $138 million for the 1988 through 1990 tax years, plus additions to tax and interest. The IRS has based its assertions on the same theories included in the 1983-1984 Notice of Deficiency. We have filed petitions in the Tax Court in response to these Notices. Based on the Tax Court opinion, we currently estimate that our maximum total after-tax exposure for the tax years 1985 through 1990 could range up to $985 million. We are in the process of analyzing our position in light of the Tax Court opinion and are evaluating our options, including continuance of the litigation or negotiation of a settlement.

We anticipate that the IRS will take positions similar to those described above for tax years subsequent to 1990. Based on the Tax Court opinion, we currently estimate that our maximum total after-tax exposure for the tax years 1991 through 1999 could range up to $1.122 billion.

In our second quarter 1999 financial statements, we have recorded a tax assessment of $1.786 billion, which includes an amount for related state tax liabilities. The charge includes interest of $871 million and taxes of $915 million. This assessment resulted in a tax benefit of $344 million related to the interest component of the assessment. As a result, our net charge to net income for the tax assessment was $1.442 billion, increasing our total after-tax reserve with respect to these matters to $1.672 billion. The tax benefit of deductible interest is included in income taxes; however, since none of the income on which this tax assessment is based is our income, we have not classified the tax charge as income taxes.

We have sufficient cash, cash equivalents and marketable securities on hand to deposit with the IRS, if we choose to do so, the full amount necessary to satisfy our total estimated maximum after-tax exposure for these tax matters, without affecting our ability to meet our foreseeable operating expenses and budgeted capital expenditures.

We are in the process of determining a new arrangement for providing excess value package insurance for our customers through a UPS subsidiary. This new arrangement will result in including in our income the total amount of excess value premiums paid by our customers. This revised arrangement, once in place, should eliminate for future periods the issues raised by the IRS in the Notices of Deficiency and increase our net income in future periods as compared to prior periods.

The IRS has also raised a number of unrelated issues regarding the timing of deductions, the characterization of expenses as capital rather than ordinary and our entitlement to the Investment Tax Credit and the Research Tax Credit in the 1985 through 1990 tax years. These issues total $88 million in tax for the 1985 through 1987 tax years and $245 million in tax for the 1988 through 1990 tax years. Additions to tax and interest are in addition to these amounts. The IRS may take similar positions for periods subsequent to 1990. The majority of these adjustments capitalize items for which depreciation deductions would be allowed in future years, and we believe their eventual resolution will not result in a material adverse effect on our financial condition.

We are a defendant in various employment-related lawsuits. In one of these actions, which alleges employment discrimination by UPS, class action status has been granted, and the United States Equal Employment Opportunity Commission has been granted the right to intervene. We are also a defendant in various other lawsuits that arose in the normal course of business. In our opinion, none of these cases is expected to have a material adverse effect upon our financial condition." *[Source: 10-Q Filed August 16, 1999]*

Requirement A: Interpreting the Excerpt

You are an intern with the Securities and Exchange Commission for the summer. Assume that during the course of your internship, this quarterly filing was received from United Parcel Service (UPS), and you are asked to prepare an analysis of the conformance of the accounting treatment and disclosures that relate to the UPS tax environment – known to have been substantially affected by the recent Tax Court Decision. Prepare an executive summary (one to two paragraphs) summarizing the tax court holdings. In addition, provide a detailed explanation of what is required by generally accepted accounting principles (GAAP) and compare those requirements to the disclosures reported by UPS. When differences are detected, explain why you believe UPS has provided the information in the filing, rather than the prescriptions by GAAP.

1. Would you propose that additional or different disclosures be requested from UPS? Why or why not?
2. In reading the excerpt, you observed that the disclosures related to the tax litigation shown in Figure 5.6-1 seem quite different from the other litigation-related disclosures. Why is this the case, and are both in accordance with GAAP? Support your position with a flowchart that explains how, through consideration of guidance available in the Financial Accounting Research System (FARS), you arrive at your conclusion.

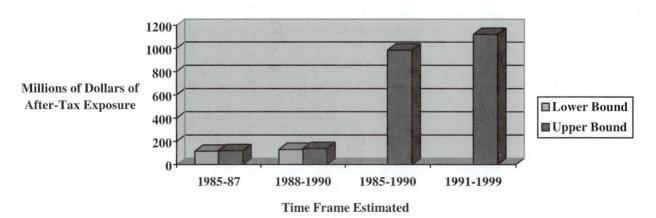

Tax Disclosures by UPS

Figure **5.6-1** A number of estimates are disclosed in the 10-Q.

Requirement B: Cash Flow Implications – Strategy Choices

1. When UPS refers to cash equivalents, to what is the company referring? The disclosure specifically refers to the company's ability to make a deposit with the IRS without affecting foreseeable operating expenses and budgeted capital expenditures. What information sources are relevant to evaluating this representation?
2. The disclosure indicates the company has a choice as to whether to make such a deposit. What other alternatives exist?
3. What strategy would you recommend to UPS regarding its handling of the current tax environment faced by the company and what would be the related cash flow implications of your suggestions?

To facilitate your evaluation of UPS, the Balance Sheet and excerpts from the Income Statement and Cash Flow Statement are provided in Tables 5.6-1, 5.6-2, and 5.6-3.

Table 5.6-1 Consolidated Balance Sheets*

Millions of $ Except Share and per Share	June 30, 1999 (unaudited)	December 31, 1998
Assets		
Current Assets:		
Cash and cash equivalents	$ 1,778	$ 1,240
Marketable securities	1,465	389
Accounts receivable	2,628	2,713
Prepaid employee benefit costs	291	703
Materials, supplies and other prepaid expenses	442	380
Total Current Assets	6,604	5,425
Property, Plant and Equipment (including aircraft under capitalized lease obligations)- at cost, net of accumulated depreciation and amortization of $8,588 in 1999 and $8,170 in 1998	11,466	11,384
Other Assets	232	258
	$ 18,302	$ 17,067
Liabilities and Shareowners' Equity		
Current Liabilities:		
Commercial paper	$ 719	$ -
Accounts payable	1,282	1,322
Accrued wages and withholdings	1,232	1,092
Dividends payable	-	247

Millions of $ Except Share and per Share	June 30, 1999 (unaudited)	December 31, 1998
Tax assessment	1,672	-
Income taxes payable	226	12
Deferred income taxes	94	114
Current maturities of long-term debt	376	410
Other current liabilities	569	520
Total Current Liabilities	6,170	3,717
Long-Term Debt (including capitalized lease obligations)	2,138	2,191
Accumulated Postretirement Benefit Obligation, Net	1,017	969
Deferred Taxes, Credits and Other Liabilities	2,855	3,017
Shareowners' Equity:		
Preferred stock, no par value, Authorized 200,000,000 shares, none	-	-
Common stock, par value $.10 per share, Authorized 900,000,000 shares, issued	56	56
Additional paid-in capital	189	325
Retained earnings	6,614	7,280
Accumulated other comprehensive loss	(147)	(63)
	6,712	7,598
Treasury stock, at cost (12,547,559 and 11,605,952 shares in 1999 and 1998)	(590)	(425)
	6,122	7,173
	$ 18,302	$ 17,067

*See notes to unaudited consolidated financial statements.

Table 5.6-2 Excerpts from Consolidated Statements of Income*

Millions of $ Except Share and per Share	Six months June 30, 1999 (unaudited)
Revenue	$12,891
Operating Profit	1,868
Other Income and (Expense):	
Investment income	70
Interest expense	(105)
Tax assessment	(1,786)
Miscellaneous, net	(22)

Millions of $ Except Share and per Share	*Six months June 30, 1999 (unaudited)*
	(1,843)
Income (Loss) Before Income Taxes	25
Income Taxes	380
Net Income (Loss)	$ (355)
Basic Earnings (Loss) Per Share	$ (0.64)
Diluted Earnings (Loss) Per Share	$ (0.64)

*See notes to unaudited consolidated financial statements.

Table 5.6-3 Excerpts from Consolidated Statements of Cash Flows*

Millions of $ Except Share and per Share	*Six months June 30, 1999 (unaudited)*	*Six months December 31, 1998*
Cash flows from operating activities:		
Net income (loss)	$ (355)	$ 810
Adjustments to reconcile net income (loss) to net cash from operating activities:…		
Net cash from operating activities	2,192	1,278
Cash flows from investing activities:		
Capital expenditures	(597)	(504)
Disposals of property, plant and equipment	50	120
…Net cash (used in) investing activities	(1,749)	(302)
Cash flows from financing activities:		
Proceeds from borrowings	999	166
Repayments of borrowings	(367)	(173)
Purchases of treasury stock	(1,140)	(418)
Issuances of treasury stock pursuant to stock awards and employee stock purchase plans	975	340
Dividends	(311)	(219)
Other transactions	(41)	(17)
Net cash from (used in) financing activities	115	(321)
Effect of exchange rate changes on cash	(20)	(12)
Net increase in cash and cash equivalents	538	643
… Cash paid during the period for:		
Interest (net of amount capitalized)	$ 85	$ 205
Income taxes	$ 423	$ 560

*See notes to unaudited consolidated financial statements.

The Rest of the Story

In its December 31, 2000, 10-K, UPS detailed in its discussion of legal proceedings that it had appealed:

> "In addition, during the first quarter of 1999, the IRS issued two Notices of Deficiency asserting that we are liable for additional tax for the 1985 through 1987 tax years, and the 1988 through 1990 tax years. The primary assertions by the IRS relate to the reinsurance of excess value package insurance, the issue raised for the 1984 tax year. The IRS has based its assertions on the same theories included in the 1983-1984 Notice of Deficiency.
>
> The IRS, in an issued report, has taken similar positions for tax years 1991 through 1994. We expect the IRS to take similar positions for tax years 1995 through 1999. Based on the Tax Court opinion, we currently estimate that our total after-tax exposure for the tax years 1984 through 1999 could be as high as $2.353 billion. We believe that a number of aspects of the Tax Court decision are incorrect, and we have appealed the decision to the U.S. Court of Appeals for the Eleventh Circuit. The Eleventh Circuit has heard oral arguments. We do not know when the court will render a decision." *[Source: 10-K for fiscal year ended December 31, 2000]*

The company explains the basis for its estimates and its action to make deposits without making concessions:

> "We determined the size of our reserve with respect to these matters in accordance with accounting principles generally accepted in the United States of America based on our estimate of our most likely liability. In making this determination, we concluded that it is more likely that we will be required to pay taxes on income reported by OPL and interest, but that it is not probable that we will be required to pay any penalties and penalty interest. If penalties and penalty interest ultimately are determined to be payable, we would have to record an additional charge of up to $681 million.
>
> On August 31, 1999, we deposited $1.349 billion, and on August 8, 2000, we deposited an additional $91 million, with the IRS related to these matters for the 1984 through 1994 tax years. We included the profit of the excess value package insurance program, using the IRS's methodology for calculating these amounts, for both 1998 and 1999 in filings we made with the IRS in 1999. In February 2000, we deposited $339 million with the IRS related to these matters for the 1995 through 1997 tax years. These deposits and filings were made in order to stop the accrual of interest, where applicable, on that amount of the IRS's claim, without conceding the IRS's positions or giving up our right to appeal the Tax Court's decision." *[Source: 10-K for fiscal year ended December 31, 2000]*

The company's "new arrangement" referenced in August of 1999 is likewise described in more details – actions to eliminate the issues considered by the Tax Court post 1999:

> "After the Tax Court decision, National Union Fire Insurance Company, a subsidiary of American International Group, Inc., notified OPL that effective September 30, 1999, it would terminate the five underlying policies that provide shippers' risk insurance for UPS customers. The termination of these policies triggered the immediate termination of the reinsurance agreement between National Union and OPL.

UPS, on behalf of our customers, and National Union agreed on a restructuring of this program, which became effective October 1, 1999. Commencing on October 1, 1999, National Union issued five new policies that include coverage for UPS customers. Glenlake Insurance Agency, Inc., a licensed insurance agency formed in 1998 and a wholly owned subsidiary of UPS Capital Corporation, now offers excess value package insurance to be issued under the five new polices.

UPS Re Ltd., a wholly owned subsidiary of UPS, has entered into a reinsurance agreement under which it will reinsure substantially all of the risks underwritten by National Union in exchange for substantially all of the premiums collected. UPS Re Ltd., is a licensed reinsurance company formed in 1999 to reinsure risks related to UPS and its subsidiaries. UPS Re Ltd., which is domiciled in Bermuda, has elected to be taxed on its income as part of UPS's consolidated income tax return for federal income tax purposes. This revised arrangement should eliminate the issues considered by the Tax Court in the Notices of Deficiency relating to OPL for the periods after September 1999." *[Source: 10-K for fiscal year ended December 31, 2000]*

When It Rains It Pours

The Internal Revenue Service additional claims are described:

"The IRS has proposed adjustments, unrelated to the OPL matters discussed above, regarding the allowance of deductions and certain losses, the characterization of expenses as capital rather than ordinary, the treatment of certain income, and our entitlement to the investment tax credit and the research tax credit in the 1985 through 1990 tax years. The proposed adjustments would result in $15 million in additional income tax expense. Also, the IRS has issued a report taking a similar position with respect to some of these issues for each of the years from 1991 through 1994. This report proposes adjustments that would result in $155 million in additional income tax expense. For the 1985 through 1994 tax years, unpaid interest on these adjustments through 2000 could aggregate up to $368 million, after the benefit of related tax deductions. We expect that we will prevail on substantially all of these issues. Specifically, we believe that our practice of expensing the items that the IRS alleges should have been capitalized is consistent with the practices of other industry participants. The IRS may take similar positions with respect to some of these issues for each of the years 1995 through 2000. The IRS's proposed adjustments include penalties and penalty interest. We believe that the possibility that such penalties and penalty interest will be sustained is remote. We believe the eventual resolution of these issues will not result in a material adverse effect on our financial condition, results of operations or liquidity." *[Source: 10-K for fiscal year ended December 31, 2000]*

In addition, the Tax Court decision has spawned related lawsuits:

"We have been named as a defendant in 23 lawsuits that seek to hold us (and, in certain cases, other defendants) liable for the collection of premiums for excess value package insurance in connection with package shipments since 1984 (or, in some of the cases, for shorter time periods). These cases generally claim that we acted as an insurer in violation of our shipping contract and without complying with state insurance laws and regulations, and that the price for excess value package insurance was excessive. Eighteen of these cases have been consolidated for pre-trial purposes in a multi-district litigation proceeding ("MDL Proceeding") before the United States District Court for the Southern District of New York. An amended consolidated complaint in the MDL Proceeding also alleges a violation of the federal RICO statute. Another complaint in the MDL Proceeding alleges violations of federal antitrust laws. We are in the process of seeking to have four of the remaining cases consolidated into the MDL Proceeding. The other remaining case was remanded from federal court to state court in Madison County, Illinois and is proceeding independent of the MDL Proceeding. No class has been certified in any of these cases. These actions all developed after the August 9, 1999 Tax Court opinion was rendered. We believe the allegations in these cases have no merit and intend to continue to defend them vigorously. The ultimate resolution of these matters cannot presently be determined." *[Source: 10-K for fiscal year ended December 31, 2000]*

Appeals Court

On June 21, 2001, UPS filed Form 8-K containing the following press release:

"APPEALS COURT SUPPORTS UPS, REVERSES U.S. TAX COURT
ATLANTA, JUNE 21, 2001 -- The 11th U.S. Circuit Court of Appeals, in an important ruling, today overturned a 1999 decision that UPS had improperly tried to avoid federal income taxes when it restructured its program for providing extra package insurance to its customers.

The appeals court said the IRS and Tax Court were wrong to brand UPS as attempting a "sham transaction" to avoid its tax obligations. After reversing the 1999 decision, the appellate court then remanded the case back to the U.S. Tax Court, saying any claims by the IRS should be analyzed under provisions of the Tax Code cited by UPS.

"The sophistication (of the insurance revisions) does not change the fact that there was a real business that served the genuine need for customers to enjoy loss coverage and for UPS to lower its liability exposure," the court majority wrote in a 16-page opinion. "We therefore conclude that UPS's restructuring of its excess-value business had both real economic effects and a business purpose, and it therefore under our precedent had sufficient economic substance to merit respect in taxation.

"For the foregoing reasons, we reverse the judgment against UPS and remand the action to the Tax Court...."

Based on the original Aug. 9, 1999, decision of a Tax Court judge that applied to the 1984 tax year, UPS estimated its potential liability at $1.8 billion for all subsequent years if his ruling were allowed to stand. The company then recorded a special tax assessment on its books of $1.786 billion, reducing its income for the second quarter of 1999 by a net $1.442 billion. Without conceding liability, UPS then paid $1.8 billion into a special account with the IRS, pending a decision by the 11th Circuit Court of Appeals. The balance will remain in place pending further proceedings on remand.

"This case was much more to us than a dispute over tax regulations and Tax Code interpretations, because we hold nothing more sacred than our reputation," said UPS Chairman and CEO Jim Kelly. "So we are extremely pleased the original opinion has been reversed."

The case, known as *UPS vs. Commissioner of Internal Revenue*, was argued before the 11th Circuit on March 7. The case focused on the manner in which UPS decided to exit the excess value coverage business in 1984, creating a new, independent company known as Overseas Partners Ltd., or OPL. OPL subsequently based itself in Bermuda and over the years, grew into one of the largest re-insurance companies in the world.

Prior to 1984, UPS provided excess value coverage itself. After creating and spinning off OPL, UPS engaged another U.S. company, National Union Fire Insurance Co., to provide the insurance purchased by UPS shippers.

The IRS argued in 1997 that UPS had created OPL solely to avoid federal taxes and that UPS must pay federal taxes on OPL's income. UPS, for its part, adamantly and consistently disputed the IRS' position, saying it had followed all applicable laws and tax regulations in establishing OPL. The appeals court ruled today "that OPL is an independently taxable entity that is not under UPS's control."

Before and after the changes, UPS offered the lowest rates in the industry for excess value coverage. To this day, a package with a value of $300 can be insured at UPS for 70-cents, compared to $4 for the U.S. Postal Service, $2.50 for FedEx and $2.10 for DHL.

UPS is the world's largest express carrier and largest package delivery company, serving more than 200 countries and territories around the world. Headquartered in Atlanta, Ga., the company is located on the Web at www.ups.com. Earlier this year, UPS was recognized by *Fortune* magazine as "America's Most Admired" package and mail delivery company for the 18th consecutive year." *[Source: Form 8-K June 21, 2001 Item 5. Other Events, Exhibit 99.1]*

Requirement C: Looking Back

Given the benefit of hindsight, how effective were the contingency-associated disclosures by UPS in 1999 and 2000? Explain.

Key Terms and Glossary

contingency "an existing condition, situation, or set of circumstances involving uncertainty as to possible gain (hereinafter a "gain contingency") or loss … (hereinafter a "loss contingency") to an enterprise that will ultimately be resolved when one or more future events occur or fail to occur." FAS 5, par. 1

Internal Revenue Service government agency charged with collection of taxes and enforcement of tax law

investment tax credit an offset to tax bills granted by Congress to encourage investment: the amount has been a function of the life of the asset acquired

probable "The future event or events are likely to occur." FAS 5, Par. 3. FAS 90, par. 45 observes: "some…respondents equated probable with certain. The Board notes that the term probable is defined in Statement 5 and is used in the same sense in this Statement. That definition is not synonymous with certain, a term that connotes a much higher level of assurance than probable."

reasonably possible "The chance of the future event or events occurring is more than remote but less than likely." FAS 5, Par. 3 [Through analogy, FAS 69, par. 72 distinguishes proved, possible, and probable mineral interests granted by Congress to encourage investment: the amount has been a function of the life of the asset acquired.]

reinsurance the practice of insurance companies selling their insurance policies to another insurance company as a risk management arrangement

remote "The chance of the future event or events occurring is slight." FAS5, Par. 4

research tax credit an offset to tax bills granted by Congress to encourage spending on research

U.S. Tax Court specialized courts handling tax disputes

Further Readings

Beaver, William H. 1968. "Market prices, financial ratios, and the prediction of failure." *Journal of Accounting Research* 6, no. 2 (Autumn), pp. 179-192.

Brazelton, J.K., and W.A. Wallace. 1999. "Taxes, inflation, and discount rates in damage computations." *CPA Expert* (Special Issue, AICPA Newsletter for Providers of Business Valuation & Litigation Services), pp. 1-5.

Brazelton, J.K., and W.A. Wallace. 1998. "How taxes are incorporated in evaluating investments: Implications for governmental financial management." *Research Supplement to Public Fund Digest* (Published by The International Consortium on Governmental Financial Management, Washington, D.C. I, no. 1 (Winter), pp. 1-25.

Brazelton, J.K., and W.A. Wallace. 1997. "Audit and accounting forum: Effects of inflation, taxes and discount rates too often ignored in courts." *Accounting Today* (June 2-15), pp. 14, 16.

Buchman, Thomas A. 1985. "An effect of hindsight on predicting bankruptcy with accounting information." *Accounting, Organizations and Society* 10, no. 3, pp. 267-285.

"Business briefs: United Parcel Service Inc., Class-action suit is settled for $38.5 million in services." 2001. *The Wall Street Journal* (August 7), p. A6.

Casey, C.J., and N.J. Barczak. 1984. "Cash flow – It's not the bottom line," *Harvard Business Review* (July-August), pp. 60-66.

Gentry, James A., Paul Newbold, and David T. Whitford. 1985. "Predicting bankruptcy: If cash flow's not the bottom line, what is?" *Financial Analysts Journal* (September-October), pp. 47-56.

Gombola, M.J., and J.E. Ketz. 1983. "A caveat on measuring cash flow and solvency." *Financial Analysts Journal* (September-October), pp. 66-72.

Greenberg, R.R., G.L. Johnson, and K. Ramesh. 1986. "Earnings versus cash flow as a predictor of future cash flow measures." *Journal of Accounting, Auditing & Finance* (Fall), pp. 266-277.

Jensen, Michael. 1986. "Agency costs of free cash flow, corporate finance, and takeovers." *AER Papers and Proceedings* 76, No. 2, pp. 323-329.

Kochanek, R.F., and C.T. Norgaard. 1988. "Analyzing the components of operating cash flow: The Charter Company." *Accounting Horizons* (March), pp. 58-66.

Langley, M. 1986. "Generous juries: In awarding damages, panels have reasons for thinking very big." *Wall Street Journal* (May 28).

Largay, J.A., and C.P. Stickney. 1980. "Cash flows, ratio analysis and the W.T. Grant bankruptcy." *Financial Analysts Journal* (July-August), pp. 51-54.

Lev, B. 1969. "Industry averages as targets for financial ratios." *Journal of Accounting Research* 7, pp. 209-299.

Wallace, Wanda A. 1989. "An early warning signal from the market: Its potential as an audit tool." *Advances in Accounting: Supplemental Volume* (Supplement 1), pp. 205-231.

Wallace, W.A., and C. Wolfe. 1995. "Do expected audit procedures prompt more ethical behavior? Evidence on tax compliance rates." *Research on Accounting Ethics*, Managing Editor: Lawrence A. Ponemon, Associate Editors Marc J. Epstein and John C. Gardner, Volume 1, pp. 145-167.

"There's an unidentified growing object on the right-hand side of the balance sheet," representatives of Shell Oil told a Financial Accounting Standards Board (FASB) hearing panel in New York City on April 23, "and it's called 'deferred taxes.' That's the item these hearings are all about."

"Unidentified growing objects, UGO," mused FASB Chair Donald J. Kirk in response, "we're in danger of inventing a new acronym here."

[Source: "Spectre of UGOs Haunts FASB Hearing," Tax Notes (April 30, 1984): 456]

CASE 7

Embezzlement Related Disclosures: Compliance with Guidance?

CASE TOPICS OUTLINE

1. Halifax Corp. SEC Filings
   A. Disclosures Relating to Embezzlement
   B. Discussion of Associated Risks

2. Reconciliation of 1999 to 2001

Halifax Corporation provides installation, maintenance and training for computer, communications, and simulator systems. The corporation provides support to state and local governments as well as to commercial customers that include military bases, prisons and office complexes. In addition, the company has offered Web site design services, on-site computer repair, and staff outsourcing. The 10-K for March 31, 2001, filed on June 28, 2001, by Halifax Corp. included the following disclosures:

> "Embezzlement Matter
> On March 18, 1999, the Company announced that an internal investigation had revealed a material embezzlement by the former controller of one of the Company's subsidiaries. The embezzlement occurred over a four year period and aggregated approximately $15.4 million of which approximately $15 million was embezzled from the Company and $400,000 prior to its acquisition by Halifax. After net recoveries through March 31, 2001, as discussed below, the cumulative net embezzlement loss to the Company was approximately $7.7 million.
>
> The embezzlement had a material effect on the Company's financial statements. During the year ended March 31, 2001, the Company recovered $1,600,000 (net of recovery costs of $1,156,000). During the year ended March 31, 2000, the Company recovered $2,250,000 (net of recovery costs of $250,000) in conjunction with its embezzlement recovery activities. The specific terms and conditions associated with the payments, including the identity of the parties, are subjects of confidentiality agreements that preclude disclosure. The embezzlement loss for fiscal 1999 was $6,093,000, offset by $3,500,000 in recoveries (net of recovery costs of $1,000,000), resulting in a net embezzlement loss for fiscal year 1999 of $2,593,000." …

"Embezzlement Recovery

During the years ended March 31, 2001 and 2000, net embezzlement recoveries were $1.6 million and $2.25 million, respectively (net of recovery costs of $1,156,000 and $250,000, respectively).

The loss of approximately $2.6 million in 1999 was net of $3.5 million of total net recoveries realized from certain recovered assets (net of recovery costs) and insurance proceeds. For additional discussion see "Embezzlement Matter" in Item 1 and Note 2 of the consolidated financial statements.

Income Taxes

As a result of the Company's historical losses (principally from the embezzlement), the Company generated significant loss carryforwards (both federal and state). At March 31, 2001 and 2000, the Company had remaining net operating loss carryforwards amounting to approximately $8.6 million and $10.2 million, respectively. Due to the uncertainty of future realization, the Company has not recorded a net benefit for these operating loss carryforwards in its financial statements." ...

"Net income (loss) from Continuing Operations

The 2001 net loss of $840,000 from continuing operations was due primarily to higher operating expenses offset by embezzlement recoveries of $1.6 million.

The 2000 net income from continuing operations of $1.4 million was principally the result of embezzlement recoveries amounting to $2.25 million.

Net losses from continuing operations in 1999 of $5.3 million were the result of embezzlement losses of $3.6 million and operating loss, in the amount of $3.6 million." ...

"The Company believes that funds generated from operations, bank borrowings, embezzlement recoveries and investing activities should be sufficient to meet its current operating cash requirements through July 1, 2002, although there can be no assurances that all the aforementioned sources of cash can be realized." ...

"2.EMBEZZLEMENT MATTER

On March 18, 1999, the Company announced that an internal investigation had revealed a material embezzlement by the former controller of one of the Company's subsidiaries. The embezzlement occurred over a four year period and aggregated approximately $15.4 million of which approximately $15 million was embezzled from the Company and $400,000 prior to its acquisition by Halifax. After net recoveries through March 31, 2001, as discussed below, the cumulative net embezzlement loss to the Company before taxes was approximately $7.7 million.

The embezzlement had a material effect on the Company's financial statements. During the year ended March 31, 2001, the Company recovered $1,600,000 (net of recovery costs of $1,156,000). During the year ended March 31, 2000, the Company recovered $2,250,000 (net of recovery costs of $250,000) in conjunction with its embezzlement recovery activities. The specific terms and conditions associated with the payments, including the identity of the parties, are subjects of confidentiality agreements that precludes disclosure. The gross embezzlement loss for fiscal 1999 was $6,093,000, which was offset by $3,500,000 in recoveries (net of recovery costs of $1,000,000), resulting in a net embezzlement loss for fiscal year 1999 of $2,593,000.

Recoveries relating to the embezzlement were as follows:

Fiscal 2001	$ 2,756,000
Fiscal 2000 and prior	7,000,000
Total recoveries	9,756,000
Recovery costs	(2,406,000)
Net recoveries	$ 7,350,000

The Company continues to pursue recovery activities from certain parties although no assurances can be given as to the timing or extent of such recoveries.

On January 9, 2001, the Securities & Exchange Commission issued a formal order of investigation of the Company and unnamed individuals concerning trading activity in the Company's securities, periodic reports filed by the Company with the SEC, certain accounting and financial matters and internal accounting controls. The Company is cooperating fully with the SEC. In addition, the Company has received an SEC subpoena for documents related to these matters. The staff of the SEC has advised that the inquiry is confidential and should not be construed as an indication by the Commission or its staff that any violation of law has occurred, or as an adverse reflection on any person, entity or security. The Company believes the investigation is primarily related to the previously reported embezzlement by one of the Company's former employees."
(SOURCE: 10-K filed June 28, 2001)

The company elsewhere in the 10-K filing states:

"Certain statements in this Annual 10-K Report constitute "forward-looking statements" within the meaning of the United States Private Securities Litigation Reform Act of 1995. Such forward-looking statements involve known and unknown risks, uncertainties and other factors which may cause the actual results, performance or achievements of the Company, or industry results, to be materially different from any future results, performance, or achievements expressed or implied by such forward-looking statements. Such factors include, among others, the following: general economic and business conditions in the Company's market area, inflation, continuation of favorable banking arrangements, the availability of capital to finance operations and planned growth, ramifications of the embezzlement referenced herein, changes in government regulations, availability of skilled personnel and competition, which may, among other things impact on the ability of the Company to implement its business strategy."

"The embezzlement matter did not involve or affect the Company's fulfillment of its Government contracts nor its accounting thereof, and it did not trigger any termination provisions under government contracts."

"Item 3. Legal Proceedings…

There are no material pending legal proceedings to which the Company is a party. The Company is engaged in ordinary routine litigation incidental to the Company's business to which the Company is a party."

"Item 9. Changes in and Disagreements with Accountants on Accounting and Financial Disclosure

Ernst & Young LLP (the "Former Accountants") resigned as the independent accountants for Halifax Corporation (the "Company") on October 19, 1999.

No report prepared by the Former Accountants on the consolidated financial position of Halifax Corporation at March 31, 1999 and 1998, and the consolidated results of operations and its cash flows of each of the three years in the period ended March 31, 1999, contained an adverse opinion or disclaimer of opinion, or was qualified or modified as to uncertainty, audit scope, or accounting principles.

In connection with the audit conducted by the Former Accountants for the fiscal year ended March 31, 1999, which was concluded on September 7,1999, and which included the consolidated balance sheets of Halifax Corporation as of March 31, 1999 and 1998, and the related consolidated statements of operations, changes in stockholders' equity (deficit) and cash flows for each of the three years in the period ended March 31, 1999, there were no disagreements between the Company and Ernst & Young LLP on any matter of accounting principles or practices, financial statement disclosure, or auditing scope or procedure, which disagreements, if not resolved to the satisfaction of Ernst & Young LLP, would have caused them to make reference thereto in their report on the financial statements for those years.

The fiscal year 1999 audit was completed on September 7, 1999 with the issuance, by Ernst & Young LLP, of an unqualified opinion as presented in the Company's Form 10-K which was filed with the SEC on September 9, 1999." *(SOURCE: 10-K filed June 28, 2001)*

Halifax Corporation reported on its balance sheets total assets of $17,966,000 as of March 31, 2001, and $27,808,000 as of March 31, 2000. Excerpts from Management Discussion and Analysis are included in Tables 5.7-1 and 5.7-2.

Table 5.7-1 EXCERPTS FROM RESULTS OF OPERATIONS

Results of Operations for Years Ended [dollars in thousands, except per share amounts]	March 31, 2001	March 31, 2000	Change	%	2000	1999	Change	%
Revenues	$51,750	$53,530	$(1,780)	-3%	$53,530	$59,071	$(5,541)	-9%
Operating (loss) Income	(1,417)	251	(1,668)	N/M*	251	(1,012)	1,263	N/M
Percent of Revenues	-3%	0%			0%	-2%		
Embezzlement (recovery) expense	(1,600)	(2,250)	(650)	-29%	(2,250)	2,593	(4,843)	NM
Income before taxes and discontinued operations	(817)	1,490	(2,307)	N/M	1,490	(5,428)	6,918	N/M
Net income	$1,098	$2,313	($1,215)	-53%	$2,313	$(5,299)	$7,612	N/M
Earnings (loss) per share – basic Continuing Operations	$(.42)	$.70			$.70	$(2.64)		

*N/M = not meaningful *(Source: 10-K as of March 31, 2001, filed June 28, 2001).*

Table 5.7-2 FACTORS THAT MAY AFFECT FUTURE RESULTS

LIQUIDITY AND CAPITAL RESOURCES	2001	2000	1999
Cash balance at March 31, 2001	$231,000	$1,800,000	$0
Working capital at March 31, 2001	$(102,000)	$3,481,000	$740,000
Net cash provided by operations before impact of embezzlement	$520,000	$1,641,000	$1,940,000
Net cash recovered (used) related to embezzlement	1,600,000	5,078,000	(5,421,000)
Net cash provided by (used in) operating activities	$2,120,000	$6,719,000	$(3,481,000)

(Source: 10-K as of March 31, 2001, filed June 28, 2001).

Halifax Corporation filed its 10-Q for the quarter ended September 30, 2001, on November 15, 2001, in which it discloses:

"Embezzlement Recovery

Embezzlement recoveries (net of settlement costs) for the three and six months ended September 30, 2000 were $2.1 million and $1.8 million, respectively. There were no embezzlement recoveries for the three and six months ended September 30, 2001." …

"Pursuant to the Company's credit facility the Company is required to satisfy two financial covenants; funded debt to EBITDA and fixed charge coverage ratio. The Company was not in compliance with the funded debt ratio as of September 30, 2001. The lender has waived the covenant violation at September 30, 2001. The Company and the lender have extended the orginal maturity date from August 31, 2002 to November 15, 2002. (See Note 4 to the condensed consolidated financial statements.)"…

"Note 4 - Debt

On December 8, 2000, the Company entered into a new revolving credit agreement with a financial institution which refinanced the Company's revolving credit line. Advances under the revolving agreement are collateralized by a first priority security interest on all the Company's assets as defined in the financing and security agreement.

The agreement also contains certain financial covenants and reporting covenants. Subsequent to September 30, 2001, the agreement, which originally matured on August 31, 2002, was extended to November 15, 2002.

The revolving credit agreement prohibits the payment of dividends or distributions as well as the payment of principal or interest on the Company's outstanding subordinated debt, which is owned by an affiliate. Interest expense on Subordinated Debt is accrued on a current basis. Pursuant to the terms of a subordination agreement related to the subordinated debt, concurrent with the extension of the revolving credit line discussed above, the due date of the subordinated debt was extended from July 1, 2002 to November 15, 2002.

The Company's credit facility requires it to satisfy two financial covenants; funded debt to earnings before interest, taxes, depreciation and amortization ("EBITDA"), and fixed charge coverage ratio. The Company was not in compliance with the funded debt to EBITDA ratio at September 30, 2001. Its lender has agreed to an amendment to waive the violations. It is the intention of the lender and the Company to restructure the covenants to assure that compliance can be achieved."

Of interest is a comparison of these disclosures to those made in the 10-Q filed as of September 9, 1999 for the period ended June 30, 1999 by Halifax Corp.:

"Note 2 – Embezzlement Matter and Restatement of Consolidated Financial Statements

On March 18, 1999, the Company announced that an internal investigation had revealed an apparent material embezzlement by the former controller of one of the Company's subsidiaries. The embezzlement occurred at, and was confined to, the Company's Richmond, VA based Halifax Technology Services Company ("HTSC"). At the time of the embezzlement, HTSC was a wholly owned subsidiary of Halifax Corporation, which resulted from a merger of CMSA (acquired by Halifax on April 1, 1996), and CCI (acquired by Halifax on November 25, 1996). On April 1, 1999, HTSC was merged into Halifax Corporation and is now a division of the Company.

The Company believes that a single individual, the former controller of HTSC, perpetrated the embezzlement. She was immediately terminated, has since been indicted, has pleaded guilty, and currently awaits sentencing. Under the terms of an agreement entered into with the Company, she is cooperating with the Company's recovery efforts.

The embezzlement occurred over a period of nearly four years and aggregated approximately $15.4 million, of which $15 million was embezzled from the Company and $400,000 from CMSA before it was acquired by Halifax. To conceal the embezzlement in the accounting records, the former controller made fraudulent adjustments totaling more than $21 million. Of the $21 million, the $15.0 million embezzled was recorded in the Company's statements of operations and balance sheets after the acquisition, approximately $2.2 million related to amounts reflected in the acquisition date balance sheet, and approximately $3.8 million related to other overstatements of operating results during the three year period subsequent to the CMSA acquisition.

Under the terms of an agreement with the Company, the embezzler has transferred certain assets back to the Company. Some of the recovered assets have been converted into approximately $1.4 million in cash as of August 31, 1999. With an estimated $1.1 million of assets awaiting conversion to cash, the Company estimates approximately $2.5 million will ultimately be recovered from the embezzler. In addition, the full policy amount of $1 million from each of two separate theft insurance policies, or an aggregate of $2 million, has been received to date.

Therefore, from these sources, the Company expects a total recovery of $4.5 million (excluding recovery costs). The Company estimates that, net of recovery costs, approximately $3.5 million will be recovered. At March 31, 1999, the Company had received approximately $670,000 from its recovery efforts and recorded a $2.83 million recovery receivable to recognize its expectation of receiving the estimated $3.5 million of total net recoveries.

Due to the corresponding overstatement of taxable income, reported by the Company during the period of the embezzlement, the Company will file for a tax refund of approximately $808,000. The receivable is recorded in "Income Taxes Receivable" in the consolidated financial statements.

The embezzlement had a material effect on the Company's financial statements for fiscal years 1999, 1998 and 1997. In addition to the correction for overstated assets and understated liabilities, the Company recorded an embezzlement loss of approximately $2,593,000, $6,044,000, and $2,892,000 for the fiscal years ended March 31, 1999, 1998 and 1997, respectively. The embezzlement loss recorded in fiscal 1999 is net of the actual and projected net recoveries aggregating $3,500,000.

In addition to the notification and involvement of the appropriate authorities, and the intensive and ongoing investigative efforts, the Company has taken other important steps as a result of the embezzlement. The Board of Directors appointed a special committee of the Board to focus on the recovery of assets taken from the Company and minimization of the damages sustained as a result of the embezzlement.

The employment contract of the HTSC president was not renewed, and he is no longer employed by the Company. Furthermore, new executives have been hired to manage the technology services division and to consolidate the Company's financial and administrative activities. The Company has also transferred key accounting and cash management functions of HTSC to Company headquarters.

The Company's financial statements for the three months ended June 30, 1998 have been restated to reflect corrections due to the embezzlement. The effect of the restatement on results of operations for the three months ended June 30, 1998 is as follows:

| Statement of Operations | Three Months Ended June 30, 1998 | |
	Previously Reported	Restated
Revenues	$17,264,000	$16,163,000
Cost of services	15,323,000	15,519,000
G&A expenses	1,306,000	865,000
Operating income	635,000	(221,000)

Interest expenses	355,000	355,000
Embezzlement loss	-	(1,798,000)
Income (loss) before taxes	280,000	(2,374,000)
Income taxes	129,000 ·	(34,000)
Net income (loss)	$151,000	$(2,340,000)
Net income (loss per share – basic	$.08	$(1.16)
Net income (loss) per share – diluted	$.07	$(1.16)"

Requirement A: Disclosure Practices

1. Do you find the disclosures in the 2001 10-K and 10-Q to be informative and sufficient as to the nature and extent of effect of the embezzlement matter? Why or why not?
2. What guidance exists to help you evaluate the sufficiency of the disclosures? Support your position with appropriate citations from the Financial Accounting Research System (FARS).
3. Reconcile the disclosures in the 1999 10-Q to those found in the 2001 filings. Do they compare reasonably? Explain.

Requirement B: Strategy-Related Considerations

1. What signals does Halifax Corp. include in its 1999 10-Q filing to indicate that it has treated the embezzlement matter seriously?
2. Do you believe this type of disclosure has particular importance to this company? Why?

Key Terms and Glossary

ebitda earnings before interest, taxes, depreciation and amortization is the general definition, but since this is not defined by generally accepted accounting principles, its application in practice has been observed to vary substantially

involuntary conversions of nonmonetary assets FIN 30, Summary explains that: "Examples of such conversions are total or partial destruction or theft of insured nonmonetary assets and the condemnation of property in eminent domain proceedings."

nonreciprocal transfer "A transaction in which an entity incurs a liability or transfers an asset to another entity (or receives an asset or cancellation of a liability) without directly receiving (or giving) value in exchange." (FAS 116, Par. 209) "In these transfers one of the two entities is often passive, a mere beneficiary or victim of the other's actions. Examples are gifts, dividends received, taxes, loss of a negligence lawsuit, imposition of fines, and theft." (superseded APS 4, par. 62)

risk "refers to any exposure to uncertainty in which the exposure has potential negative consequences" according to CON 7, Par. 64. The FASB describes various risks in FAS 133, par. 408: "The Board recognizes that entities are commonly exposed to a variety of risks in the course of their activities, including interest rate, foreign exchange, market price, credit, liquidity, theft, weather, health, catastrophe, competitive, and business cycle risks. The Exposure Draft did not propose detailed guidance on what risks could be designated as being hedged, other than to note in the basis for conclusions that special hedge accounting for certain risk management transactions, such as hedges of strategic risk, would be precluded. In redeliberating the issue of risk, the Board reaffirmed that hedge accounting cannot be provided for all possible risks and decided to be more specific about the risks for which hedge accounting is available."

Further Readings

Cohen, Jeffrey R., Laurie W. Pant and David J. Sharp. 1993. "Culture-Based Ethical Conflicts Confronting Multinational Accounting Firms." *Accounting Horizons* 7, no. 3, pp. 1-13.

Cravens, K.S. and Wallace, W.A. 2001. A Framework for Determining the Influence of the Corporate Board of Directors in Accounting Studies. *Corporate Governance: An International Review.* 9, no. 1 (January), pp. 2-24.

Financial Executives International and National Investor Relations. 2001. "Best practice" guidelines for earnings releases (April): see http://www.fei.org.

Finley, David R. 1994, "Game Theoretic Analysis Of Discovery Sampling For Internal Fraud Control Auditing." *Contemporary Accounting Research* 11, 1, pp. 91-114.

Healy, Paul M. and Krishna G. Palepu. 1993. "The Effect of Firms' Financial Disclosure Strategies on Stock Prices." *Accounting Horizons* 7, no. 1, pp. 1-11.

Licata, Michael P., Wayne G. Bremser, and Theresa P. Rollins. 1997. "A SEC Enforcement Actions Against Auditors: Auditing Education Linked to the Pitfalls of Audit Practice." *Issues in Accounting Education* 12, no. 2 (Fall), pp. 537-560.

Menon, Krishnagopal and David D. Williams. 1994. "The Insurance Hypothesis And Market Prices." *The Accounting Review* 69, no. 2, pp. 327-342.

Morton, Sanford. 1993. "Strategic Auditing for Fraud." *The Accounting Review* 68, no. 4, pp. 825-839.

National Commission of Fraudulent Financial Reporting (the Treadway Commission). 1987. *Report of the National Commission on Fraudulent Financial Reporting.* Washington, D.C.: U.S. Government Printing Office.

Ross, S. 1979. "Disclosure Regulations in Financial Markets: Implications of Modern Finance Theory and Signaling Theory." *Key Issues in Financial Regulation:*, pp. 177-201.

Walker, R.G. and S.P. Robinson. 1994. "Related Party Transactions: A Case Study Of Inter-Organizational Conflict Over The 'Development' Of Disclosure Rules." *Abacus* 30, no. 1, pp. 18-43.

Wallace, Wanda A. 2000. "Reporting Practices: Potential Lessons From Cendant," *European Management Journal* 18, no. 3 (June), pp. 328-333.

Wallace, Wanda A. 2000. "The Value Relevance of Accounting: The Rest of the Story." *European Management Journal* 18, no. 6 (December), pp. 675-682.

Wright, Arnold and Sally Wright. 1996. "The Relationship Between Assessments of Internal Control Strength and Error Occurrence, Impact and Cause." *Accounting and Business Research* 27, no. 1, pp. 58-71.

"The hardest crossword puzzle to solve is the one in which we have penciled in a wrong word and are too stubborn or fixated to erase it; in much the same way, it is often easier to solve a problem when you are merely ignorant than when you are wrong." **Sidney J. Harris** *[Cited by George W. Downs and Patrick D. Larkey in* The Search for Government Efficiency: From Hubris to Helplessness *(Philadelphia: Temple University Press, 1986), p. 49.]*

CASE 8

What Constitutes a Subsequent Event? Related Gain Contingency Considerations

CASE TOPICS OUTLINE

1. Subsequent Event for Euronet Worldwide, Inc.
   A. Extinguishment of Debt
   B. Extraordinary Gain

2. Gain Contingency Considerations

Euronet Worldwide, Inc. provides both software and service solutions related to secure electronic financial transactions. A press release was issued by Euronet Worldwide, Inc. on September 10, 2001, in which it announced the appointment of Daniel R. Henry as President, in addition to his Chief Operating Officer (COO) role. The release elaborated on the fact that Mr. Henry co-founded the company with Michael Brown in 1994 and that Mr. Brown would continue as Chairman and Chief Executive Officer--no longer holding the title of President. This same release identifies the realization of a subsequent event reported in its Form 10-Q for the period ended June 30, 2001. Specifically, since that date, it had exchanged senior discount notes for shares of its common stocks. The release quantifies implications of the exchange as of August 31, 2001 as decreasing the indebtedness since June 30, 2001, thereby resulting in an annual interest expense savings of approximately $2 million per year.

In its quarterly filing, Euronet Worldwide included the following notes among its disclosures:

"EURONET WORLDWIDE, INC. AND SUBSIDIARIES
NOTES TO THE UNAUDITED CONSOLIDATED FINANCIAL STATEMENTS
SEPTEMBER 30, 2001 AND 2000

NOTE 1 - FINANCIAL POSITION AND BASIS OF PRESENTATION

The accompanying unaudited consolidated financial statements of Euronet Worldwide, Inc. and subsidiaries (collectively, "Euronet" or the "Company")(formerly Euronet Services Inc.), have been prepared from the records of the Company, pursuant to the rules and regulations of the Securities and Exchange Commission. In the opinion of management, such unaudited consolidated financial statements include all adjustments (consisting only of normal, recurring accruals) necessary to present fairly the financial position of the Company at September 30, 2001, the results of its operations for the three-month periods and nine-month periods ended September 30, 2001 and 2000 and cash flows for the nine-month periods ended September 30, 2001 and 2000.

The unaudited consolidated financial statements should be read in conjunction with the audited consolidated financial statements of Euronet Worldwide, Inc and subsidiaries for the year ended December 31, 2000, including the notes thereto, set forth in the Company's Form 10-K.

The results of operations for the three-month and nine-month periods ended September 30, 2001 are not necessarily indicative of the results to be expected for the full year.

The Company generated an operating loss of $6.2 million for the nine months ended September 30, 2001 primarily due to the significant costs associated with the expansion of its ATM network and investment support and research and development in its software. In addition, the Company generated negative cash flows from operations of $0.3 million for the nine months ended September 30, 2001, as a result of these same factors. Based on the Company's current business plan and financial projections, the Company expects to reduce operating losses and net cash used in operating activities during the remainder of 2001. In the Processing Services Segment, the Company anticipates that increased transaction levels in its ATM network will result in additional revenues without a corresponding increase in expenses. In addition, the Company expects to further expand its ATM outsourcing services and offer new value-added services, which will provide continued revenue growth without significantly increasing direct operating expenses or capital investments. In the Software Solutions Segment, the Company expects to continue its strategic repositioning of its software business from direct software sales to software-only customers to more integrated solutions combining the strengths of the Company's electronic financial transaction network system with its software development strengths.

The Company has a $4.0 million credit facility under an unsecured revolving credit agreement (see Note 5). As of September 30, 2001, the Company had drawn $2.0 million against such credit agreement. In addition, the Company holds repurchased notes payable with a face value of DEM 139.7 million ($65.0 million) and a fair value at September 30, 2001 of $52.0 million. The Company believes that cash and cash equivalents at September 30, 2001, and the revolving credit agreement described above, will provide the Company with sufficient cash resources until it achieves positive cash flow. The Company nevertheless has a policy of assessing opportunities for additional debt and equity financing as they arise, and will pursue any such opportunities if the Company considers that they may contribute to fulfilling its financial and strategic business objectives.

Based on the above, management is confident that the Company will be able to continue as a going concern. Accordingly, these consolidated financial statements have been prepared on a going concern basis which contemplates the continuation and expansion of trading activities as well as the realization of assets and liquidation of liabilities in the ordinary course of business....

NOTE 6 - EXTINGUISHMENT OF DEBT

During the three months ending March 31, 2001, in a single transaction, the Company exchanged 8,750 Senior Discount Notes (principal face amount of DEM 8.75 million) of its Senior Discount Notes for two new Senior discount notes having an aggregate face amount of $2.9 million (the "New Notes"). The interest, repayment and other terms of the New Notes are identical to those of the Senior Discount Notes for which they were exchanged, except that (i) the principal amount was reduced as indicated in the previous sentence, (ii) the Company has the right to prepay the New Notes at any time at its option by paying the "Accreted Value" of the Notes, and (iii) the new notes are governed by a new Note Purchase Agreement rather than the indenture under which the Senior Discount Notes were issued and the New Notes therefore are not covered by any of the provisions of such indenture relating to action by the trustee, voting or maintenance of listing on a stock exchange. This exchange has been accounted for as an extinguishment of debt and issuance of new debt with a resulting $0.4 million (net of applicable income taxes of $0.3 million) recognized as an extraordinary gain on such extinguishment. The extinguishment gain (pre-tax) represents the difference between the allocated carrying value of the debt extinguished ($3.3 million) and the fair market value of the New Notes issued ($2.5 million), offset by the write-off of the allocated unamortized deferred financing costs ($0.1 million). This transaction was exempt from registration in accordance with Section 3(a)9 of the Act.

During the six months ending June 30, 2001, in eight separate transactions, the Company exchanged 48,600 units (principal amount of DEM 48.6 million) of its Senior Discount Notes and 145,800 warrants for 1,691,000 shares of its common stock, par value $0.02 per share. This exchange has been accounted for as an extinguishment of debt with a resulting $7.0 million (net of applicable income taxes of $1.0 million) recognized as an extraordinary gain on such extinguishment. The extinguishment gain (pre-tax) represents the difference between the allocated carrying value of the debt and any related warrants extinguished ($19.0 million) and the fair market value of the common stock issued ($10.5 million), offset by the write-off of the allocated unamortized deferred financing costs ($0.5 million). These transactions were exempt from registration in accordance with Section 3(a)9 of the Act.

During the three months ending September 30, 2001, in five separate transactions, the Company exchanged 34,000 units (principal amount of DEM 34.0 million) of its Senior Discount Notes and 102,000 warrants for 1,157,000 shares of its common stock, par value $0.02 per share. This exchange has been accounted for as an extinguishment of debt with a resulting $2.1 million (inclusive of an applicable income tax benefit of $1.0 million) recognized as an extraordinary gain on such extinguishment. The extinguishment gain (pre-tax) represents the difference between the allocated carrying value of the debt and any related warrants extinguished ($13.6 million) and the fair market value of the common stock issued ($12.2 million), offset by the write-off of the allocated unamortized deferred financing costs ($0.3 million). These transactions were exempt from registration in accordance with Section 3(a)9 of the Act.

The Senior Discount Notes that were acquired by the Company in the above exchanges have not been retired. The Company will consider additional repurchases of its Senior Discount Notes if opportunities arise to complete such transactions on favorable terms....

NOTE 9 - SUBSEQUENT EVENTS

As of November 9, 2001, in a single transaction, the Company exchanged an aggregate of face value DEM 3.0 million of its Senior Discount Notes for 79,500 shares of its common stock, par value $0.02 per share. This exchange will be accounted for as an extinguishment of debt with the resulting extraordinary gain on such extinguishment calculated as the difference between the allocated carrying value of the debt and any related warrants extinguished and the fair market value of the common stock issued, offset by the write-off of the allocated unamortized deferred financing costs. The transaction is exempt from registration in accordance with Section 3(a)9 of the Act. The Senior Discount Notes that were acquired by the Company in the above exchange have not been retired.

As of October 22, 2001, the Hungarian American Enterprise Fund exercised warrants to purchase a total of 102,500 shares of Euronet common stock, par value $0.02 per share, for an aggregate strike price of $598,500. The warrants had been issued under the Credit Agreement referred to in Note 5.

As of November 13, 2001, DST Systems, Inc. exercised warrants to purchase a total of 246,000 shares of Euronet common stock, par value $0.02 per share, for an aggregate strike price of $1,436,520. The warrants had been issued under the Credit Agreement referred to in Note 5.

Total proceeds to the Company of the above warrant exercises were $2,034,520."

(Source: 10-Q/A for the period ended September 30, 2001, filed November 21, 2001)

Elsewhere in the 10-Q/A filing, financial statements are presented, excerpts from which appear in Table 5.8-1 and Table 5.8-2.

Table 5.8-1 LIABILITIES AND STOCKHOLDERS' DEFICIT EXCERPTS FROM CONSOLIDATED BALANCE SHEET (UNAUDITED)

(In thousands of U.S. Dollars, except share and per share data)	Sept. 30, 2001	Dec. 31, 2000
LIABILITIES AND STOCKHOLDERS' DEFICIT		
Current liabilities:		
Trade accounts payable	$ 5,009	$ 5,223
Current installments of obligations under capital leases	4,295	3,466
Accrued expenses and other current liabilities	6,201	6,747
Short-term borrowings	531	-
Advance payments on contracts	1,838	2,155
Billings in excess of costs and estimated earnings on software Installation contracts	1,752	2,875
Total current liabilities	19,626	20,466
Total current liabilities	19,626	20,466
Obligations under capital leases, excluding current installments	7,624	8,034
Notes payable	46,217	77,191
Other long-term liabilities	2,000	-
Total liabilities	75,467	105,691
Stockholders' deficit:		
Common stock, $0.02 par value. Authorized 60,000,000 shares; issued and outstanding 21,121,448 shares at September 30, 2001 and 17,814,910 at December 31, 2000	422	356
Additional paid in capital	105,924	81,327
Treasury stock	(145)	(140)
Employee loans for stock	(463)	(561)
Subscription receivable	-	(59)
Accumulated deficit	(122,566)	(123,811)
Restricted reserve	779	784
Accumulated other comprehensive loss	(2,906)	(2,697)
Total stockholders' deficit	(18,955)	(44,801)
Total liabilities and stockholders' deficit	$ 56,512	$ 60,890

(Source: 10-Q/A for the period ended September 30, 2001, filed on November 21, 2001)

Table 5.8-2 EXCERPTS FROM EURONET WORLDWIDE, INC. AND SUBSIDIARIES
CONSOLIDATED STATEMENTS OF OPERATIONS AND COMPREHENSIVE INCOME / (LOSS)
(UNAUDITED)

(In thousands of U.S. Dollars, except share and per share data)	Three Months Ended Sept. 30, 2001	Three Months Ended Sept. 30, 2000
Total revenues	$ 15,681	$ 14,026
Total operating expenses	16,619	30,921
Operating loss	(938)	(16,895)
Other (expense)/income:		
Interest income	71	187
Interest expense	(2,063)	(2,505)
Foreign exchange gain/(loss), net	(3,560)	4,202
Loss before income taxes and extraordinary item	(6,490)	(15,011)
Income taxes	(1,015)	(767)
Loss before extraordinary item	(7,505)	(15,778)
Extraordinary gain on extinguishment of debt, net of applicable income taxes	2,097	-
Net income/(loss)	(5,408)	(15,778)
Other comprehensive loss:		
Translation adjustment	(3)	(65)
Comprehensive income/(loss)	($ 5,411)	($ 15,843)
Loss per share - basic and diluted:	$ (0.37)	$ (0.90)
Loss before extraordinary item		
Extraordinary gain on early retirement of debt	0.10	-
Net income/(loss)	$ (0.27)	$ (0.90)
Weighted average number of shares outstanding	20,426,648	17,541,079

(Source: 10-Q/A for the period ended September 30, 2001, filed on November 21, 2001)

Requirement A: Subsequent Events

1. Using the Financial Accounting Research System (FARS), identify guidance that might help a company such as Euronet Worldwide, Inc. determine whether something ought to be disclosed as a subsequent event.
2. Is there any relationship between subsequent event disclosures and gain contingencies? Support your position.

Requirement B: Strategy-Related Considerations

Company management determines press-release content, which is not restricted in the same manner as either 10-Q or 10-K filings, as long as nothing fraudulent is included.

1. Do you find the disclosure in the press release of Euronet Worldwide, Inc. on September 10, 2001 regarding interest savings resulting from the subsequent event reported in the June 30, 2001 10-Q filing to be of assistance to capital market participants? Why or why not?
2. Should such consequences of subsequent events be included within the note to the financial statement itself? Why or why not? Is such a communication implicit in any case?

Key Terms and Glossary

Type I subsequent event "Those events that provide additional evidence with respect to conditions that existed at the date of the balance sheet and affect the estimates inherent in the process of preparing financial statements…The financial statements should be adjusted for any change in estimates resulting from the use of such evidence."
Source: AU Section 560.06 of SAS No. 1

Type II subsequent event "Those events that provide evidence with respect to conditions that did not exist at the date of the balance sheet being reported on but arose subsequent to that date. These events should not result in adjustment of the financial statements. Some of these events, however, may be of such a nature that disclosure of them is required to keep the financial statements from being misleading."
Source: AU Section 560.06 of SAS No. 1

Further Readings

American Institute of Certified Public Accountants (AICPA). 1998. *AICPA Professional Standards, Volume 1. U.S. Auditing Standards.* New York, NY: AICPA –AU Section 561 "Subsequent Discovery of Facts Existing at the Date of the Auditor's Report" (June 1).

Dechow, P., A. Hutton, R. Sloan. 1996. "Causes and Consequences of Earnings Manipulation: An Analysis of Firms Subject to Enforcement Actions by the SEC." *Contemporary Accounting Research* 13, pp. 1-36.

Gigler, F. 1994. "Self-Enforcing Voluntary Disclosures." *Journal of Accounting Research* 32, pp. 224-241.

Healy, Paul M. and Krishna G. Palepu. 2001. "Information Asymmetry, Corporate Disclosure, and the Capital Markets: A Review of the Empirical Disclosure Literature." *Journal of Accounting and Economics* 31, pp. 405-440.

Skinner, D. 1994. "Why Firms Voluntarily Disclose Bad News." *Journal of Accounting Research* 32, pp. 38-61.

Wallace, Wanda A. and C. Kermit Littlefield. 1994. "What is the Nature of Subsequent Event Disclosures? Are Good News and Bad News Symmetrically Disclosed?" *The Auditor's Report* 17, no. 3 (Summer), pp. 12-14

"The basic difference between a technician and a professional person is that the former possess the know-how, while the latter, in addition to the know-how, understands why it should be done."   **- Janusz Santocki**

[Source:"Educating Tomorrow's Accountants," <u>Management Accounting</u> (January, 1987), pp. 45-46.]

CASE 9

Reconciling International Practices to Those of the FASB: Cash Flow

CASE TOPICS OUTLINE

1. Anglo American plc
   A. Differences in Terminology
   B. Press Release: Interim Results for 2001

2. Cash Flow Comparison

Anglo American plc is a global company, with an investor relations office in London, within the United Kingdom (UK). The company operates in the mining and natural resource sectors—including gold, platinum, diamonds, coal, base and ferrous metals, industrial minerals, and forest products. Its operations are geographically diverse, with operations in Africa, Europe, South and North America, and Australia.

The language found in financial statements varies between the UK and the United States (U.S.). This is evidenced in Table 5.9-1 that provides a comparison of certain basic terminology. Such financial statement terminology must be mastered to effectively read financial reports from each of these countries.

Table 5.9-1 Financial Statement Terminology

United Kingdom (UK)	United States (U.S.)
Turnover	Sales
Operating Costs	Operating Expenses
Provision for Depreciation	Depreciation Expense
Profit for the Year	Net Income
Profit and Loss Account	Retained Earnings
Depreciation	Accumulated Depreciation
Stocks	Inventory
Debtors	Accounts Receivable
Creditors Due in 1 Year	Accounts Payable
Other Creditors	Other Liabilities
Share Capital	Common Stock
Share Premium Account	Additional Paid-in Capital

Anglo American plc reports interim results for 2001 in a news release on September 7, 2001. Among the disclosures is mention of cash flow:

"Cash flow from operations was US$1,506 million compared with US$1,068 million in the prior period. This inflow was after a US$419 million increase in working capital.

Purchases of tangible fixed assets amounted to US$772 million, an increase of US$168 million. Tax payments were US$347 million compared with US$180 million. The acquisition of businesses, primarily an additional small interest in Anglo Platinum, resulted in a cash outflow of US$154 million."

The Consolidated Cash Flow Statement for the six months ended 30 June 2001 is reported in Table 5.9-2. It is followed by the two notes referenced on the face of the statement. The news release indicates that the financial information was prepared in accordance with generally accepted accounting principles (GAAP) in the UK.

Table 5.9-2 Consolidated cash flow statement for the six months ended 30 June 2001

US$ million	Note	6 months ended 30.06.01
Net cash inflow from operating activities	8	1,506
Expenditure relating to fundamental reorganisations		(20)
Dividends from joint ventures and associates		223
Returns on investments and servicing of finance		
Interest received and other financial income		144
Interest paid		(254)
Dividends received from fixed asset investments		41
Dividends paid to minority shareholders		(281)
Net cash outflow from returns on investments and servicing of finance		(350)
Taxes paid		(347)
Capital expenditure and financial investment		
Payments for fixed assets		(772)
Proceeds from the sale of fixed assets		199
Payments for other financial assets (1)		(79)
Proceeds from the sale of other financial assets (1)		1,019
Net cash inflow/(outflow) for capital expenditure and financial investment		367
Acquisitions and disposals		
Acquisition of subsidiaries (2)		(154)
Disposal of subsidiaries		135
Investment in associates		(189)
Sale of interests in associates		(1,148)
Investment in proportionally consolidated joint arrangements		(51)
Investment in joint ventures		(22)
Net cash inflow/(outflow) from acquisitions and disposals		867
Equity dividends paid to Anglo American shareholders		(509)
Cash inflow/(outflow) before use of liquid resources and financing		1,737
Management of liquid resources (3)		(977)
Financing		(795)
Decrease in cash in the period	10	(35)

(1) Disposal and acquisition of other financial assets included in fixed assets.
(2) Net of assets resold of US$709 million in the second half of 2000 in respect of the acquisition of Tarmac plc.
(3) Cash flows in respect of current asset investments.
(SOURCE: Anglo American plc News Release on 7 September 2001)

Note 8 Reconciliation of group operating profit to net cash flow from operating activities

US$ million	6 months ended 30.06.01
Group operating profit--subsidiaries	1,326
Depreciation and amortisation charges	517
Decrease/(increase) in stocks	21
Increase in debtors	(302)
(Decrease)/increase in creditors	(138)
Other items	82
Net cash inflow from operating activities	1,506

Note 10 Reconciliation of net cash flow to movement in net (debt)/funds

US$ million	6 months ended 30.06.01
Decrease in cash in the period	(35)
Cash outflow/(inflow) from debt financing	824
Cash outflow/(inflow) from management of liquid resources	977
Change in net debt arising from cash flows	1,766
Loans and current asset investments acquired with subsidiaries	(42)
Loans and current asset investments disposed with subsidiaries	11
Currency translation differences	88
Movement in net funds/(debt)	1,823
Net (debt)/funds at start of the period	(3,590)
Net debt at the end of the period	(1,767)

Requirement A: Reconciliation to GAAP

1. Compare and contrast the presentation of cash flow information by this company operating in the United Kingdom to that required by generally accepted accounting principles (GAAP) in the United States. Specifically, access FAS No. 95 and compare and contrast the examples provided for presentation of cash flow to the contents of Table 5-9.2 and related notes.
2. Within the press release, mention is made of working capital. What is meant by this term and how does it relate, historically, to reporting practices in the United States?

Requirement B: Strategy-Related Considerations

1. Do you find the content of cash flow-associated disclosures by Anglo American plc to be of more or less use in understanding the strategy of management when compared with the practices common in the U.S.? Explain.
2. The FASB 95 content includes the following phrasing:
   "Cash Flow per Share
   FAS95, Par. 33
   Financial statements shall not report an amount of cash flow per share. Neither cash flow nor any component of it is an alternative to net income as an indicator of an enterprise's performance, as reporting per share amounts might imply."
   Do you believe this proscription is in the best interest of financial statement users? Why or why not?

Key Terms and Glossary

cash "cash includes not only currency on hand but demand deposits with banks or other financial institutions. Cash also includes other kinds of accounts that have the general characteristics of demand deposits in that the customer may deposit additional funds at any time and also effectively may withdraw funds at any time without prior notice or penalty. All charges and credits to those accounts are cash receipts or payments to both the entity owning the account and the bank holding it. For example, a bank's granting of a loan by crediting the proceeds to a customer's demand deposit account is a cash payment by the bank and a cash receipt of the customer when the entry is made." (FAS 95, par. 7, footnote 1)

cash equivalents "cash equivalents are short-term, highly liquid investments that are both:

a. Readily convertible to known amounts of cash
b. So near their maturity that they present insignificant risk of changes in value because of changes in interest rates.

Generally, only investments with original maturities* of three months or less qualify under that definition." *Original maturity means original maturity to the entity holding the investment. For example, both a three-month U.S. Treasury bill and a three-year Treasury note purchased three months from maturity qualify as cash equivalents. However, a Treasury note purchased three years ago does not become a cash equivalent when its remaining maturity is three months." (FAS 95, Par. 8, including footnote 2)

financial flexibility Concept Statement 5, Footnote 13 states: "Financial flexibility is the ability of an entity to take effective actions to alter amounts and timing of cash flows so it can respond to unexpected needs and opportunities."

liquidity Concept Statement 4, Par. 54 states: "Financial reporting should provide information about how an organization obtains and spends cash or other liquid resources, about its borrowing and repayment of borrowing, and about other factors that may affect its liquidity. Information about those resource flows may be useful in understanding the operations of an enterprise, evaluating its financing activities, assessing its liquidity, or interpreting performance information provided. Information about performance and economic resources, obligations, and net resources also may be useful in assessing an enterprise's liquidity." Concept Statement 5, Footnote 13 states: "Liquidity reflects an asset's or liability's nearness to cash."

working capital current assets less current liabilities FAS 6, paragraph 20 notes that Chapter 3A of ARB No. 43, Paragraph 7 "defines current liabilities as those whose liquidation "is reasonably expected to require the use of existing resources properly classified as current assets, or the creation of other current liabilities." That paragraph goes on to say that the current liabilities classification "is intended to include obligations for items which have entered into the operating cycle . . . and debts which arise from operations directly related to the operating cycle. . . ."

Further Readings

Kochanek, Richard F. and Corine T. Norgaard. 1988. "Analyzing the Components of Operating Cash Flow: The Charter Company." *Accounting Horizons* 2, no. 1, pp. 58-66.

Casey, Cornelius J. and Norman J. Bartczak. 1984. "Cash Flow—It's Not the Bottom Line." *Harvard Business Review* (July-August), pp. 60-66.

Collins, W., E.S. Davies and P. Weetman. 1992. "Management Discussion and Analysis: An Evaluation of Practice in UK and US Companies." *Accounting and Business Research* 23, no. 90, pp. 123-137.

Cummins, J. David, Martin F. Grace, and Richard D. Phillips. 1999. "Regulatory Solvency Prediction in Property-Liability Insurance: Risk-Based Capital, Audit Ratios, and Cash Flow Simulation." *Journal of Risk and Insurance* 66, no. 3, September, pp. 417-458.

Jensen, Michael. 1986. "Agency Costs of Free Cash Flow, Corporate Finance, and Takeovers." *AER Papers and Proceedings* 76, no. 2, pp. 323-329.

Kaplan, S.N. and R.S. Ruback. 1995. "The Valuation of Cash Flow Forecasts: An Empirical Analysis." *Journal of Finance* 50, pp. 1059-1093.

Laitinen, Erkki K. and T. Laitinen. 1998. "Cash Management Behavior and Failure Prediction." *Journal of Business Finance and Accounting* 25, no. 7-8 (September-October), pp. 893-920.

Nurnberg, Hugo. 1993. "Inconsistencies And Ambiguities In Cash Flow Statements Under FASB Statement No. 95." *Accounting Horizons* 7, no. 2, pp. 60-75.

Opler, Tim and Sheridan Titman. 1993. "The Determinants of Leveraged Buyout Activity: Free Cash Flow vs. Financial Distress Costs." *Journal of Finance* 48, no. 5 (December), pp. 1985-1999.

Dhumale, Rahul. 1998. "Earnings Retention as a Specification Mechanism in Logistic Bankruptcy Models: A Test of the Free Cash Flow Theory." *Journal of Business Finance and Accounting* 25, no. 7-8 (September-October), pp. 1005-1024.

Gentry, James A., Paul Newbold, and David T. Whitford. 1985. "Predicting Bankruptcy: If Cash Flow's Not the Bottom Line, What Is?" *Financial Analysts Journal* (September-October), pp. 47-56.

Stephens, Ray G. and Vijay Govindarajan. 1990. "Small Sample Studies: On Assessing a Firm's Cash Generating Ability." *The Accounting Review* 65, no. 1 (January), pp. 242-257.

Wells, Brenda P., Larry A. Cox, and Kenneth M. Gaver,. 1995. "Free Cash Flow in the Life Insurance Industry." *Journal of Risk and Insurance* 62, Issue 1 (March), pp. 50-66.

**"Out of sight, out of mind,"
when translated into Russian [by computer], then back again into English became
"invisible maniac."**

--Arthur Calder-Marshall

CASE 10

Is the Asset Impaired – Or Perhaps A Big Bath?

CASE TOPICS OUTLINE

1. Analyst Expectations for FleetBoston Financial
   A. 8-K Filings for FleetBoston Financial
   B. 10-Q Financial Statements for FleetBoston

2. Asset Impairment or Big Bath?

On December 21, 2001, the *Connecticut Post* reported that a kitchen-sink quarter had been expected by analysts and that FleetBoston Financial indeed was providing such a clean up of its balance sheet. On December 19, 2001, FleetBoston Financial Corp. filed an 8-K with the SEC which contained the following diclosures:

> "FLEETBOSTON TO TAKE A SERIES OF ACTIONS TO STRENGTHEN BALANCE SHEET Boston, Massachusetts, December 19, 2001: Recognizing the ongoing economic slowdown, FleetBoston Financial (FBF-NYSE) today announced a series of actions to strengthen the company's balance sheet. These actions will result in an after-tax charge of approximately $650 million ($.62 E.P.S.) to fourth quarter earnings. The Corporation expects to report a net profit of approximately $30 million ($.03 E.P.S.) in the fourth quarter inclusive of these actions and to release complete details of its fourth quarter results on January 16, 2002. "Our financial strength allows us to take actions now that will position FleetBoston to fully realize the benefits of the improved economic conditions we expect to see in the second half of 2002," said Chad Gifford, FleetBoston's president and chief operating officer. "It is our practice to address economic uncertainty up front and we are fortunate to have the financial capacity to take action now." The specific actions and estimated pre-tax charges are summarized as follows:
> - - ARGENTINA - A charge of approximately $150 million is being taken on our portfolio of Argentine government securities and loans. This brings to $200 million the total impairment charges taken against the Argentine portfolio this year, of which $75 million will go to bolster loan loss reserves and $125 million relates to the recently-announced government sponsored bond swap program. The Corporation has operated in Argentina for 85 years with great success and strong profitability. Its very experienced management team is well equipped to deal with the financial adjustment that is occurring in that country.
> - - - PRINCIPAL INVESTING - The Corporation has operated in this business for over 40 years and has generated strong returns over that period. The current environment is unprecedented in the confluence of negative factors affecting the

principal investing industry. Writedowns of approximately $475 million will be taken to the carrying value of the portfolio in the fourth quarter, primarily in the technology and telecom sectors. This action follows a review of the portfolio in light of the pronounced weakness that has severely impacted market liquidity and the operating performance of the underlying investments, coupled with our intent to maintain a cautious stance on the economy. The principal investing portfolio of $3.6B is currently carried at a discount of approximately 25% of Fleet's original investment with discounts approaching 50% in the direct technology and telecom portfolio.

- - - CREDIT ACTIONS - The current recessionary environment continues to strain a number of our domestic commercial and industrial customers. The Corporation continues to take an aggressive approach to recognizing these pressures and is committed to maintaining its established reserve strength. The Corporation expects to incur incremental credit costs of $175 million to strengthen the loan loss reserve to the $3 billion level and charges of $150 million related to the movement of approximately $350 million of problem credits to accelerated disposition status. During the quarter, writedowns were taken on a number of our larger troubled credits, including a well-publicized energy-related credit. As a result of these actions, the reserve-to-loans ratio is expected to rise to the range of 2.3% to 2.4% at year-end.

- - - RESTRUCTURING CHARGE - The Corporation continues to be responsive to the current weak operating environment and wants to ensure that its expense base remains aligned with its revenue expectations, particularly in a weak capital markets environment. Approximately $100 million of charges are being taken to primarily cover severance and related costs for various businesses and is expected to further reduce staff by 700 individuals against our employee base of approximately 55,000 employees. Eugene M. McQuade, FleetBoston's vice chairman and chief financial officer stated: "The strength of our operating earnings as well as capital and reserves in excess of $20 billion afford us ample capacity to take these actions. We expect to end the year with healthy capital ratios of approximately 7.7% for Tier 1 capital and 6.5% for tangible common equity. Our expectation to achieve the analyst consensus estimate of $3.26 for 2002 earnings per share remains intact." Mr. Gifford further commented: "We have great confidence in the underlying strength of our franchise and we draw on that strength in taking these actions. Our greatest priority lies in seizing the potential of our extensive customer base and continuing the growth initiatives underway in our mainstream businesses."

- FleetBoston Financial is the seventh-largest financial holding company in the United States. A $200 billion diversified financial services company, it offers a comprehensive array of innovative financial solutions to 20 million customers in more than 20 countries and territories. FleetBoston Financial is headquartered in Boston and listed on the New York Stock Exchange (NYSE: FBF) and the Boston Stock Exchange (BSE: FBF).

- ************

- This release contains forward-looking statements that involve risks and uncertainties that could cause actual results to differ materially from estimates. These risks and uncertainties include, among other things, (1) changes in general political and economic conditions, either domestically or internationally, including the economic effects of the September 11, 2001 terrorist attacks against the United States and the response of the United States to those attacks, the continuing weakness in the Latin American economies, particularly Argentina, and a further deterioration in credit quality, including the resultant effect on the level of the Corporation's nonperforming assets and chargeoffs; (2) interest rate and currency fluctuations, equity and bond market fluctuations and perceptions, including continued weakness in the global capital markets and the impact of such weakness on the Corporation's Principal Investing and other capital markets businesses; (3) changes in the competitive environment for financial services organizations and the Corporation's ability to manage those changes; (4) legislative or regulatory developments, including changes in laws concerning taxes, banking, securities, insurance and other aspects of the financial services industry; (5) technological changes, including the impact of the Internet on the Corporation's businesses; (6) the ability of the Corporation to fully realize expected cost savings and realize those savings within the expected timeframes; and (7) the level of costs related to the integration of acquired businesses. For further information, please refer to the Corporation's reports filed with the SEC." *(Source: 8-K filing on December 19, 2001)*

Earlier, the company had issued an 8-K/A that included a press release containing the following related discussion:

"FLEETBOSTON REPORTS THIRD QUARTER EARNINGS OF $766 MILLION OR $.70 PER SHARE
COMMON DIVIDEND INCREASED BY 6%

Boston, Massachusetts, October 17, 2001: FleetBoston Financial (FBF-NYSE) today reported third quarter earnings of $766 million, or $.70 per share, compared with $969 million, or $.87 per share in the third quarter of 2000. Earnings from the Corporation's primary capital markets units – Principal Investing, Robertson Stephens, and Quick & Reilly – fell by $239 million or $.22 per share from their level in the third quarter of last year reflecting continued slowness in the capital markets, exacerbated by the tragic events of September 11.

Offsetting these declines were earnings growth from several business lines including Retail Banking, Latin America, and Small Business; higher cash management fees; merger-related cost savings; and expense reductions from the corporate cost containment program. The current quarter's results included a gain on the sale of an equity investment, net of merger related charges, totaling $60 million ($.05 per share), while the third quarter of 2000 included divestiture gains, net of merger related charges, totaling $59 million ($.05 per share).

Return on assets and return on equity for the quarter were 1.47% and 15.56%, respectively, compared with 1.78% and 21.6% a year ago. For the first nine months of 2001, earnings before strategic charges were $2.2 billion, or $1.96 per share, versus $3.02 billion, or $2.72 per share, in the first nine months of 2000.

FleetBoston also announced today a 6% increase in its quarterly common dividend to $.35 per share for shareholders of record on December 3, 2001.

Terrence Murray, Chairman and Chief Executive Officer of FleetBoston commented, "We have all been affected and, in many ways, transformed by the events of September 11. While Fleet was fortunate to not have lost any of our employees from this tragedy, we nonetheless grieve with the rest of the country over the many lives that were lost, including those of friends, relatives and business associates. During the past few weeks, I've spent quite a bit of time meeting with employees in many of our businesses, including those in and around New York City who were personally affected by the tragedy. It was truly inspiring to see first hand how incredibly well our employees in the area were handling the adversity and we can all learn a valuable lesson from their courage and determination to serve the customer."

Murray continued, "These are certainly difficult times for our economy and corporate America. An economic slowdown was well underway prior to September 11 and has now worsened. For Fleet, the biggest impact has been seen in our capital markets businesses, which continued weak throughout the third quarter. Despite the economy's performance of late, we remain very optimistic that our country will meet the economic challenges that we face and return to a period of growth and prosperity. We also remain enthusiastic about the future of FleetBoston as evidenced by our dividend increase. Our customer service efforts are gaining traction in our consumer businesses and in wholesale banking we are really beginning to leverage our lead relationships. These positive developments, coupled with our expense discipline and balance sheet strength, position us well to capitalize when economic conditions improve."

Chad Gifford, President and Chief Operating Officer said, "The Corporation moved ahead on a number of fronts during the third quarter. In an effort to support our country's financial markets and our shareholders in the wake of September 11, we announced a plan to repurchase up to $4 billion of our stock by December 31, 2002 and began executing on this program immediately. We also continued with our efforts to improve the customer experience. Specifically, we announced plans to open 28 new branches and 23 new ATMs in Massachusetts, while upgrading 27 other branches and ATM locations. In addition, we also opened an Investment Access Center in the MetLife building adjacent to Grand Central Station in New York City. This location not only provides our customers with traditional Fleet and Quick & Reilly products and services but also gives our customers self-service on-line access to their accounts. A milestone was reached with the recent enrollment of our two millionth HomeLink on-line banking customer. Finally, work continued during the third quarter on our announced acquisition of Liberty Financial's Asset Management unit and we expect to close shortly. We remain committed to our top priority of building shareholder value through strengthening our existing business lines and seizing the potential of our extensive customer base. We are intensely focused on execution and customer service-driven revenue growth."

Credit Quality/Balance Sheet

Nonperforming assets were $1.56 billion, or 1.22% of total loans, at September 30, 2001, up 12% from June 30, 2001. The provision for credit losses was $325 million in the current quarter, which matched net chargeoffs. In the third quarter of 2000, the provision was $325 million and net chargeoffs were $321 million. The reserve for credit losses was $2.73 billion at September 30, 2001, representing 2.14% of total loans and leases.

Total assets at September 30, 2001 were $202 billion, compared with $218 billion at September 30, 2000. The decline from a year ago is due, in part, to the sale/run-off of low-margin assets in connection with the Summit merger, and the sale of our mortgage company in June. Stockholders' equity amounted to $20 billion at September 30, 2001, with a common equity to assets ratio of 9.6%.

A detailed financial package containing supplemental information on the third quarter financial results can be found by accessing the Corporation's web site (http://www.fleet.com). ..." *(Source: 8-K/A filed October 17, 2001)*

The Company filed its 10-Q for the period ended September 30, 2001 on November 14, 2001, which contained the following observations:

"Decreases in earnings from the prior year in both the three and nine month comparisons resulted from a significant drop in capital markets revenue due to the pronounced fallout experienced in U.S. capital markets which began in the second half of 2000. Declines in current year revenues reflect the continued slowdown in these markets during 2001. These revenue declines were partly offset by improved results in Retail Banking and International Banking, as well as lower operating expenses resulting from a corporate-wide cost containment program and a drop in revenue-related compensation costs.

Although certain branch and other operations were affected by the September 11 terrorist attacks, and some employees were relocated from their New York locations to alternate sites in New Jersey following the attacks, FleetBoston's overall operations were only modestly impacted, and its consolidated results of operations for the third quarter and its overall financial condition were not materially impacted by these events. These events caused, and may continue to cause, additional weakness in the economy and in general business activities. FleetBoston continues to evaluate the effects of these events on the Corporation's fourth quarter and future results of operations.

Results for the three and nine months ended September 30, 2001 and 2000 included the following:

Three months ended September 30, 2001:

• Gain of $146 million ($91 million after-tax) from the sale of FleetBoston's investment in the NYCE Corporation.

• Summit merger-related costs of $52 million ($31 million after-tax), composed of $35 million of merger integration costs and $17 million of accelerated depreciation of assets to be disposed of at a later date.

Three months ended September 30, 2000:

• Branch divestiture gains of $164 million ($84 million after-tax) associated with the previously disclosed BankBoston merger.

• Merger integration costs of $40 million ($25 million after-tax) incurred in connection with the BankBoston merger.

Nine months ended September 30, 2001:

• Gains of $333 million ($204 million after-tax) from branch divestitures associated with the BankBoston merger and $146 million ($91 million after-tax) from the above-mentioned sale of the investment in the NYCE Corporation.

• Write-downs of $602 million ($370 million after-tax) taken against the carrying value of the Principal Investing portfolio.

• Summit merger-related costs of $863 million ($542 million after-tax), consisting of $463 million ($302 million after-tax) of merger- and restructuring-related charges, $135 million ($82 million after-tax) of merger integration costs and a $265 million ($158 million after-tax) loss from the sale of low-margin securities following the merger.

• Restructuring charges of $79 million ($50 million after-tax) primarily related to a reorganization of capital markets-related businesses.

• An aggregate loss of $428 million ($285 million after-tax) from the sale of the mortgage banking business." *(Source: 10-Q filing for the period ended September 30, 2001 on November 14, 2001)*

The Consolidated Statements of Income in the quarterly filing are reported in Table 5.10-1.

Table 5.10-1 FLEETBOSTON FINANCIAL CORPORATION
CONSOLIDATED STATEMENTS OF INCOME
(unaudited)

Dollars in millions, except per share amounts	*Three months ended September 30, 2001*	*Three months ended September 30, 2000*	*Nine months ended September 30, 2001*	*Nine months ended September 30, 2000*
Interest income:				
Interest and fees on loans and leases	$ 2,601	$ 3,323	$ 8,517	$ 9,865
Interest on securities and trading assets	446	658	1,536	1,915
Other	302	128	781	508
Total interest income	3,349	4,109	10,834	12,288
Interest expense:				
Deposits of domestic offices	590	817	2,025	2,402
Deposits of International offices	274	332	849	926
Short-term	243	406	863	1,216

Dollars in millions, except per share amounts	Three months ended September 30, 2001	Three months ended September 30, 2000	Nine months ended September 30, 2001	Nine months ended September 30, 2000
borrowings				
Long-term debt	363	558	1,300	1,535
Other	32	67	130	208
Total interest expense	1,502	2,180	5,167	6,287
Net interest income	1,847	1,929	5,667	6,001
Provision for credit losses	325	325	955	980
Net interest income after provision for credit losses	1,522	1,604	4,712	5,021
Noninterest income:				
Capital markets revenue	460	752	455	2,632
Banking fees and commissions	406	400	1,201	1,207
Investment services revenue	348	423	1,099	1,399
Credit card revenue	193	186	520	529
Processing-related revenue	68	154	330	467
Gains on branch divestitures	—	164	353	843
Other	135	185	503	475
Total noninterest income	1,610	2,264	4,461	7,552
Noninterest expense:				
Employee compensation and benefits	979	1,178	3,008	3,995
Occupancy and equipment	283	294	847	903
Intangible asset amortization	96	97	294	291
Marketing and public relations	63	82	184	238
Legal and other professional	51	88	182	266
Merger- and restructuring-related charges	17	6	542	68
Loss on sale of mortgage banking business	—	—	428	—
Other	408	545	1,324	1,741
Total noninterest expense	1,897	2,290	6,809	7,502
Income before income taxes	1,235	1,578	2,364	5,071
Applicable income	469	609	926	2,055

Dollars in millions, except per share amounts	Three months ended September 30, 2001	Three months ended September 30, 2000	Nine months ended September 30, 2001	Nine months ended September 30, 2000
taxes				
Net income	$ 766	$ 969	$ 969	$ 3,016
Diluted weighted average common shares outstanding (in millions)	1,091.8	1,101.5	1,094.1	1,099.7
Net income applicable to common shares	$ 760	$ 959	$ 1,415	$ 2,987
Basic earnings per share	.70	.89	1.31	2.76
Diluted earnings per share	.70	.87	1.29	2.72
Dividends declared	.33	.30	.99	.90

*See accompanying Condensed Notes to Consolidated Financial Statements; Note 6 is reported within this case. *(Source: FleetBoston Financial Corp. 10-Q for quarterly period ended September 30, 2001)*

"NOTE 6. MERGER- AND RESTRUCTURING-RELATED CHARGES

In the first quarter of 2001, FleetBoston recorded aggregate merger- and restructuring-related charges of $487 million in connection with the Summit merger and a restructuring of its capital markets-related businesses. Of the $487 million, $408 million related to Summit and $79 million primarily related to capital markets. The $408 million charge was composed of $73 million of merger-related charges, $322 million of restructuring-related charges, and $13 million of accelerated depreciation of assets to be disposed of at a later date, which resulted from revisions to the estimated useful lives of assets currently in use that will be disposed when the Summit integration has been completed.

In addition to the merger- and restructuring-related charges, FleetBoston incurred $45 million of merger integration costs in the first quarter. These integration costs, which are expensed as incurred, include the costs of converting duplicate computer systems, training and relocation of employees and departments, consolidation of facilities and customer communications. During the second and third quarters of 2001, aggregate costs of $145 million, composed of $55 million and $90 million of additional accelerated depreciation and integration costs, respectively, were recorded.

In 1999, the Corporation recorded $467 million of restructuring charges in connection with the BankBoston merger. Additional information concerning these 1999 charges is included in Note 14 to the Consolidated Financial Statements included in the Corporation's Current Report on Form 8-K dated May 4, 2001. During the second quarter of 2001, $14 million of such charges were reversed, primarily related to severance and facilities accruals which were not fully utilized.

Restructuring-Related Charges
Summit

Of the $322 million restructuring-related charge, $150 million related to personnel, $96 million related to asset write-downs and contract cancellations, $60 million related to facilities and $16 million related to other restructuring expenses.

Personnel-related costs of $150 million included severance to be paid in a lump sum or over a defined period, benefit program changes and outplacement services for approximately 2,700 positions identified during the first quarter for elimination in connection with restructuring, principally as a result of the elimination of duplicate functions within the combined company. During the first nine months of 2001, approximately $89 million of personnel-related benefits were paid and approximately 2,500 employees were terminated and left the Corporation.

Asset write-downs and contract cancellation costs of $96 million related to costs to dispose of duplicate or obsolete equipment and computer software, and penalties incurred to cancel leases and other contracts. During the first nine months of 2001, $20 million of costs were paid and $51 million of write-downs were recorded.

Facilities-related charges of $60 million represented minimum lease payments related to duplicate branch and other facilities. During the first nine months of 2001, $1 million of facilities-related charges were paid and $8 million accrued for such charges, which were not fully utilized, was reversed. Other costs of $16 million included expenses and various other costs incurred to merge the two companies. During the first nine months of 2001, $9 million of other costs were paid.

Capital Markets

Of the $79 million charge, $52 million related to severance to be paid in a lump sum or over a defined period, benefit program changes and outplacement services for approximately 750 positions identified during the first quarter for elimination in connection with the restructuring; $23 million of costs related to future lease obligations and write-downs of capitalized assets; and $4 million of other restructuring expenses. During the first nine months of 2001, approximately 740 employees were terminated and left the Corporation, and $43 million of related benefits were paid.

The following table presents activity in restructuring-related accruals during the nine months ended September 30, 2001.

FLEETBOSTON FINANCIAL CORPORATION
CONDENSED NOTES TO CONSOLIDATED FINANCIAL STATEMENTS
SEPTEMBER 30, 2001

Restructuring Accrual Activity

	Summit & Capital Markets	BankBoston
Balance at December 31, 2000	$ —	$ 146
Restructuring accrual	401	—
Restructuring reversal	(8)	(14)
Cash payments	(162)	(104)
Noncash write-downs	(51)	—
Balance at September 30, 2001	$ 180	$ 28

The $104 million of cash payments included in the table above related to the BankBoston merger consisted of $89 million of personnel benefits, $14 million in facilities charges, and $1 million of other restructuring expenses. The remaining accrual at September 30, 2001 is composed primarily of expected cash outlays related to severance and facilities obligations." *(Source: FleetBoston Financial Corp. 10-Q for quarterly period ended September 30, 2001)*

The assets reported on the Consolidated Balance Sheets in the quarterly filing are itemized in Table 5.10-2.

Table 5.10-2 EXCERPT FROM FLEETBOSTON FINANCIAL CORPORATION
CONSOLIDATED BALANCE SHEETS
(unaudited)

Dollars in millions, except per share amounts	September 30, 2001	December 31, 2000
Assets		
Cash, due from banks and interest-bearing deposits	$ 15,001	$ 12,826
Federal funds sold and securities purchased under agreements to resell	7,500	1,959
Trading assets	6,663	7,108
Mortgages held for sale	539	2,138
Securities (market value: $22,255 and $34,932)	22,251	34,964
Loans and leases	127,820	134,834
Reserve for credit losses	(2,734)	(2,709)
Net loans and leases	125,086	132,125
Due from brokers/dealers	4,059	2,987
Premises and equipment	2,896	2,867
Mortgage servicing rights	—	2,695
Intangible assets	4,198	4,557
Other assets	13,669	14,859
Total assets	$ 201,862	$ 219,085

(Source: FleetBoston Financial Corp. 10-Q for quarterly period ended September 30, 2001)

The derivation of net cash flow provided by operating activities in the FLEETBOSTON FINANCIAL CORPORATION CONSOLIDATED STATEMENTS OF CASH FLOWS included the line items (in millions): "Depreciation and amortization of premises and equipment" $ 445 and $437, "Merger- and restructuring-related charges" of $542 and $68, and "Write-downs of principal investing investments" in the amount of $ 602 and —, for the nine months ended September 30, 2001 and 2000, respectively.

Requirement A: Impairment of Assets and Write-downs

1. What accounting guidance applies to the determination of whether an asset is impaired? What guidance applies to quantifying the amount of a write-down, when it is deemed to be appropriate? Does the nature of the asset being written down influence such adjustments? How?

2. Using the disclosures by FleetBoston, write an executive summary as to the nature of the write-downs taken, and the likely implications of these actions for future periods. Provide the basis for your expectations in specific terms, detailing the types of accounts affected and estimated amounts. Support your position with appropriate citations from the Financial Accounting Research System (FARS).

Requirement B: Strategy-Related Considerations

Significant effects of write-offs in a single quarter have prompted the business press to dub such practices as "Rumpelstilzchen accounting" (i.e., turning future 'straw' into 'gold' by hitting current year's income with a large write-down) or "big bath accounting."

1. What are the circumstances in which Company management may be more likely to take a write-down?
2. Should such a declaration be presumed to be a "big bath"? What differentiates the occasional write-off from a management strategy of a "big bath"?
3. Do you believe such practices result in effective financial reporting? Explain.

Key Terms and Glossary

big bath large write-downs of assets

capital market transactions hypothesis drawn from the theory that investors' perceptions of a firm are of importance to the corporate managers because they expect to issue public debt or equity or to make an acquisition of another company, especially when the latter involves a stock transaction

corporate control hypothesis is a theory motivated by empirical evidence that both boards of directors and investors hold managers accountable for current stock performance

impairment "the condition that exists when the carrying amount of a long-lived asset (asset group) exceeds its fair value" (FAS 144, par. 7)

"lemons" problem information problem that arises from differences in information and conflicts in the incentives between managers and capital providers; signaling is viewed as one approach to addressing the challenge of asymmetric information, whereby managers use voluntary disclosure practices and similar tools to inform the market participants of their expectations and accomplishments to date

Further Readings

Aboody, D., M. E. Barth, R. Kasznik. 1999. "Revaluations of Fixed Assets and Future Firm Performance." *Journal of Accounting and Economics* 26, pp. 149-178.

Ambrosini, Dana. 2001. "FleetBoston Financial Cutting 700 Jobs Out of 55,000 Workforce.*" Connecticut Post*. Knight-Ridder/Tribune Business News (December 21). PITEM01355017, Infotrac Business Index.

Bartov, E. 1993. "The Timing of Asset Sales and Earnings Manipulation." *The Accounting Review* 68, pp. 840-855.

Beneish, M.D. 1999. "Incentives and Penalties Related to Earnings Overstatements that Violate GAAP.*" The Accounting Review* 74, pp. 425-457.

Brown, P.D., H.Y. Izan, A.L. Loh. 1992. "Fixed Asset Revaluations and Managerial Incentives." *Abacus* 28, pp. 36-57.

Dechow, P., A. Hutton, R. Sloan. 1996. "Causes and Consequences of Earnings Manipulation: An Analysis of Firms Subject to Enforcement Actions by the SEC." *Contemporary Accounting Research* 13, pp. 1-36.

Dillon, G. J. 1979. "Corporate Asset Revaluations, 1925-1934." *The Accounting Historians Journal* 6, pp. 1-15.

Easton, P.D., P.H. Eddey, and T.S. Harris 1993. "An Investigation of Revaluations of Tangible Long-Lived Assets." *Journal of Accounting Research* 31, pp. 1-38.

Gaver, J., K. Gaver. 1998. "The Relation Between Nonrecurring Accounting Transactions and CEO Cash Compensation." *The Accounting Review* 73, pp. 235-253.

Gigler, F. 1994. "Self-Enforcing Voluntary Disclosures." *Journal of Accounting Research* 32, pp. 224-241.

Healy, Paul. 1985. "The Effect of Bonus Schemes on Accounting Decisions." *Journal of Accounting and Economics* 7, no. 1/3, pp. 85-107.

Healy, Paul M. and Krishna G. Palepu. 2001. "Information Asymmetry, Corporate Disclosure, and the Capital Markets: A Review of the Empirical Disclosure Literature." *Journal of Accounting and Economics* 31, pp. 405-440.

Holthausen, R.W., Larcker, D.F., Sloan, R.G. 1995. "Annual Bonus Schemes and the Manipulation of Earnings." *Journal of Accounting and Economics* 19, pp. 29-74.

"Numbers Game: Big Bath? Or a Little One." 1986. *Forbes* (October 6).

Ohlson, J.A. 1995. "Earnings, Book Values, and Dividends in Security Valuation." *Contemporary Accounting Research* 11, pp. 161-182.

Rees, L., S. Gill, and R. Gore. 1996. "An Investigation of Asset Write-Downs and Concurrent Abnormal Accruals." *Journal of Accounting Research* 34 (Suppl.), pp. 157-169.

Saito, S. 1983. "Asset Revaluations and Cost Basis: Capital Revaluation in Corporate Financial Reports." *The Accounting Historians Journal* 10, pp. 1-23.

Skinner, D. 1994. "Why Firms Voluntarily Disclose Bad News." *Journal of Accounting Research* 32, pp. 38-61.

Strong, J. and J. Meyer. 1987. "Asset Write-downs: Managerial Incentives and Security Returns." *Journal of Finance* 42, pp. 643-661.

Walker, R.G. 1992. "The SEC's Ban on Upward Asset Revaluations and the Disclosure of Current Values." *Abacus* 28, pp. 3-35.

Weberman, Ben. 1986. "Rumpelstilzchen Accounting." *Forbes* (February 24), pp. 30-31.

"Far better an approximate answer to the right question, is often vague, than an exact answer to the wrong question, which can always be made precise."

John Tukey

[Source: Cited by George W. Downs and Patrick D. Larkey, <u>The Search for Government Efficiency: From Hubris to Helplessness</u> (Philadelphia: Temple University Press, 1986), p. 95.]

CASE 11

Financial Instruments and Hedging: Measurement Challenges

CASE TOPICS OUTLINE

1. Enron Corp.
   A. 8-K Filing
   B. Inclusion of Press Release
   C. C. 10-K Filing in 2000

2. Analysis
3. Enron Corp. Files for Chapter 11

On November 8, 2001, Enron Corp. filed an 8-K:

"Enron Corp. (NYSE: ENE) is providing information to investors concerning several important matters:

    o   A required restatement of prior period financial statements to reflect: (1) recording the previously announced $1.2 billion reduction to shareholders' equity reported by Enron in the third quarter of 2001; and (2) various income statement and balance sheet adjustments required as the result of a determination by Enron and its auditors (which resulted from information made available from further review of certain related-party transactions) that three unconsolidated entities should have been consolidated in the financial statements pursuant to generally accepted accounting principles. The restatement is outlined in TABLE 1 [Table 5.11-1 in this case];

    o   Enron intends to restate its financial statements for the years ended December 31, 1997 through 2000 and the quarters ended March 31 and June 30, 2001. As a result, the previously-issued financial statements for these periods and the audit reports covering the year-end financial statements for 1997 to 2000 should not be relied upon;

    o   The accounting basis for the $1.2 billion reduction to shareholders' equity mentioned above;

    o   The Special Committee appointed by Enron's Board of Directors to review transactions between Enron and related parties;

    o   Information regarding the LJM1 and LJM2 limited partnerships formed by Enron's then Chief Financial Officer, the former CFO's role in the partnerships, the business relationships and transactions between Enron and the partnerships, and the economic results of those transactions as known thus far to Enron, which are outlined in TABLE 2 [Table 5.11-2 in this case]; and

     o   Transactions between Enron and other Enron employees.

The restatements discussed below affect prior periods. After taking into account Enron's previously disclosed $1.2 billion adjustment to shareholders' equity in the third quarter of 2001, these restatements have no effect on Enron's current financial position.

As used herein, "Enron" means Enron Corp. or one or more of its subsidiaries or affiliates. The dollar amounts and percentages set forth herein are rounded amounts and percentages.

....

1.   Background on Special Purpose Entities and Related-Party Transactions

Enron, like many other companies, utilizes a variety of structured financings in the ordinary course of its business to access capital or hedge risk. Many of these transactions involve "special purpose entities," or "SPEs." Accounting guidelines allow for the non-consolidation of SPEs from the sponsoring company's financial statements in certain circumstances. Accordingly, certain transactions between the sponsoring company and the SPE may result in gain or loss and/or cash flow being recognized by the sponsor, commonly referred to by financial institutions as "monetizations."

LJM Cayman, L.P. ("LJM1") and LJM2 Co-Investment, L.P. ("LJM2") (collectively "LJM") are private investment limited partnerships that were formed in 1999. Andrew S. Fastow, then Executive Vice President and Chief Financial Officer of Enron, was (from inception through July 2001) the managing member of the general partners of LJM1 and LJM2. Enron believes that the LJM partnerships have as limited partners a significant number of institutions and other investors that are not related parties to Enron. These partnerships are a subject of the Special Committee's investigation and it is possible that the Committee's review will identify additional or different information concerning matters described herein.

2. Restatement of Prior Period Financial Statements

Enron will restate its financial statements from 1997 to 2000 and the first and second quarters of 2001 to: (1) reflect its conclusion that three entities did not meet certain accounting requirements and should have been consolidated, (2) reflect the adjustment to shareholders' equity described below, and (3) include prior-year proposed audit adjustments and reclassifications (which were previously determined to be immaterial in the year originally proposed). Specifically, Enron has concluded that based on current information:

     o   The financial activities of Chewco Investments, L.P. ("Chewco"), a related party which was an investor in Joint Energy Development Investments Limited Partnership ("JEDI"), should have been consolidated beginning in November 1997;

     o   The financial activities of JEDI, in which Enron was an investor and which was consolidated into Enron's financial statements during the first quarter of 2001, should have been consolidated beginning in November 1997; and

     o   The financial activities of a wholly-owned subsidiary of LJM1, which engaged in derivative transactions with Enron to permit Enron to hedge market risks of an equity investment in Rhythms NetConnections, Inc., should have been consolidated into Enron's financial statements beginning in 1999.

The effects of the restatements are outlined in Table 1 [Table 5.11-1 in this case]. A description of the restatements follows the table." *(Source: Enron Corp. 8-K filed November 8, 2001)*

Table 5.11-1 ENRON CORP. RESTATEMENTS UNAUDITED

IN MILLIONS EXCEPT FOR PER SHARE	1997	1998	1999	2000	1ST QTR 2001	2ND QTR 2001	3RD QTR 2001
Net income as reported	$ 105(a)	$ 703	$ 893	$ 979	$ 425	$ 404	$ (618)
Restatements:							
Consolidation of JEDI and Chewco	(45)	(107)	(153)	(91)	--	--	--
Consolidation of LJM1 subsidiary	--	--	(95)	(8)	--	--	--
Raptor equity adjustment	--	--	--	--	--	--	--
Prior year proposed audit adjustments and reclassifications	(51)	(6)	(2)	(33)	17	5	(17)
NET INCOME RESTATED	9	590	643	847	442	409	(635)
Diluted EPS as reported	0.16	1.01	1.10	1.12	0.49	0.45	(0.84)
DILUTED EPS RESTATED	(0.01)	0.86	0.79	0.97	0.51	0.46	(0.86)
Recurring net income as reported	515	698	957	1,266	406	404	393
Restatements:							
Consolidation of JEDI and Chewco	(45)	(107)	(153)	(91)	--	--	--
Consolidation of LJM1 subsidiary	--	--	(95)	(8)	--	--	--
Raptor equity adjustment	--	--	--	--	--	--	--
Prior year proposed audit adjustments and reclassifications	(51)	(6)	(2)	(33)	17	5	(17)
RECURRING NET INCOME RESTATED	419	585	707	1,134	423	409	376
Diluted recurring EPS as reported	0.87	1.00	1.18	1.47	0.47	0.45	0.43
DILUTED RECURRING EPS RESTATED	0.71	0.85	0.87	1.33	0.49	0.46	0.41
Total assets as reported	22,552	29,350	33,381	65,503	67,260	63,392	--
Restatements:							
Consolidation of JEDI and	447	160	187	(192)	--	--	--

IN MILLIONS EXCEPT FOR PER SHARE	1997	1998	1999	2000	1ST QTR 2001	2ND QTR 2001	3RD QTR 2001
Chewco Consolidation of LJM1 subsidiary	--	--	(222)	--	--	--	--
Raptor equity adjustment	--	--	--	(172)	(1,000)	(1,000)	--
Prior year proposed audit adjustments and reclassifications	(79)	(87)	(147)	(364)	(1,249)	247	--
TOTAL ASSETS RESTATED	22,920	29,423	33,199	64,775	65,011	62,639	61,177(b)
Debt as reported	6,254	7,357	8,152	10,229	11,922	12,812	--
Restatements: Consolidation of JEDI and Chewco	711	561	685	628	--	--	--
Consolidation of LJM1 Subsidiary	--	--	--	--	--	--	--
Raptor equity adjustment	--	--	--	--	--	--	--
Prior year proposed audit adjustments and reclassifications	--	--	--	--	--	--	--
DEBT RESTATED	6,965	7,918	8,837	10,857	11,922	12,812	12,978(b)
Equity as reported	5,618	7,048	9,570	11,470	11,727	11,740	--
Restatements: Consolidation of JEDI and Chewco	(262)	(391)	(540)	(810)	--	--	--
Consolidation of LJM1 subsidiary	--	--	(166)	60	60	60	--
Raptor equity adjustment	--	--	--	(172)	(1,000)	(1,000)	--
Prior year proposed audit adjustments and reclassifications	(51)	(57)	(128)	(242)	(286)	11	--
EQUITY RESTATED	5,305	6,600	8,736	10,306	10,501	10,811	9,491(b)

(a) After effect of significant contract restructuring charge totaling $463 million (after tax)
(b) Represents estimated balances pending completion of September 30, 2001 financial statements
(Source: Enron Corp. 8-K filed November 8, 2001)

"A.   Restatement Number 1

Enron's decision that Chewco should be consolidated beginning in November 1997 is based on current information that Chewco did not meet the accounting criteria to qualify as an unconsolidated SPE. As a result of Chewco's failure to meet the criteria, JEDI, in which Chewco was a limited partner, also did not qualify for nonconsolidation treatment. Because of those consolidations, Enron's prior-year reported debt amounts will be increased by both JEDI's and Chewco's borrowings. The net effect will reduce Enron's prior-years' reported net income and shareholders' equity amounts. In addition, Enron's net income is reduced for specific JEDI revenues previously allocated to Chewco, relating to the appreciation in value of Enron stock, which eliminate upon consolidation. This, in effect, reduces Enron's share of JEDI's earnings.

B. Restatement Number 2

Enron's decision that the LJM1 subsidiary should be consolidated in 1999 and 2000 is based on Enron's current assessment that the subsidiary did not qualify for nonconsolidation treatment because of inadequate capitalization. Accordingly, Enron now believes that the hedging transactions in which Enron engaged with the LJM1 subsidiary (related to Enron's investment in the stock of Rhythms NetConnections, Inc.) should have been consolidated into Enron's financial statements for 1999 and 2000. This consolidation has the effect of reducing Enron's net income in 1999 and 2000 and shareholders' equity in 1999 and increasing shareholders' equity in 2000, thus eliminating the income recognized by Enron on these derivative transactions.

C. Restatement Number 3

As discussed in Section 3 below, concerning Enron's recent disclosure of a $1.2 billion reduction to shareholders' equity in the third quarter of 2001, shareholders' equity will be reduced by $172 million beginning as of June 30, 2000, and by an additional $828 million beginning as of March 31, 2001, to properly record notes receivable (described in Section 3 below) as a reduction to equity.

D. Restatement Number 4

The restatements will also include prior-year proposed audit adjustments and reclassifications which were determined to be immaterial in the year originally proposed.

3. Accounting Basis for $1.2 Billion Reduction in Shareholders' Equity

Enron's previously-announced $1.2 billion reduction of shareholders' equity primarily involves the correction of the effect of an accounting error made in the second quarter of 2000 and in the first quarter of 2001. As described in more detail below, four SPEs known as Raptor I-IV (collectively, "Raptor") were created in 2000, permitting Enron to hedge market risk in certain of its investments. (LJM2 invested in these entities, but the related-party nature of the transaction is not relevant to the accounting correction). As part of the capitalization of these entities, Enron issued common stock in exchange for a note receivable. Enron increased notes receivable and shareholders' equity to reflect this transaction. Enron now believes that, under generally accepted accounting principles, the note receivable should have been presented as a reduction to shareholders' equity (similar to a shareholder loan). This treatment would have resulted in no net change to shareholders' equity. The net effect of this initial accounting entry was to overstate both notes receivable and shareholders' equity by approximately $172 million (which represented less than 2% of shareholders' equity at the time) in each of the second quarter, third quarter, and year-end financial statements of Enron for the year 2000.

In the first quarter of 2001, Enron entered into contracts with Raptor that could have obligated Enron to issue Enron common stock in the future in exchange for notes receivable. Enron accounted for these transactions using the accounting treatment described in the preceding paragraph. This resulted in an additional overstatement of both notes receivable and shareholders' equity by $828 million. As a result of these errors, shareholders' equity and notes receivable were overstated by a total of $1 billion in the unaudited financial statements of Enron at March 31 and June 30, 2001.

In the third quarter of 2001, Enron purchased LJM2's equity interests in Raptor for $35 million. As previously discussed, Enron accounted for this transaction as a reduction to Enron shareholders' equity and notes receivable by $1.2 billion. Enron recorded a $200 million equity reduction (which was part of the $1.2 billion reduction) related to the excess of the fair value of contracts deliverable by Enron over the notes receivable recorded in shareholders' equity, as adjusted.

Prior period financials will be restated to adjust shareholders' equity for all periods affected as shown in Section 2.

4. The Special Committee

Based on various reports and information concerning Enron's transactions with certain related parties, on October 31, 2001, the Board of Directors elected William Powers, Dean of the University of Texas School of Law, to the Board, and appointed Dean Powers as Chairman of a newly formed Special Committee of the Board to conduct an independent investigation and review of transactions between Enron and certain related parties. The Special Committee also was charged with taking any disciplinary action that it deems appropriate, communicating with the Securities and Exchange Commission (which has commenced a formal investigation of these matters), and recommending to the Board any other appropriate actions. The other members of the Special Committee are independent directors Frank Savage, CEO of Savage Holdings LLC, Paulo Ferraz Pereira, Executive Vice President of investment bank Group Bozano, and Herbert S. Winokur, Jr., Chairman and CEO of Capricorn Holdings, Inc.

The Special Committee has retained the law firm of Wilmer, Cutler & Pickering as its counsel. The firm's representation is led by William R. McLucas, former head of the Division of Enforcement of the SEC. Wilmer, Cutler has retained Deloitte & Touche to provide related accounting advice to the law firm. The Special Committee's review is in its early stages. It will include an analysis of both the underlying substance and business purposes of the transactions, as well as an analysis of their financial impact on Enron and, to the extent information is available, on the related parties. The duration of the Special Committee's review, and the ultimate results of that review, have not yet been determined. While the information provided herein reflects Enron's current understanding of the relevant facts, it is possible that the Special Committee's review will identify additional or different information concerning these matters.

5. The LJM Limited Partnerships and Transactions with Enron

A. The LJM Partnerships.

As discussed above, LJM1 and LJM2 are private investment limited partnerships. Enron believes that, under the LJM1 and LJM2 limited partnership agreements (as with many similar agreements in private equity investing), the general partners are entitled to receive a percentage of the profits in excess of their portions of total capital contributed to the partnerships depending upon the performance of the partnerships' investments. Enron also believes that the general partners are entitled to receive annual management fees based in part on formulas that take into account the total amount of capital committed and/or invested by the limited partners. Enron now believes that Mr. Fastow received in excess of $30 million relating to his LJM management and investment activities. Enron believes that the initial capital commitments to LJM1 were $16 million, and the aggregate capital commitments to LJM2 were $394 million.

LJM1 and LJM2 were described to the Enron Board of Directors as potential sources of capital to buy assets from Enron, potential equity partners for Enron investments, and counterparties to help mitigate risks associated with Enron investments. The Board also was informed that LJM1 and LJM2 intended to transact business with third parties. Prior to approving Mr. Fastow's affiliation with LJM1 and LJM2, the Board determined that Mr. Fastow's participation in the partnerships would not adversely affect the interests of Enron. The Board approved the initial transaction with LJM1 and recognized that Enron may (but was not required to) engage in additional transactions with LJM1.

The Board directed that certain controls be put into place relating to Mr. Fastow's involvement with the partnerships and transactions between Enron and the partnerships. The Board required review and approval of each transaction by the Office of the Chairman, the Chief Accounting Officer and the Chief Risk Officer. The Board also recognized the ability of the Chairman of the Board to require Mr. Fastow to resign from the partnerships at any time, and directed that the Audit and Compliance Committee conduct annual reviews of transactions between Enron and LJM1 and LJM2 completed during the prior year. Whether these controls and procedures were properly implemented is a subject of the Special Committee's investigation.

Enron believes that, as of July 31, 2001, Mr. Fastow sold his interests in LJM1 and LJM2 to Michael J. Kopper, and that Mr. Fastow ceased to be the managing member of their general partners. Prior to that time, Mr. Kopper reported to Mr. Fastow as a non-executive officer of an Enron division. Enron believes Mr. Kopper resigned from Enron immediately before purchasing Mr. Fastow's interests in LJM2. Mr. Fastow is no longer working for Enron.

B. General Summary of LJM Transactions.

From June 1999 through September 2001, Enron and Enron-related entities entered into 24 business relationships in which LJM1 or LJM2 participated. These relationships were of several general types, including: (1) sales of assets by Enron to LJM2 and by LJM2 to Enron; (2) purchases of debt or equity interests by LJM1 or LJM2 in Enron-sponsored SPEs; (3) purchases of debt or equity interests by LJM1 or LJM2 in Enron affiliates or other entities in which Enron was an investor; (4) purchases of equity investments by LJM1 or LJM2 in SPEs designed to mitigate market risk in Enron's investments; (5) the sale of a call option and a put option by LJM2 on physical assets; and (6) a subordinated loan to LJM2 from an Enron affiliate. The financial results of these transactions are summarized in Table 2 [Table 5.11-2 in this case] below." *(Source: Enron Corp. 8-K filed November 8, 2001)*

Table 5.11-2 UNAUDITED SUMMARY OF LJM TRANSACTIONS

DOLLARS IN MILLIONS	LJM INVESTMENT	CASH AND OTHER VALUE RECEIVED BY LJM	LJM NET CASH FLOW	IMPACT OF LJM TRANSACTIONS ON ENRON'S PRE-TAX EARNINGS
2001:				
Sale of Assets	--	--	--	$ 0.7
Purchases of Equity/Debt in Enron-Sponsored Special Purpose Entities	--	52.5	52.5	--
Investments in Enron Affiliates	3.4	49.7	46.3	--
Portfolio Special Purpose Entities	--	75.5	75.5	(166.2)(a)
Call Option	--	--	--	--
Transactions with LJM and Other Entities	--	--	--	--
Transaction with LJM and Whitewing	--	--	--	--
Total	$ 3.4	$ 177.7	$ 174.3	$ (165.5)
2000:				
Sale of Assets	$ 30.0(b)	$ 32.4	$ 2.4	$ 86.6
Purchases of Equity/Debt	100.7	64.4	(36.3)	--

DOLLARS IN MILLIONS	LJM INVESTMENT	CASH AND OTHER VALUE RECEIVED BY LJM	LJM NET CASH FLOW	IMPACT OF LJM TRANSACTIONS ON ENRON'S PRE-TAX EARNINGS
in Enron-Sponsored Special Purpose Entities				
Investments in Enron Affiliates	66.5	19.3	(47.2)	--
Portfolio Special Purpose Entities	127.1	148.5	21.4	517.9(a,c)
Call Option	11.3	12.5	1.2	--
Transactions with LJM and Other Entities	7.5	11.7	4.2	--
Transaction with LJM and Whitewing	40.3	--	(40.3)	--
Total	$ 383.4	$ 288.8	$ (94.6)	$ 604.5
1999:				
Sale of Assets	--	--	--	--
Purchases of Equity/Debt in Enron-Sponsored Special Purpose Entities	73.8	15.4	(58.4)	2.4
Investments in Enron Affiliates	44.5	1.0	(43.5)	16.9
Portfolio Special Purpose Entities	64.0	95.2(d)	31.2	119.5(c)
Call Option	--	--	--	--
Transactions with LJM and Other Entities	--	--	--	--
Transaction with LJM and Whitewing	--	38.5	38.5	--
Total	$ 182.3	$ 150.1	$ (32.2)	$ 138.8
Summary Totals:				
Sale of Assets	$ 30.0	$ 32.4	$ 2.4	$ 87.3
Purchases of Equity/Debt in Enron-Sponsored Special Purpose Entities	174.5	132.3	(42.2)	2.4
Investments in Enron Affiliates	114.4	70.0	(44.4)	16.9
Portfolio Special Purpose Entities	191.1	319.2	128.1	471.2
Call Option	11.3	12.5	1.2	--
Transactions with LJM and Other Entities	7.5	11.7	4.2	--
Transaction with LJM and Whitewing	40.3	38.5	(1.8)	--
Total	$ 569.1	$ 616.6	$ 47.5	$ 577.8
Estimated Fair Value of Existing LJM Investments		$ 43.6(e)		

(a) The pre-tax earnings impact of transactions with LJM2 through the Raptor SPEs was approximately $532 million in 2000 and $545 million for the nine months ended September 30, 2001. During 2000 and the nine months ended September 30, 2001, the Raptor SPEs hedged losses related to Enron investments of $501 million and $453 million respectively. The 2001 pre-tax earnings amount includes a $711 million pre-tax charge in the quarter ended September 30, 2001 related to the termination of the Raptor SPEs.

(b) This amount excludes a seller financed note from Enron to LJM of approximately $70 million.

(c)　These pre-tax earnings resulted from a transaction with an LJM1 affiliate related to Enron's equity investment in Rhythms Netconnections, Inc. As previously stated, Enron now believes, based on current information, that the financial activities of the LJM1 affiliate should have been consolidated into its financial statements in 1999 and 2000 and will be restating prior years' financial statements to reflect this change. The pre-tax earnings / (loss) impact of this transaction was approximately $119.5 million and ($14.1) million in 1999 and 2000 respectively.

(d)　This amount represents Enron's estimate of the value received in Enron common stock, a portion of which was restricted. The estimate was based on a 36% discount off of the screen price on the date of issuance for shares that were restricted and estimated proceeds received by LJM from the sale of the unrestricted shares.

(e)　This amount represents Enron's estimated fair value of the six investments made by LJM that remain outstanding. *(Source: Enron Corp. 8-K filed November 8, 2001)*

> "C. Sale of Assets.
> In June 2000, LJM2 purchased dark fiber optic cable from Enron for a purchase price of $100 million. LJM2 paid Enron $30 million in cash and the balance in an interest-bearing note for $70 million. Enron recognized $67 million in pre-tax earnings in 2000 related to the asset sale. Pursuant to a marketing agreement with LJM2, Enron was compensated for marketing the fiber to others and providing operation and maintenance services to LJM2 with respect to the fiber. LJM2 sold a portion of the fiber to industry participants for $40 million, which resulted in Enron recognizing agency fee revenue of $20.3 million. LJM2 sold the remaining dark fiber for $113 million in December 2000 to an SPE that was formed to acquire the fiber. In December 2000, LJM2 used a portion of the proceeds to pay in full the note and accrued interest owed to Enron. At the time of LJM2's sale of the fiber to the SPE, Enron entered into a derivative contract which served as credit support for the benefit of some of the debt holders of a third-party investor in the SPE. This credit support provided the lender with a specified rate of return. As a result, Enron's credit exposure under the $70 million note was replaced with $61 million in remaining exposure under the derivative contract. LJM2 earned $2.4 million on its resale of the fiber.
> D. Purchases of Equity/Debt in Enron-Sponsored SPEs.
> Between September 1999 and December 2000, LJM1 or LJM2 purchased equity or debt interests in nine Enron-sponsored SPEs. LJM1 and LJM2 invested $175 million in the nine SPEs. These transactions enabled Enron to monetize assets and generated pre-tax earnings to Enron of $2 million in 1999.
>
> 　Enron believes that LJM received cash of $15 million, $64 million and $53 million in 1999, 2000 and 2001, respectively, relating to its investments in these entities. In three instances, third-party financial institutions also invested in the entities. LJM invested on the same terms as the third-party investors. In one of these nine transactions, Enron entered into a marketing agreement with LJM2 that provided Enron with the right to market the underlying equity. This arrangement gave Enron profit potential in proceeds received after LJM2 achieved a specified return level. In six of these nine transactions, Enron repurchased all or a portion of the equity and debt initially purchased by LJM.
>
> 　The SPEs owned, directly or indirectly, a variety of operating and financial assets. For example, Yosemite Securities Trust was a finance entity which facilitated Enron's ability to raise funds in the capital markets through the use of credit-linked notes, a standard financing arrangement offered by investment banks. Osprey Trust is beneficially-owned by a number of financial institutions and is a limited partner in Whitewing Associates, L.P., an Enron unconsolidated affiliate ("Whitewing"). Enron is the other partner. Whitewing purchased certain Enron investments for future sale.
>
> 　In addition, as a result of these transactions, Enron was able to monetize equity interests with investment banks. These monetizations resulted in Enron's recognizing $146 million and $5 million in pre-tax earnings in 2000 and 2001, respectively, and $252 million in cash inflows, all in 2000.

E. Investment in Enron Affiliates.

In two transactions, LJM2 made direct and indirect investments in stock (and warrants convertible into stock) of New Power Holdings, Inc. ("NPW"). NPW initially was a wholly-owned subsidiary of Enron, subsequently included other strategic and financial investors, and in October 2000 became a public company. NPW is engaged in the retail marketing and retail sale of natural gas, electricity and other commodities, products and services to residential and small commercial customers in the United States. In January 2000, LJM2 invested $673,000 in Cortez Energy Services LLC ("Cortez"), a limited liability company formed by Enron and LJM2, and Enron contributed five million shares of NPW stock to Cortez. In July 2000, in a private placement, LJM2 purchased warrants exercisable for NPW stock for $50 million on the same terms as third-party investors. Enron believes that LJM2 still owns these investments.

In September 1999, LJM1 acquired from Enron a 13% equity interest in a company owning a power project in Brazil for $10.8 million, and acquired redeemable preference shares in a related company for $500,000. Enron recognized a $1.million loss on the sale of these interests to LJM1. Enron recognized revenues of $65 million, $14 million and $5 million from a commodity contract with the company owning the power project in 1999, 2000 and 2001, respectively. As part of an exclusive marketing arrangement to sell LJM1's equity in the project to third-parties and to limit LJM1's return, Enron paid LJM1 a $240,000 fee in May 2000. In 2001, Enron repurchased LJM1's 13% equity interest and the redeemable preference shares for $14.4 million. Enron currently owns this equity interest.

In December 1999, LJM2 paid Enron $30 million for a 75% equity interest in a power project in Poland. Enron recognized a $16 million gain in 1999 on the sale. Enron paid $750,000 to LJM2 as an equity placement fee. In March 2000, Enron repurchased 25% of the equity in the Polish power project from LJM2 for $10.6 million, and Whitewing acquired the remaining 50% from LJM2 for $21.3 million. Enron and Whitewing still own their respective equity interests.

In December 1999, LJM2 acquired a 90% equity interest in an Enron entity with ownership rights to certain natural gas reserves for $3 million. As a result, Enron recognized $3 million in revenue from an existing commodity contract. Subsequently, LJM2 assigned a portion of its ownership interest in the entity to Enron and Whitewing at no cost (to achieve certain after-tax benefits). Enron believes LJM2 continues to own its remaining interest.

F. Portfolio SPEs.

Enron and LJM established a series of SPEs in order to mitigate market exposures on Enron investments, including investments in NPW, Rhythms NetConnections, Inc., and other technology, energy, and energy-related companies. LJM made $191 million in equity investments in five separate SPEs, three of which (Raptor I, II and IV) were also capitalized with Enron stock and derivatives which could have required the future delivery of Enron stock. Raptor III was capitalized with an economic interest in warrants convertible into stock of NPW. The fifth SPE is discussed in Section 2B above. Enron subsequently engaged in hedging transactions with these SPEs, which included price swap derivatives, call options and put options. The derivatives and options generally were intended to hedge Enron's risk in certain investments having an aggregate notional amount of approximately $1.9 billion.

With respect to the four Raptor SPEs, Enron acquired LJM2's equity in the SPEs during the third quarter of 2001 for $35 million. Enron recognized pre-tax earnings (losses) relating to risk management activities of $119 million, $518 million and ($166) million in 1999, 2000 and 2001, respectively, including the effect of a $711 million pre-tax charge recognized in 2001, related to the termination of the Raptor SPEs. During 2000 and the nine months ended September 30, 2001, the Raptor SPEs hedged losses of $501 million and $453 million, respectively. The fifth SPE was used to hedge Enron's exposure arising from an investment in the stock of Rhythms NetConnections, Inc. However, it was subsequently determined that it did not meet the criteria to qualify for unconsolidated treatment. (See Section 2B for a discussion of the restatement related to the fifth SPE.)

In total, LJM1 and LJM2 invested $191 million and received $319 million (an estimated $95 million of which is non-cash value from the receipt of 3.6 million shares of Enron restricted stock) related to their investments in these five SPEs.

G. Call Option.

In May 2000, Enron purchased a call option from LJM2 on two gas turbines, at the same time that LJM2 contracted to purchase the gas turbines from the manufacturer. Enron paid LJM2 $1.2 million for this right during a seven-month period in 2000. The call option gave Enron the right to acquire these turbines from LJM2 at LJM2's cost, which was $11.3 million. The call option was subsequently assigned from Enron to an Enron-sponsored SPE capitalized by a third-party financial institution. In December 2000, the call option was exercised by the SPE and it acquired the turbines from LJM2 at cost.

H. Transactions with LJM and Other Entities.

Enron sold its contractual right to acquire a gas turbine to a utility for $15.8 million in July 2000. Enron recognized a pre-tax gain of $3.5 million on the transaction. At the same time, the utility entered into a put option agreement with LJM2 relating to the turbine under which the utility paid LJM2 $3.5 million. Subsequently, upon the execution of an engineering, procurement and construction contract with a wholly-owned subsidiary of Enron, the utility assigned the contractual right to acquire the gas turbine to that subsidiary.

In December 1999, Enron sold an equity investment in Enron Nigeria Barge Ltd. to an investment bank and provided seller financing. In June of 2000, LJM2 purchased this equity investment directly from the investment bank for $7.5 million and the assumption of the seller-financed note from Enron. In September 2000, LJM2 sold the equity investment to an industry participant for $31.2 million. The proceeds from LJM2's sale were used by LJM2 to repay the principal and interest on the note from Enron in the amount of $23.0 million. The remaining $8.2 million repaid LJM2's $7.5 million purchase price and provided a profit of $700,000 to LJM2.

I. Transaction between LJM and Whitewing.

In December 1999, a wholly-owned subsidiary of Whitewing entered into a $38.5 million credit agreement with LJM2, the borrower. The loan had a term of one year and carried an interest rate of LIBOR+2.5%. The loan amount (including interest) of $40.3 million was repaid by LJM2 in 2000.

J. Currently Outstanding LJM2 Transactions.

Enron believes that LJM2 currently has interests in six of the investments described above in which LJM2 originally invested $124 million, and that LJM2 has received cash inflows of $27 million from these investments. These investments include $23 million in equity in two Enron-sponsored SPEs, $32.5 million in equity in Osprey Trust $3 million in equity in an Enron affiliate, and $50.7 million in direct equity investments in NPW (representing two transactions).

Enron and LJM2 also entered into various agreements relating to cash management services, employee services, and office space provided by Enron to LJM2. In addition, Enron paid LJM2 a management fee for certain transactions, and other transaction fees described above. Enron also reimbursed LJM2 for transaction-related expenses (such as legal and tax fees and other costs) associated with some of the transactions described above.

6. Other Transactions

Like many other companies involved in trade and finance, Enron (through affiliates, subsidiaries, and SPEs) routinely engages in financing arrangements with third-party financial institutions, including commercial banks, investment banks and institutional investors, to fund acquisitions of assets or businesses, project development activities, and similar business arrangements. These activities are transacted with third parties using structures similar in some respects to the arrangements entered into with LJM. Enron provides credit support to the creditors of SPEs through the use of financial guarantees and hedging contracts. The payment of fees to third-party financial institutions and institutional investors, such as debt and equity placement fees and structuring fees, is common in debt and equity syndications.

7. Other Employee Transactions

From June 1993 through November 1997, an Enron subsidiary was the general partner of JEDI and a third-party, the California Public Employees' Retirement System ("CalPERS"), was the limited partner. In November 1997, JEDI made a liquidating distribution to CalPERS of $383 million. Concurrently, Chewco purchased a limited partnership interest in JEDI for $383 million, $132 million of which was financed by an interest-bearing loan from JEDI to Chewco, and $240 million of which was borrowed from a third-party financial institution (supported by a guarantee from Enron). The restatement resulting from the Chewco transaction is discussed in 2A. Based on current information, Enron believes that a non-executive officer of an Enron division, Michael J. Kopper, was an investor in the general partner of Chewco and, at the time of the purchase, also was the manager of the Chewco general partner.

From December 1997 to December 2000, Chewco received distributions of $433 million from JEDI. Among other things, Chewco used a portion of these distributions to make repayments on its JEDI loan and to repay an additional borrowing from the third-party financial institution.

In December 1999, Chewco purchased a $15 million equity interest in Osprey Trust, an Enron-sponsored SPE, from LJM1.

In March 2001, Enron purchased Chewco's limited partnership interest in JEDI for $35 million. In September 2001, Enron paid an additional $2.6 million to Chewco in connection with a tax indemnification agreement between JEDI, Chewco and Enron. Of the total purchase consideration, $26 million was used by Chewco to make a payment on the JEDI loan. Chewco currently has an outstanding balance due on the JEDI loan of $15 million. JEDI is currently a wholly-owned subsidiary of Enron.

Enron now believes that Mr. Kopper also was the controlling partner of a limited partnership that (through another limited partnership) in March 2000 purchased interests in affiliated subsidiaries of LJM1. Enron also now believes that four of the six limited partners of the purchaser were, at the time of the investment, non-executive officers or employees of Enron, and a fifth limited partner was an entity associated with Mr. Fastow. These officers and employees, and their most recent job titles with Enron, were Ben Glisan, Managing Director and Treasurer of Enron Corp.; Kristina Mordaunt, Managing Director and General Counsel of an Enron division; Kathy Lynn, Vice President of an Enron division; and Anne Yaeger, a non-officer employee. Enron is terminating the employment of Mr. Glisan and Ms. Mordaunt. Ms. Lynn and Ms. Yaeger are no longer associated with Enron and Enron believes they are now associated with LJM2. At the time these individuals invested in the limited partnership, LJM1 had ceased entering into new transactions with Enron. However, some pre-existing investments involving LJM1 and Enron were still in effect, and Enron believes that these investments resulted in distributions or payments to LJM1 and to the limited partnership in which these individuals invested.

Pursuant to a services agreement among Enron, LJM1, and LJM2, Enron made available to LJM1 and LJM2 a portion of the time of certain of its employees to provide administrative assistance to the general partners of LJM1 and LJM2. Mr. Kopper, Ms. Lynn and Ms. Yaeger, among other Enron employees, were made available to LJM1 or LJM2 from time to time during their employment by Enron.

This statement includes forward-looking statements within the meaning of Section 27A of the Securities Act of 1933 and Section 21E of the Securities Exchange Act of 1934. The Private Securities Litigation Reform Act of 1995 provides a safe harbor for forward-looking statements made by Enron or on its behalf. These forward-looking statements are not historical facts, but reflect Enron's current expectations, estimates and projections. All statements contained herein which address future operating performance, events or developments that are expected to occur in the future (including statements relating to earnings expectations) are forward-looking statements. Important factors that could cause actual results to differ materially from those in the forward-looking statements herein include results of the Special Committee's review and results of the SEC investigation." *(Source: Enron Corp. 8-K filed November 8, 2001)*

The 8-K filing of November 8, 2001 by Enron Corp. also includes a press release dated November 8, 2001 regarding related party and off-balance sheet transactions and restatement of earnings. The content of that press release follows:

"ENRON PROVIDES ADDITIONAL INFORMATION ABOUT RELATED PARTY AND OFF-BALANCE SHEET TRANSACTIONS; COMPANY TO RESTATE EARNINGS FOR 1997-2001

FOR IMMEDIATE RELEASE: Thursday, Nov. 8, 2001

HOUSTON - Enron Corp. (NYSE: ENE) today provided additional information about various related party and off-balance sheet transactions in which the company was involved. The information was posted today on the company's website at www.enron.com/corp/sec and also made available in a Form 8-K Report filed today with the Securities and Exchange Commission (SEC).

Specifically, Enron's filing provides information about:

o   a required restatement of prior period financial statements to reflect the previously disclosed $1.2 billion reduction to shareholders' equity, as well as various income statement and balance sheet adjustments required as the result of a determination by Enron and its auditors, based on current information, that certain off-balance sheet entities should have been included in Enron's consolidated financial statements pursuant to generally accepted accounting principles;

o   the restatement of its financial statements for 1997 through 2000 and the first two quarters of 2001. As a result, financial statements for these periods and the audit reports relating to the year-end financial statements for 1997 through 2000 should not be relied upon;

o   the accounting basis for the above-mentioned reduction to shareholders' equity;

o   the special committee appointed by the Enron Board of Directors to review transactions between Enron and related parties;

o   information regarding the two LJM limited partnerships formed by Enron's then Chief Financial Officer, his role in the partnerships, the business relationships and transactions between Enron and the partnerships, and the economic results of those transactions as known thus far; and

o   transactions between Enron and certain other Enron employees.

"We believe that the information we have made available addresses a number of the concerns that have been raised by our shareholders and the SEC about these matters," said Ken Lay, Enron Chairman and CEO. "We will continue our efforts to respond to investor requests for information about our operational and financial condition so they can evaluate, appreciate and appropriately value the strength of our core businesses."

Restatement of Earnings

As further described on Enron's website, and its Form 8-K Report, Enron will restate prior years' financial statements to reflect its review of current information concerning the transactions discussed below. After taking into account Enron's previously disclosed adjustment to shareholders' equity in the third quarter of 2001, these restatements have no effect on Enron's current financial position.

Based on this review, Enron has determined that:

o Enron's current assessment indicates that the restatement will include a reduction to reported net income of approximately $96 million in 1997, $113 million in 1998, $250 million in 1999 and $132 million in 2000, increases of $17 million for the first quarter of 2001 and $5 million for the second quarter and a reduction of $17 million for the third quarter of 2001. These changes to net income are the result of the retroactive consolidation of JEDI and Chewco beginning in November 1997, the consolidation of the LJM1 subsidiary for 1999 and 2000 and prior year proposed audit adjustments. The consolidation of JEDI and Chewco also will increase Enron's debt by approximately $711 million in 1997, $561 million in 1998, $685 million in 1999 and $628 million in 2000. The restatement will have no negative impact on Enron's reported earnings for the nine month period ending Sept. 2001.

o Enron is one of the world's leading energy, commodities and services companies. The company markets electricity and natural gas, delivers energy and other physical commodities, and provides financial and risk management services to customers around the world. Enron's Internet address is www.enron.com. The stock is traded under the ticker symbol "ENE."… ″

(Source: Enron Corp. 8-K filed November 8, 2001 included press release)

Moving backwards in time, consider a sample of the disclosures found in the year-end 10-K filing by Enron Corp. for 2000:

"In 2000 and 1999, Enron entered into various transactions with related parties, which resulted in an exchange of assets and an increase in common stock of $171 million in 2000. See Note 16.

In 2000, a partnership in which Enron was a limited partner made a liquidating distribution to Enron resulting in a non-cash increase in current assets of $220 million, a decrease of $20 million in non-current assets and an increase in current liabilities of $160 million."…

" 9 UNCONSOLIDATED EQUITY AFFILIATES

Enron's investment in and advances to unconsolidated affiliates which are accounted for by the equity method is as follows:

(In millions)	Net Voting Interest(a)	December 31, 2000	1999
Azurix Corp.	34%	$ 325	$ 762
Bridgeline Holdings	40%	229	-
Citrus Corp.	50%	530	480
Dabhol Power Company	50%	693	466
Joint Energy Development Investments L.P. (JEDI)(b)	50%	399	211
Joint Energy Development Investments II L.P. (JEDI II)(b)	50%	220	162
SK - Enron Co. Ltd.	50%	258	269
Transportadora de Gas del Sur S.A.	35%	479	452
Whitewing Associates, L.P.(b)	50%	558	662
Other		1,603	1,572
		$5,294(c)	$5,036(c)

(a) Certain investments have income sharing ratios which differ from Enron's voting interests.

(b) JEDI and JEDI II account for their investments at fair value. Whitewing accounts for certain of its investments at fair value. These affiliates held fair value investments totaling $1,823 million and $1,128 million, respectively, at December 31, 2000 and 1999.

(c) At December 31, 2000 and 1999, the unamortized excess of Enron's investment in unconsolidated affiliates was $182 million and $179 million, respectively, which is being amortized over the expected lives of the investments.

Enron's equity in earnings (losses) of unconsolidated equity affiliates is as follows:

(In millions)	2000	1999	1998
Azurix Corp.(a)	$(428)	$ 23	$ 6
Citrus Corp.	50	25	23
Dabhol Power Company	51	30	-
Joint Energy Development Investments L.P.	197	11	(45)
Joint Energy Development Investments II, L.P.	58	92	(4)
TNPC, Inc. (The New Power Company)	(60)	-	-
Transportadora de Gas del Sur S.A.	38	32	36
Whitewing Associates, L.P.	58	9	-
Other	123	87	81
	$ 87	$ 309	$ 97

(a) During the fourth quarter of 2000, Azurix Corp. (Azurix) impaired the carrying value of its Argentine assets, resulting in a charge of approximately $470 million. Enron's portion of the charge was $326 million.

Summarized combined financial information of Enron's unconsolidated affiliates is presented below:

December 31, (In millions)	2000	1999
Balance sheet		
Current assets(a)	$ 5,884	$ 3,168
Property, plant and equipment, net	14,786	14,356
Other noncurrent assets	13,485	9,459
Current liabilities(a)	4,739	4,401
Long-term debt(a)	9,717	8,486
Other noncurrent liabilities	6,148	2,402
Owners' equity	13,551	11,694

(a) Includes $410 million and $327 million receivable from Enron and $302 million and $84 million payable to Enron at December 31, 2000 and 1999, respectively.

(In millions)	2000	1999	1998
Income statement(a)			
Operating revenues	$15,903	$11,568	$8,508
Operating expenses	14,710	9,449	7,244
Net income	586	1,857	142
Distributions paid to Enron	137	482	87

(a) Enron recognized revenues from transactions with unconsolidated equity affiliates of $510 million in 2000, $674 million in 1999 and $563 million in 1998.

In 2000 and 1999, Enron sold approximately $632 million and $192 million, respectively, of merchant investments and other assets to Whitewing. Enron recognized no gains or losses in connection with these transactions. Additionally, in 2000, ECT Merchant Investments Corp., a wholly-owned Enron subsidiary, contributed two pools of merchant investments to a limited partnership that is a subsidiary of Enron. Subsequent to the contributions, the partnership issued partnership interests representing 100% of the beneficial, economic interests in the two asset pools, and such interests were sold for a total of $545 million to a limited liability company that is a subsidiary of Whitewing. See Note 3. These entities are separate legal entities from Enron and have separate assets and liabilities. In 2000 and 1999, the Related Party, as described in Note 16, contributed $33 million and $15 million, respectively, of equity to Whitewing. In 2000, Whitewing contributed $7.1 million to a partnership formed by Enron, Whitewing and a third party. Subsequently, Enron sold a portion of its interest in the partnership through a securitization. See Note 3.

In 2000, The New Power Company sold warrants convertible into common stock of The New Power Company for $50 million to the Related Party (described in Note 16).

From time to time, Enron has entered into various administrative service, management, construction, supply and operating agreements with its unconsolidated equity affiliates. Enron's management believes that its existing agreements and transactions are reasonable compared to those which could have been obtained from third parties."…

Derivative Instruments. At December 31, 2000, Enron had derivative instruments (excluding amounts disclosed in Note 10) on 54.8 million shares of Enron common stock, of which approximately 12 million shares are with JEDI and 22.5 million shares are with related parties (see Note 16), at an average price of $67.92 per share on which Enron was a fixed price payor. Shares potentially deliverable to counterparties under the contracts are assumed to be outstanding in calculating diluted earnings per share unless they are antidilutive. At December 31, 2000, there were outstanding non-employee options to purchase 6.4 million shares of Enron common stock at an exercise price of $19.59 per share.…

16 RELATED PARTY TRANSACTIONS

In 2000 and 1999, Enron entered into transactions with limited partnerships (the Related Party) whose general partner's managing member is a senior officer of Enron. The limited partners of the Related Party are unrelated to Enron. Management believes that the terms of the transactions with the Related Party were reasonable compared to those which could have been negotiated with unrelated third parties.

In 2000, Enron entered into transactions with the Related Party to hedge certain merchant investments and other assets. As part of the transactions, Enron (i) contributed to newly-formed entities (the Entities) assets valued at approximately $1.2 billion, including $150 million in Enron notes payable, 3.7 million restricted shares of outstanding Enron common stock and the right to receive up to 18.0 million shares of outstanding Enron common stock in March 2003 (subject to certain conditions) and (ii) transferred to the Entities assets valued at approximately $309 million, including a $50 million note payable and an investment in an entity that indirectly holds warrants convertible into common stock of an Enron equity method investee. In return, Enron received economic interests in the Entities, $309 million in notes receivable, of which $259 million is recorded at Enron's carryover basis of zero, and a special distribution from the Entities in the form of $1.2 billion in notes receivable, subject to changes in the principal for amounts payable by Enron in connection with the execution of additional derivative instruments. Cash in these Entities of $172.6 million is invested in Enron demand notes. In addition, Enron paid $123 million to purchase share-settled options from the Entities on 21.7 million shares of Enron common stock. The Entities paid Enron $10.7 million to terminate the share-settled options on 14.6 million shares of Enron common stock outstanding. In late 2000, Enron entered into share-settled collar arrangements with the Entities on 15.4 million shares of Enron common stock. Such arrangements will be accounted for as equity transactions when settled.

In 2000, Enron entered into derivative transactions with the Entities with a combined notional amount of approximately $2.1 billion to hedge certain merchant investments and other assets. Enron's notes receivable balance was reduced by $36 million as a result of premiums owed on derivative transactions. Enron recognized revenues of approximately $500 million related to the subsequent change in the market value of these derivatives, which offset market value changes of certain merchant investments and price risk management activities. In addition, Enron recognized $44.5 million and $14.1 million of interest income and interest expense, respectively, on the notes receivable from and payable to the Entities.

In 1999, Enron entered into a series of transactions involving a third party and the Related Party. The effect of the transactions was (i) Enron and the third party amended certain forward contracts to purchase shares of Enron common stock, resulting in Enron having forward contracts to purchase Enron common shares at the market price on that day, (ii) the Related Party received 6.8 million shares of Enron common stock subject to certain restrictions and (iii) Enron received a note receivable, which was repaid in December 1999, and certain financial instruments hedging an investment held by Enron. Enron recorded the assets received and equity issued at estimated fair value. In connection with the transactions, the Related Party agreed that the senior officer of Enron would have no pecuniary interest in such Enron common shares and would be restricted from voting on matters related to such shares. In 2000, Enron and the Related Party entered into an agreement to terminate certain financial instruments that had been entered into during 1999. In connection with this agreement, Enron received approximately 3.1 million shares of Enron common stock held by the Related Party. A put option, which was originally entered into in the first quarter of 2000 and gave the Related Party the right to sell shares of Enron common stock to Enron at a strike price of $71.31 per share, was terminated under this agreement. In return, Enron paid approximately $26.8 million to the Related Party.

In 2000, Enron sold a portion of its dark fiber inventory to the Related Party in exchange for $30 million cash and a $70 million note receivable that was subsequently repaid. Enron recognized gross margin of $67 million on the sale.

In 2000, the Related Party acquired, through securitizations, approximately $35 million of merchant investments from Enron. In addition, Enron and the Related Party formed partnerships in which Enron contributed cash and assets and the Related Party contributed $17.5 million in cash. Subsequently, Enron sold a portion of its interests in the partnerships through securitizations. See Note 3. Also, Enron contributed a put option to a trust in which the Related Party and Whitewing hold equity and debt interests. At December 31, 2000, the fair value of the put option was a $36 million loss to Enron.

In 1999, the Related Party acquired approximately $371 million, merchant assets and investments and other assets from Enron. Enron recognized pre-tax gains of approximately $16 million related to these transactions. The Related Party also entered into an agreement to acquire Enron's interests in an unconsolidated equity affiliate for approximately $34 million....

18 ACCOUNTING PRONOUNCEMENTS...

Recently Issued Accounting Pronouncements. In 1998, the Financial Accounting Standards Board (FASB) issued SFAS No. 133, "Accounting for Derivative Instruments and Hedging Activities," which was subsequently amended by SFAS No. 137 and SFAS No. 138. SFAS No. 133 must be applied to all derivative instruments and certain derivative instruments embedded in hybrid instruments and requires that such instruments be recorded in the balance sheet either as an asset or liability measured at its fair value through earnings, with special accounting allowed for certain qualifying hedges. Enron will adopt SFAS No. 133 as of January 1, 2001. Due to the adoption of SFAS No. 133, Enron will recognize an after-tax non-cash loss of approximately $5 million in earnings and an after-tax non-cash gain in "Other Comprehensive Income," a component of shareholders' equity, of approximately $22 million from the cumulative effect of a change in accounting principle. Enron will also reclassify $532 million from "Long-Term Debt" to "Other Liabilities" due to the adoption.

The total impact of Enron's adoption of SFAS No. 133 on earnings and on "Other Comprehensive Income" is dependent upon certain pending interpretations, which are currently under consideration, including those related to "normal purchases and normal sales" and inflation escalators included in certain contract payment provisions. The interpretations of these issues, and others, are currently under consideration by the FASB. While the ultimate conclusions reached on interpretations being considered by the FASB could impact the effects of Enron's adoption of SFAS No. 133, Enron does not believe that such conclusions would have a material effect on its current estimate of the impact of adoption.

(Source: Enron Corp. 10-K for December 31, 2000, filed on April 2, 2001)

Requirement A: The Relationship of Generally Accepted Accounting Principles to Issues In the Restatement

1. Identify the guidance upon which Enron Corp. relies in its restatement. Using the Financial Accounting Research System (FARS), be specific as to the aspect of each pronouncement that ties to the key determinant of each restatement item.

2. The media noted that Enron's disclosures in mid-October first indicated a reduction in shareholder equity of $1.2 billion because the corporation had decided to unwind certain transactions with some limited partnerships with which it had done business. However, the elaboration on the situation led to the disclosure that the original accounting for the transactions was not in accordance with generally accepted accounting principles. The media has pointed out that the early 2000 issuance by Enron of shares of its own common stock to four "special-purpose entities" (SPEs) in exchange for a notes receivable would not qualify as an issuance of stock until cash was received. Explain why this is the case.

3. The media has discussed Enron Corp., pre-restatement, as being innovative in tailoring contracts, making new positions valued at over $4 billion each day. The point has been made that trading losses were not the focus of the bad news from the corporation, but rather that the erosion of the equity base of Enron Corporation through the restatement became the issue. Fears among trading partners arose as to Enron Corp.'s ability to finance its trading activity, since counterparties are expected to look to equity base for assurance. The reported rating downgrades—as they reached junk status, due to their below investment grade levels' effects on various transactions—were expected to force Enron to produce hundreds of millions of dollars in cash or stock. An estimated $3.9B of debt could come due, according to various media discussions, and Enron Corp. was not viewed as sufficiently liquid to meet such demands. Somewhat expected was the 8-K filed by Enron Corp, on December 2, 2001:

"ENRON FILES VOLUNTARY PETITIONS FOR CHAPTER 11 REORGANIZATION; SUES DYNEGY FOR BREACH OF CONTRACT, SEEKING DAMAGES OF AT LEAST $10 BILLION

FOR IMMEDIATE RELEASE: Sunday, December 2, 2001
-   Proceeds of Lawsuit Would Benefit Enron's Creditors

- Company in Active Discussions to Receive Credit Support For, Recapitalize and Revitalize Its North American Wholesale Energy Trading Operations Under New Ownership Structure
- Enron Will Downsize Operations and Continue Sales of Non-Core Assets

HOUSTON -- Enron Corp. (NYSE: ENE) announced today that it along with certain of its subsidiaries have filed voluntary petitions for Chapter 11 reorganization with the U.S. Bankruptcy Court for the Southern District of New York. As part of the reorganization process, Enron also filed suit against Dynegy Inc. (NYSE: DYN) in the same court, alleging breach of contract in connection with Dynegy's wrongful termination of its proposed merger with Enron and seeking damages of at least $10 billion. Enron's lawsuit also seeks the court's declaration that Dynegy is not entitled to exercise its option to acquire an Enron subsidiary that indirectly owns Northern Natural Gas Pipeline. Proceeds from the lawsuit would benefit Enron's creditors.

In a related development aimed at preserving value in its North American wholesale energy trading business, Enron said that it is in active discussions with various leading financial institutions to provide credit support for, recapitalize and revitalize that business under a new ownership structure. It is anticipated that Enron would provide the new entity with traders, back office capabilities and technology from Enron's North American wholesale energy business, and that the new entity would conduct counterparty transactions through EnronOnline, the company's existing energy trading platform. Any such arrangement would be subject to the approval of the Bankruptcy Court.

In connection with the company's Chapter 11 filings, Enron is in active discussions with leading financial institutions for debtor-in-possession (DIP) financing and expects to complete these discussions shortly. Upon the completion and court approval of these arrangements, the new funding will be available immediately on an interim basis to supplement Enron's existing capital and help the company fulfill obligations associated with operating its business, including its employee payroll and payments to vendors for goods and services provided on or after today's filing.

Filings for Chapter 11 reorganization have been made for a total of 14 affiliated entities, including Enron Corp.; Enron North America Corp., the company's wholesale energy trading business; Enron Energy Services, the company's retail energy marketing operations; Enron Transportation Services, the holding company for Enron's pipeline operations; Enron Broadband Services, the company's bandwidth trading operation; and Enron Metals & Commodity Corp.

Enron-related entities not included in the Chapter 11 filing are not affected by the filing. These non-filing entities include Northern Natural Gas Pipeline, Transwestern Pipeline, Florida Gas Transmission, EOTT, Portland General Electric and numerous other Enron international entities.

To conserve capital, Enron will implement a comprehensive cost-saving program that will include substantial workforce reductions. These workforce reductions primarily will affect the company's operations in Houston, where Enron currently employs approximately 7,500 people.

In addition, the company will continue its accelerated program to divest or wind down non-core assets and operations. Details of the units to be affected will be communicated shortly.

The Dynegy Lawsuit

In its lawsuit filed today in U.S. Bankruptcy Court in New York, Enron alleges, among other things, that Dynegy breached its Merger Agreement with Enron by terminating the agreement when it had no contractual right to do so; and that Dynegy has no right to exercise its option to acquire the entity that indirectly owns the Northern Natural Gas pipeline because that option can only be triggered by a valid termination of the Merger Agreement.

The Chapter 11 Filings

In conjunction with today's petitions for Chapter 11 reorganization, Enron will ask the Bankruptcy Court to consider a variety of "first day motions" to support its employees, vendors, trading counterparties, customers and other constituents. These include motions seeking court permission to continue payments for employee payroll and health benefits; obtain interim financing authority and maintain cash management programs; and retain legal, financial and other professionals to support the company's reorganization actions. In accordance with applicable law and court orders, vendors and suppliers who provided goods or services to Enron Corp. or the subsidiaries that have filed for Chapter 11 protection before today's filing may have pre-petition claims, which will be frozen pending court authorization of payment or consummation of a plan of reorganization.

The Wholesale Energy Trading Business

The discussions currently underway with various leading financial institutions are aimed at obtaining credit support for, recapitalizing and revitalizing Enron's North American wholesale energy trading operations under a new ownership structure in which Enron would continue to have a significant ownership interest.

"If these discussions are successful, they could result in the creation of a new trading entity with a strong and unencumbered balance sheet, the industry's finest trading team, and its leading technology platform, all backed by one or more of the world's leading financial institutions," said Greg Whalley, Enron president and chief operating officer. "We understand that it may take time for counterparties to resume normal trading levels with this entity, but we are confident that this business can be put back on a solid footing. Obviously, our potential partners share our confidence or they would not be at the table with us. We intend to take steps to retain employees who are key to the future success of our wholesale energy trading business and to regain the support and confidence of its trading counterparties."

Comment by Ken Lay

"From an operational standpoint, our energy businesses-including our pipelines and utilities-are conducting normal operations and will continue to do so, " said Kenneth L. Lay, chairman and CEO of Enron. "While uncertainty during the past few weeks has severely impacted the market's confidence in Enron and its trading operations, we are taking the steps announced today to help preserve capital, stabilize our businesses, restore the confidence of our trading counterparties, and enhance our ability to pay our creditors."

Enron's principal legal advisor with regard to the proposed merger with Dynegy, Enron's Chapter 11 filings, the Dynegy lawsuit, and related matters is Weil, Gotshal & Manges LLP. Enron's principal financial advisor with regard to its financial restructuring is The Blackstone Group.

About Enron Corp.

Enron Corp. markets electricity and natural gas, delivers energy and other physical commodities, and provides financial and risk management services to customers around the world. Enron's Internet address is www.enron.com.

Forward-looking Statements

This press release contains statements that are forward-looking within the meaning of Section 27A of the Securities Act of 1933 and Section 21E of the Securities Exchange Act of 1934. Investors are cautioned that any such forward-looking statements are not guarantees of future performance and that actual results could differ materially as a result of known and unknown risks and uncertainties, including: various regulatory issues, the outcome of the Chapter 11 process, the outcome of the litigation discussed above, the outcome of the discussions referred to above, general economic conditions, future trends, and other risks, uncertainties and factors disclosed in the Company's most recent reports on Forms 10-K, 10-Q and 8-K filed with the Securities and Exchange Commission."

(Source: 8-K filed by Enron Corp. on December 2, 2001)

a. What is meant by counterparty?
b. Why would you expect counterparties to care about the equity of a company such as Enron?
c. What is meant by "unwinding" and how does this relate to the Enron Corp.'s filing of Chapter 11, if at all?
d. The partnerships attracting attention in the restatement were involved with derivative and hedging transactions. What is it about such transactions that makes the creation of partnerships as discussed in the 10-K of 2000 and in subsequent disclosures desirable? Do unique accounting implications for the recording of financial instrument and hedging transactions arise in this case setting? Explain.
e. The media has pointed out that a decade ago, 80 percent of Enron's revenues came from the regulated gas-pipeline business, and that by 2000, around 95 percent of its revenues and more than 80 percent of its profits came from trading energy and both buying and selling stakes in energy producers. Commodities trading in gas in 1989, moved to electrons in 1994, and to bandwidth in 1999. Pulp, paper, plastics, metal, and transportation were among its trading operations. Enron traded interest rates, credit risks, and even weather. EnronOnline's trading floor has been characterized as a sophisticated dot.com, engaged in commodity barter and arbitrage. At one point, Enron was trading at 55 times its earnings. Do these observations influence your analysis of the risk situation, both historical and future for Enron Corp. How?
f. In the 10-K disclosure on new accounting developments, mention is made of pending interpretations by the Financial Accounting Standards Board. Is this commonplace? Why or why not? What does it suggest about the accounting for derivatives and hedging? Explain.

Requirement B: Strategy-Related Considerations

The media has raised issues about the corporate governance structure and decisions made with regard to related party transactions by the Board of Directors. It has been alleged that there was insufficient transparency about potential conflicts of interest. The very idea that dealings with private partnerships run by its own officers may have created half of pretax earnings created questions as to the quality of earnings.

1. Why would a Board of Directors authorize transactions with a related party?
2. Did the Enron Board of Directors create any control structure relative to these transactions?
3. In the wake of the developments detailed in this case, how would you evaluate the actions to date of the directors?

Key Terms and Glossary

basis swaps "are derivative instruments that are used to modify the receipts or payments associated with a recognized, variable-rate asset or liability from one variable amount to another variable amount. They do not eliminate the variability of cash flows; instead, they change the basis or index of variability." (FAS 133, Par. 391)

legal risk recognizes the possibility of legal responsibilities being altered due to legislative action; since derivatives markets are international, counterparties to the same contract may be expected to have different legal responsibilities toward one another, especially in the case of bankruptcy; this is more threatening due to the fact that many laws governing the over-the-counter (OTC) securities were

call options (or put options) on debt instruments can accelerate the repayment of principal on a debt instrument

contractually specified servicing fees "All amounts that, per contract, are due to the servicer in exchange for servicing the financial asset and would no longer be received by a servicer if the beneficial owners of the serviced assets (or their trustees or agents) were to exercise their actual or potential authority under the contract to shift the servicing to another servicer. Depending on the servicing contract, those fees may include some or all of the difference between the interest rate collectible on the asset being serviced and the rate to be paid to the beneficial owners of those assets." (FAS 140, Par. 364)

credit risk the risk that counterparty will not pay what is owed (this can be reduced through use of exchange-traded futures, since the risk becomes distributed throughout the exchange, whereas in a contract, a counterparty's default or insolvency will result in delay or nonreceipt of the obligation); the risk of counterparty default is said to be more difficult to evaluate when it applies further into the future. The result of this difference in timing of payments is that the credit risk generally is greater for currency forwards than it is judged to be for rate swaps. Current credit risk of an interest rate swap is set at its replacement cost. Future credit risk rises and falls in proportion to the fluctuation in the instruments' values. A dome-shaped risk curve is typical, rising from origination and falling toward expiration. The idea underlying this shape is that at origination, interest rate uncertainty is an increasing function of the length of the forecast. Then, as time passes, the contract matures and fewer future payments remain at risk. Hence, the dome shape emerges. In contrast, the currency risk profiles are said to increase steadily, since the primary cash flow arises at the contract's end. Net arrangements and master agreements, increasingly common, help reduce credit risk. Regulators also have an influence on credit risk. As an example, the Central Banks of several countries including the U.S. Federal Reserve are on record warning that controls are essential before increasing credit. If global standards and policies emerge, the cooperation will no doubt lead to some reduction in both legal and settlement risks.

currency-sharing agreements divide foreign currency risk between two counterparties who may have long-term contracting arrangements, such as selling a component between manufacturers located in two different countries. Issues of whether to price in U.S. dollars or, for example, deutsche marks are common. The resolution can matter substantially in terms of the implications of foreign currency fluctuations. By sharing such risks, both parties effectively reduce risks.

derivative instrument "is a financial instrument or other contract with all three of the following

written prior to the advent of OTC derivatives. In the late 1980s, the London borough of Hammersmith and Fulhan used interest-rate swaps to speculate on interest rates' direction, earning superior returns from volatile derivatives until interest turned against them. At that point, with big losses faced, the local officials declared that they were not allowed to invest in swaps and therefore should not have to bear the losses. The reality of legal risks was highlighted in 1990 when Britain's highest court, the House of Lords in the United Kingdom ruled for the municipalities, instantly transferring more than $150 million in losses from more than 70 local governments to the dealers. When the House of Lords nullified swap contracts that the municipality of Hammersmith and Fulham had opened, this action was reported to have destroyed contracts between 130 government entities and 75 of the largest banks in the world. Over half of all the realized derivative losses in 1991 were a direct result of this action by the House of Lords.

LIBOR swap rate "the fixed rate on a single-currency, constant-notional interest rate swap that has its floating-rate leg referenced to the London Interbank Offered Rate (LIBOR) with no additional spread over LIBOR on that floating-rate leg. That fixed rate is the derived rate that would result in the swap having a zero fair value at inception because the present value of fixed cash flows, based on that rate, equate to the present value of the floating cash flows." (FAS 138, Par. 40)

liquidity risk reduction of trades, perhaps stemming from turbulence in the markets, that reduces liquidity, i.e., the ability to convert into cash--reduction in liquidity can lead to more price volatility, less certainty, less trading, even less liquidity, continuing in a cycle

market risk any market-related factor that can change the value of the instrument; components that ought to be considered across the term structure include: absolute price or rate change (referred to as delta risk); convexity (gamma risk); change in price volatility (vega risk); time decay (theta); basis or correlation; and discount rate (rho); market risk management should take into account possible abnormal conditions and reduced liquidity

monetizing a financial concept of breaking economic markets into very small pieces that can be sold forward, hedged, borrowed against, and otherwise traded, as a tool for creating competitive markets

net arrangements and master agreements The Group of Thirty suggests a single master agreement rather than multiple master agreements, since the latter can permit "cherry-picking." In other words, a risk arises that the right to set off amounts due under different master agreements might be delayed. A master agreement should provide for full rather than limited two-way payments. This results in the net amount calculated through the netting provisions being due whether it is to, or from, the defaulting party. The

characteristics:

a. It has (1) one or more underlyings and (2) one or more notional amounts...or payment provisions or both. Those terms determine the amount of the settlement or settlements, and, in some cases, whether or not a settlement is required. ...

b. It requires no initial net investment or an initial net investment that is smaller than would be required for other types of contracts that would be expected to have a similar response to changes in market factors.

c. Its terms require or permit net settlement, it can readily be settled net by a means outside the contract, or it provides for delivery of an asset that puts the recipient in a position not substantially different from net settlement." (FAS 133, Par. 6)

derivatives transaction is a contract whose value depends on (or derives from) the value of an underlying asset, reference rate or index.

embedded call "A call option held by the issuer of a financial instrument that is part of and trades with the underlying instrument. For example, a bond may allow the issuer to call it by posting a public notice well before its stated maturity that asks the current holder to submit it for early redemption and provides that interest ceases to accrue on the bond after the early redemption date. Rather than being an obligation of the initial purchaser of the bond, an embedded call trades with and diminishes the value of the underlying bond." (FAS 140, Par. 364)

fair value "The amount at which an asset (liability) could be bought (incurred) or sold (settled) in a current transaction between willing parties, that is, other than in a forced or liquidation sale. Quoted market prices in active markets are the best evidence of fair value and should be used as the basis for the measurement, if available. If a quoted market price is available, the fair value is the product of the number of trading units times that market price. If a quoted market price is not available, the estimate of fair value should be based on the best information available in the circumstances. The estimate of fair value should consider prices for similar assets or similar liabilities and the results of valuation techniques to the extent available in the circumstances. Examples of valuation techniques include the present value of estimated expected future cash flows using discount rates commensurate with the risks involved, option-pricing models, matrix pricing, option-adjusted spread models, and fundamental analysis. Valuation techniques for measuring assets and liabilities should be consistent with the objective of measuring fair value. Those techniques should incorporate assumptions that market participants would use in their estimates of values, future revenues, and future expenses, including assumptions about interest rates, default, prepayment, and volatility. In measuring forward contracts, such as foreign currency forward contracts, at fair value by discounting estimated future cash flows, an entity should base the estimate of future cash flows on the changes in the forward rate (rather

benefits of increasing the certainty about the value of a net position under full two-way payments dominates alternative arrangements, based on the judgments of The Group of Thirty.

notional amount "a number of currency units, shares, bushels, pounds, or other units specified in a derivative instrument." (FAS 138, Par. 40)

operating risk refers to losses stemming from inadequate risk management and internal controls by those firms that use derivatives; if there is incomplete involvement in or understanding of derivative portfolios by management, then operating risks increase. Operating risks involve inadequacies in documentation, credit controls, or position limits, as well as a lack of control over the use of leverage. Trading and exposure limits ought to be strictly applied, and leverage effects should be continuously monitored by considering liability exposures (analyzed by multiplying percentage changes in rates by the leverage factor to get one's hands around the entire exposure).

option contract provides one party with a right, but not an obligation, to buy or sell something at an agreed-on price on or before a set date, which presents one-sided risk. This is an important dimension of option-type instruments which is significant because the counterparty, the writer of the option, has only a potentially unfavorable outcome: at best, it retains the premium paid by the option holder while at worst, its losses could be virtually unlimited.

securitization the process by which financial assets are transformed into securities (FAS 140, Par. 364)

settlement risk risk that arises when one party settles the contract before the other party does and the latter does not receive what is owed; this is referred to as Herstatt risk, with the namesake of Bank Herstatt which was a German bank closed by German regulators at the close of business on June 26, 1974--since U.S. banks paid the bank German marks specified in forward contracts before the other side of the contract was paid in U.S. dollars, losses resulted. Settlement risks can be sidestepped through the use of transfer agents and escrow agents or through a simple act of simultaneous transfers. Similarly, derivatives transactions such as rate swaps and other contracts that do not involve principal payments reduce Herstatt risk, as do master agreements and netting arrangements. If netting applies, current credit exposure is the sum of negative and positive exposures on transactions in the portfolio. However, for potential credit exposure, simulation of the entire portfolio is necessary because a summation will not effectively treat offsets or give credit for different timing of peak exposures, meaning that the exposure is overstated by a mere summation.

short sales (sales of borrowed securities). "Short sales typically involve the following activities:

(1)   Selling a security (by the short seller to the purchaser)

(2)   Borrowing a security (by the short seller from

than the spot rate). In measuring financial liabilities and nonfinancial derivatives that are liabilities at fair value by discounting estimated future cash flows (or equivalent outflows of other assets), an objective is to use discount rates at which those liabilities could be settled in an arm's-length transaction." (FAS 138, Par. 40)

financial instrument "Cash, evidence of an ownership interest in an entity, or a contract that both:

a. Imposes on one entity a contractual obligation* (1) to deliver cash or another financial instrument† to a second entity or (2) to exchange other financial instruments on potentially unfavorable terms with the second entity

b. Conveys to that second entity a contractual right‡ (1) to receive cash or another financial instrument from the first entity or (2) to exchange other financial instruments on potentially favorable terms with the first entity.

*Contractual obligations encompass both those that are conditioned on the occurrence of a specified event and those that are not. All contractual obligations that are financial instruments meet the definition of liability set forth in Concepts Statement 6, although some may not be recognized as liabilities in financial statements—may be "off-balance-sheet"—because they fail to meet some other criterion for recognition. For some financial instruments, the obligation is owed to or by a group of entities rather than a single entity.

†The use of the term financial instrument in this definition is recursive (because the term financial instrument is included in it), though it is not circular. The definition requires a chain of contractual obligations that ends with the delivery of cash or an ownership interest in an entity. Any number of obligations to deliver financial instruments can be links in a chain that qualifies a particular contract as a financial instrument.

‡Contractual rights encompass both those that are conditioned on the occurrence of a specified event and those that are not. All contractual rights that are financial instruments meet the definition of asset set forth in Concepts Statement 6, although some may not be recognized as assets in financial statements—may be "off-balance-sheet"—because they fail to meet some other criterion for recognition. For some financial instruments, the right is held by or the obligation is due from a group of entities rather than a single entity." (FAS 138, Par. 40)

firm commitment "agreement with an unrelated party, binding on both parties and usually legally enforceable, with the following characteristics:

a. The agreement specifies all significant terms, including the quantity to be exchanged, the fixed price, and the timing of the transaction. The fixed price may be expressed as a specified amount of an entity's functional currency or of a foreign currency. It may also be expressed as a specified interest rate or specified effective yield.

the lender)

(3) Delivering the borrowed security (by the short seller to the purchaser)

(4) Purchasing a security (by the short seller from the market)

(5) Delivering the purchased security (by the short seller to the lender).

Those five activities involve three separate contracts. A contract that distinguishes a short sale involves activities (2) and (5), borrowing a security and replacing it by delivering an identical security." (FAS 133, Par. 59)

systemic risk is the risk that any disruption will lead to widespread difficulties in firms, markets, or the financial system as a whole, such as a computer software problem within world financial markets and exchanges. Systemic risks in the derivatives market appear more problematic due to the domination of the market by a few large players; two U.S. banks accounted for 95 percent of the notional amount of derivatives in the U.S. banking system in 1992, whereas such domination is not at this scale in most other markets. Since derivatives are growing and the market is beginning to get standard-setters' and regulators' attention, systemic risk is expected to decline.

take-or-pay contracts. "Under a take-or-pay contract, an entity agrees to pay a specified price for a specified quantity of a product whether or not it takes delivery." (FAS 133, Par. 59)

The Group of Thirty, Consultative Group on International Economic & Monetary Affairs, Inc., 1990 M Street, N.W., Suite 450, Washington, D.C. 20036

transferee "An entity that receives a financial asset, a portion of a financial asset, or a group of financial assets from a transferor." (FAS 140, Par. 364)

transferor "An entity that transfers a financial asset, a portion of a financial asset, or a group of financial assets that it controls to another entity." (FAS 140, Par. 364)

underlying "a specified interest rate, security price, commodity price, foreign exchange rate, index of prices or rates, or other variable. An underlying may be a price or rate of an asset or liability but is not the asset or liability itself." (FAS 138, Par. 40) "An underlying usually is one or a combination of the following:

(1) A security price or security price index

(2) A commodity price or commodity price index

(3) An interest rate or interest rate index

(4) A credit rating or credit index

(5) An exchange rate or exchange rate index

(6) An insurance index or catastrophe loss index

(7) A climatic or geological condition (such as temperature, earthquake severity, or rainfall), another physical variable, or a related index." (FAS 133, Par. 57)

b. The agreement includes a disincentive for nonperformance that is sufficiently large to make performance probable." (FAS 138, Par. 40)

floors, caps, and collars "Floors or caps (or collars, which are combinations of caps and floors) on interest rates and the interest rate on a debt instrument are considered to be clearly and closely related, provided the cap is at or above the current market price (or rate) and the floor is at or below the current market price (or rate) at issuance of the instrument." (FAS 133, Par. 61); an embedded derivative instrument in which the underlying is an interest rate or interest rate index-- examples of which are interest rate cap or an interest rate collar--that alters net interest payments that otherwise would be paid or received on an interest-bearing host contract

forecasted transaction "A transaction that is expected to occur for which there is no firm commitment. Because no transaction or event has yet occurred and the transaction or event when it occurs will be at the prevailing market price, a forecasted transaction does not give an entity any present rights to future benefits or a present obligation for future sacrifices." (FAS 133, Par. 540)

forward-type derivative obligates one party to buy and a counterparty to sell something (that is, a financial instrument, foreign currency, or commodity) at a future date at an agreed-on price

undivided interest "Partial legal or beneficial ownership of an asset as a tenant in common with others. The proportion owned may be pro rata, for example, the right to receive 50 percent of all cash flows from a security, or non–pro rata, for example, the right to receive the interest from a security while another has the right to the principal." (FAS 140, Par. 364)

unilateral ability "A capacity for action not dependent on the actions (or failure to act) of any other party." (FAS 140, Par. 364)

value at risk is the most commonly recommended method for valuing portfolios. The idea is to determine a portfolio's change in value due to adverse market movements of any factor, such as volatility or price, for a specified period of time--preferably one day as the time frame for assessing change in value. The Group of Thirty contends that dealers should mark their derivatives positions to market on at least a daily basis for risk management purposes. Intraday or even real time valuation is cited as potentially helpful in managing market risk of some option portfolios. The value-at-risk uses probability analysis based on common confidence intervals, such as 95% representing two standard deviations for a specified time horizon (e.g., a one-day exposure). The phrasing of the result of analysis might be at 95%, it can be determined that any change in portfolio value outside of a predicted range over one day from adverse market movement would be a specified amount.

Further Readings

"A Tale of Two Banks: Events in Paris Cast a Fresh Light on the Drama in London." 1995. *The Economist* (March 11), p. 20.

Abken, Peter 1994. "Over-the-Counter Financial Derivatives: Risky Business?" *Economic Review-- Federal Reserve Bank of Atlanta* (March/April), p. 12.

Achenbach, Joel. 2001. "Enron, We Hardly Knew Ye." *Washington Post* (December 6, 12:31 p.m. .

Adams, Jane B. 1995. "Simplifying Accounting for Derivative Instruments, Including Those Used for Hedging." *Highlights of Financial Reporting Issues* (Financial Accounting Standard Board, January), pp. 1-7.

Ascarelli, Silvia and Deborah Ball. 2001. "Behind Shrinking Deficits: Derivatives? Report Suggests Italy Used Swaps to Meet EU Targets on Budget" *The Wall Street Journal* (November 6), p. A22.

Barrionuevo, Alexei, and Rebecca Smith. 2001. "Dynegy Hits Back at Enron With Lawsuit: Claim Is Failed Merger Deal Entitles Concern to Get Northern Natural Gas." *The Wall Street Journal* (December 4), p. A10.

"Berardino Congressional Testimony." 2001. "Remarks of Joseph F. Berardino, Managing Partner, Chief Executive Officer, Andersen." U.S. House of Representatives, Committee on Financial Services (Chairman Oxley, Congressman LaFalce, Chairman

Lowenstein, Roger. 1995. "Intrinsic Value: As Orange County Blames Others, Guess Where Latest Report Points." *The Wall Street Journal* (September 7).

Lucas, Timothy S. and Janet Danola. 1993. "Improving Disclosures about Derivatives." *FASB Viewpoints* (December 31), pp. 1,2.

Lucchetti, Aaron. 2001. "When Bad Stocks Happen to Good Mutual Funds: Enron Could Spark New Attention to Accounting." *The Wall Street Journal* (December 13), pp. C1, C19.

McGee, Suzanne. 1995. "Farmers May Be Next Victims of Derivatives," *The Wall Street Journal* (December 11), pp. C1, C14.

Mellino, Angelo and Stuart Turnbull. 1995. "Misspecification and the Pricing and Hedging of Long-Term Foreign Currency Options." *Journal of International Money and Finance* (June), pp. 373-393.

Melloan, George. 1995. "Leeson's Law: Too Much Leverage Can Wreck a Bank." *The Wall Street Journal* (March 6), p. A15.

Michaels, Adrian. 2001. "Andersen Chief Calls for Revamp of Accounting System." *The Financial Times* (December 4).

Mills, Mark and Peter Huber. 2001. "Deregulation Will Survive Enron." *The Wall Street Journal* (December

Baker, Congressman Kanjorski, Chairwoman Kelly, Congressman Gutierrez) (December 12).

Berardino, Joe. 2001. "Enron: A Wake-Up Call." *The Wall Street Journal* (December 4), p. A18.

Bodily, Samuel, and Robert Bruner. 2001. "What Enron Did Right." *The Wall Street Journal* (November 19), p. A20.

Brauchli, Marcus W., Nicholas Bray, and Michael R. Sesit. 1995. "Broken Bank: Barings PLC Officials May Have Been Aware Of Trader's Position: Investigators Say Firm Knew Extent of Its Exposure, But Failed to Respond--Leeson Was 'Hero' to Some." *The Wall Street Journal* (March 6), pp. A1, A7.

Bryan-Low, Cassell, and Suzanne McGee. 2001. "Enron Short Seller Detected Red Flags in Regulatory Filings." *The Wall Street Journal* (November 5), p. C1.

Conover, Teresa L., and Wanda A. Wallace. 2000. "Accounting Hedges: Should We Expect Changes Under SFAS No. 133?" *Advances in International Accounting* (Volume 13) (Stamford, Connecticut: JAI Press; Editor J. Timothy Sale; Associate Editors Stephen B. Salter and David J. Sharp), pp. 119-132.

Craig, Suzanne and Jonathan Weil. 2001. "Most Analysts Remain Plugged In to Enron." *The Wall Street Journal* (October 26), pp. C1, C2.

Dhanani, Slpha and Roger Groves. 2001. "The Management of Strategic Exchange Risk: Evidence From Corporate Practices." *Accounting and Business Research* 31, no. 4 (Autumn), pp. 275-290.

Edwards, Gerald, and Gregory Eller. 1995. "Overview of Derivatives Disclosures by Major U.S. Banks," *Federal Reserve Bulletin* (September), p. 820.

Emshwiller, John R. 2002. "Documents Track Enron's Partnerships: Top Officers Viewed Deals As Integral to Ensuring Growth in Recent Years." *The Wall Street Journal* (January 2), pp. A3, A8.

Emshwiller, John R. 2001. "Enron Transaction With Entity Run By Executive Raises Questions." *The Wall Street Journal* (November 5), p. A3.

Emshwiller, John R. and Rebecca Smith. 2001. "Corporate Veil: Behind Enron's Fall, A Culture of Operating Outside Public's View; Hidden Deals With Officers and Minimal Disclosure Finally Cost It Its Trust; Chewco and JEDI Warriors." *The Wall Street Journal* (December 5), pp. A1, A10.

Emshwiller, John and Rebecca Smith. 2001. "Dynegy's Enron Deal Faces Uncertainties: Potential Antitrust Worries Or New Enron Liabilities Could Upset Agreement." *The Wall Street Journal* (November 12), pp. A3,A12.

Emshwiller, John R. and Rebecca Smith. 2001. "Enron Did Business With a Second Entity Operated by Another Company Official: No Public Disclosure Was Made of Deals." *The Wall Street Journal* (October 26), pp. C1, C14.

"Five Accounting Firms Issue Statement on Enron." 2001. Joint Press Release (December 4).

Francis, Theo and Ellen Schultz. 2001. "Enron Faces Suits by 401(K) Plan Participants." *The Wall Street*

6), editorial page.

Molvar, Roger H.D. and James F. Green. 1995. "The Question of Derivatives," *The Journal of Accountancy* (March), p. 55.

Nobes, Christopher W., Editor. 2001. *GAAP 2000: A Survey of National Accounting Rules in 53 Countries.* Arthur Andersen, BDO, Deloitte Touche Tohmatsu, Ernst & Young International, Grant Thornton, KPMG, and PricewaterhouseCoopers.

Pacelle, Mitchell and Cassell Bryan-Low. 2001. "Enron's Collapse Roils Insiders and Wall Street: Belfer Family Is a Big Loser As Stock Dive." *The Wall Street Journal* (December 5), pp. C1, C13.

Pacelle, Mitchell, Michael Schroeder, and John Emshwiller. 2001. "Enron Would Restructure Around 'Core.'" *The Wall Street Journal* (December 13), pp. A3, A6.

Pitt, Harvey L. 2001. "How to Prevent Future Enrons." *The Wall Street Journal* (December 11), p. A18.

Pretzlik, Charles and Gary Silverman. 2001. "Enron is Regulators' Nightmare Come True. Banks on the Hook. Companies & Finance The Collapse of Enron." *The Financial Times* (November 30), p. 29.

"Review & Outlook: What Was Enron?" 2001. *The Wall Street Journal* (December 12), p. A18.

Richardson, Karen. 2001. "Hong Kong May Give Investors Broader Reach to Hedge Funds." *The Wall Street Journal* (December 13), p. C10.

Sapsford, Jathon and Alexei Barrionuevo. 2001. "Reviving Enron Requires Return Of Old Clients." *The Wall Street Journal* (December 5), pp. A3, A10.

Schroeder, Michael. 2001. "Enron Debacle Will Test Leadership of SEC's New Chief: Harvey Pitt's Handling of Energy-Trading Firm's Collapse to Be Watched Closely." *The Wall Street Journal* (December 31), p. A.10.

Schroeder, Michael. 2001. "Enron Debacle Spurs Calls for Controls." *The Wall Street Journal* (December 14), p. A4.

Schroeder, Michael and Greg Ip. 2001. "Out of Reach: The Enron Debacle Spotlights Huge Void In Financial Regulation—Energy Firm Lobbied Hard To Limit the Oversight Of Its Trading Operations—Keeping Ms. Born at Bay." *The Wall Street Journal* (December 13), pp. A1, A6.

Securities and Exchange Commission (SEC). 2001. "SEC Issues Financial Disclosure Cautionary Advice." For Immediate Release 2001-147. "Action: Cautionary Advice Regarding Disclosure About Critical Accounting Policies." Release No. 33-8040; 34-45149; FR 60 (December 12). Accessible at http://www.sec.gov/pdf/33-8040.pdf.

Skinner, D.J. 1996. "Are Disclosures About Bank Derivatives and Employee Stock Options Value-Relevant?" *Journal of Accounting and Economics* 22, pp. 393-405.

Smith, Randall. 2001. "Lehman Faced Possible Conflict As Merger Failed." *The Wall Street Journal* (December 5), pp. C1, C11.

Smith, Randall and Steven Lipin. 1994. "Beleaguered

Journal (November 23), pp. C1, C10.

French, Kenneth.1988. "Pricing Financial Futures Contracts: An Introduction," *Financial Markets and Portfolio Management*, Spring.

Goldberg, Stephen, Charles Tritschler, and Joseph Godwin. 1995. "Financial Reporting for Foreign Exchange Derivatives," *Accounting Horizons* (June), pp. 1-15.

Herz, Robert. 1994. "Hedge Accounting, Derivatives, and Synthetics: The FASB Starts Rethinking the Rules." *Journal of Corporate Accounting and Finance* (Spring), pp. 323-333.

Hill, Andrew and Peter Thal Larsen. 2001. "Enron Promised Dollars 1.5bn in Emergency Funding." *The Financial Times* (December 4), p. 1.

Hill, Andrew, Sheila Mcnulty, Elizabeth Wine. 2001. "A Chaotic Collapse: Enron's Demise Stems From a Lethal Combination of Abundant Financing and Media Hype. Investors' Blind Belief Inflated An Ultimately Unsustainable Bubble, Says Andrew Hill." *The Financial Times* (November 30), p. 20.

Jarrow, Robert and Stuart Turnbull. 1995. "Pricing Derivatives on Financial Securities Subject to Credit Risk." *The Journal of Finance* (March), pp. 53-85.

Jereski, Laura. 1994. "The Wrong Stuff: Good Connections Put Hedge Fund in Business But a Bad Bet Sank It—Manager David Weill, Suave and Impressive, Drew in Europe's Wealthy Class--Adieu to a Gilded World." *The Wall Street Journal* (September 28), pp. A1, A8.

Kedrosky, Paul. 2001. "How Enron Ran Out of Gas." *The Wall Street Journal* (October 29), p. A22.

Kessler, Andy. 2001. "Lying Is a Capital Crime." *The Wall Street Journal* (November 30), p. A14.

Knecht, G. Bruce. 1994."The Lawyers' Turn: Derivatives Are Going Through Crucial Test: A Wave of Lawsuits." *The Wall Street Journal* (October 28), p. A1.

Lipin, Steven. 1994. "Gibson Greetings Reaches Accord in Suit Against Bankers Trust Over Derivatives." *The Wall Street Journal* (November 25), p. A2.

Giant: As Derivatives Losses Rise, Industry Fights To Avert Regulation--Stigma Has Already Stalled 'Exotic' End of Business, Where Most of Profit Is--Now a $35 Trillion Market," *The Wall Street Journal* (August 25), pp. A1, A4.

The Group of Thirty. 1994. *Defining the Roles of Accountants, Bankers and Regulators in the United States: A Study Group Report* (Washington, D.C.).

Venkatachalam, M. 1996. "Value Relevance of Banks Derivatives Disclosures." *Journal of Accounting and Economics* 17, pp. 327-355.

Wallace, Wanda A. 1999. *Performance Measurement and Risk Monitoring* (Boston, New York: Warren Gorham & Lamont, RIA Group).

Wallace, Wanda. 1999-2000. "How Important are Thin-Market Considerations?" Assurance Forum, *Accounting Today* (Vol. 13, No. 22, December 13-January 2), pp. 16, 68.

Wallace, Wanda A. 1999. "Risk Evaluation: Just who is minding the store?" Assurance Forum, *Accounting Today* (August 23-September 5), pp. 16, 45, 46.

Wallace, Wanda A. 1996. "FASB Hedge Accounting Rule Blurs Fact," Audit & Accounting Forum, *Accounting Today* (June 3-16), pp. 16, 17, 20.

Weil, Jonathan. 2001. "After Enron, 'Mark to Market' Accounting Gets Scrutiny." *The Wall Street Journal* (December 4), pp. C1, C2.

Weil, Jonathan. 2001. "Basic Principle of Accounting Tripped Enron." *The Wall Street Journal* (November 12), pp. C1, C2.

Weil, Jonathan. 2001. "Arthur Andersen Could Face Scrutiny on Clarity of Enron Financial Reports." *The Wall Street Journal* (November 5), p. C1.

Wilson Arlette C. 1998. "The Decision on Derivatives (Accounting Standards for Derivative Instruments and Hedging Activities)." *Journal of Accountancy* (November).

Winograd, Barry N., and Robert H. Herz. 1995. "Derivatives: What's An Auditor To Do?" *Journal of Accountancy* (June), pp. 75-80.

Zuckerman, Gregory. 2001. "Hedge Funds Now Frown Upon Anonymity." *The Wall Street Journal* (December 13), pp. C1, C10.

"If accounting is important and you change the accounting rules, then the play of the game changes."   **- William R. Kinney, Jr.**

[Source: "Commentary on 'The Relation of Accounting Research to Teaching and Practice: A 'Positive' View," <u>Accounting Horizons</u> (March 1989), p. 123]

CASE 12

Emerging Issues: The Agenda of FASB

CASE TOPICS OUTLINE

1. Priorities of the Financial Accounting Standards Board—Annual Survey of the Financial Accounting Standards Advisory Council
    A. Board Members' Rankings
    B. Your Rankings

2. Strategy-Related Considerations

The Financial Accounting Standards Board (FASB) evaluates potential agenda projects by considering the pervasiveness of the issue, alternative solutions, technical feasibility, cost-benefit relationship, and practical consequences. Annually, the Financial Accounting Standards Advisory Council (FASAC) administers a survey to solicit FASB members' and Council members' views about future FASB agenda priorities. This survey is also sent to former members of FASAC.

After describing a topic, comments are elicited from respondents, as to need and scope, and then the respondent is requested to evaluate each of the topics on a scale of 1 to 3, with "1" being the highest priority and "3" the lowest. A score of "1" would indicate that the Board should add this topic to the agenda now. A score of "2" would indicate that the Board should place the topic on the agenda in the near future, when current agenda projects have been completed and resources are available. A score of "3" would indicate that the Board should not add this topic to the agenda." Toward the end of the survey, relative rankings are sought.

Excerpts from the 2001 Annual FASAC Survey: Priorities of the Financial Accounting Standards Board administered in August of 2001, including ranking and scoring results from FASB members as reported in November 2001, are listed in Table 5.12.1. The descriptions of the scope of various projects are excerpted from various discussions in the survey form; such a synopsis is not provided for each potential agenda item. In contrast with the Board, members of FASAC ranked Business Combinations—Application of the Purchase Method first (with a 1.14 score) and the Reporting of Financial Performance as fifth (with a 1.74 score). Former FASAC members cited Accounting for Interests in Joint Ventures, Cost-Sharing Arrangements, etc. as first (with a 1.64 score). Hence, some diversity of opinion in the rankings is apparent.

Table 5.12-1 EXCERPTS FROM 2001 ANNUAL FASAC SURVEY FORM AND
REPORTED RESULTS FOR FASB MEMBERS

Instructions provided as to reported rank: "Please indicate the order in which you would rank those topics using "1" to indicate the topic you believe is the most important future agenda project for the FASB to address and "22" to indicate the least important."

Potential Agenda Projects	Rank* (score)
Business Combinations—Application of the Purchase Method Accounting for noncontrolling interests Determining the aggregate amount paid in an acquisition (including accounting for contingent consideration) Identifying assets acquired and liabilities assumed Accounting for preacquisition contingencies	3 (1.00)
Business Combinations—Fresh-Start (New Basis) Issues The scope of the project also would include the issue of gain recognition in the financial statements of the entity that has transferred or lost control over net assets for which a new basis of accounting is recognized.	6 (1.50)
Disclosure about Intangibles A possible scope would focus on identifying the major classes of unrecognized intangible assets and consider the potential relevance and reliability of information about expenditures, values, and changes in them.	4 (1.63)
Reporting Financial Performance A minimum scope would address the classification and display of information in all basic financial statements, both annual and interim (but would exclude a reconsideration of segment reporting). That approach would include a study of financial measures that users of financial statements find most useful with the goal of providing the information with which those measures can be determined. A broader approach would include determining and defining how key financial measures should be calculated. An even broader scope would require that certain specific financial measures be provided in the financial statements. A project on performance reporting likely would include a reconsideration of cash flow reporting.	1 (1.00)
Liability and Revenue Recognition If added to the agenda, a project on liabilities could lead to an amendment of Concepts Statement 6, Concepts Statement 5, or both-- clarifying the definition of liabilities and the nature of the different classes of liabilities, as well as by sharpening the guidance for recognizing liabilities. A project on liability recognition likely would include consideration of lease accounting. Conceptual issues surrounding both liability and revenue recognition need to be addressed.	2 (1.13)
Disclosure of Nonfinancial Metrics (recall the Jenkins Report)	19 (2.75)

Potential Agenda Projects	Rank* (score)
Recognition of Project Intangibles A project on recognition of project intangibles most likely would include a reconsideration of the accounting for research and development costs.	10 (2.00)
Recognition of Embedded Intangibles and Service Obligations	15 (2.29)
Accounting for Leases	11 (2.00)
Share-Based Payments	18 (2.5)
Insurance Accounting	16 (2.63)
R&D Costs (Reconsideration of FASB Statement No. 2)	8 (2.00)
Cash Flow Reporting (Reconsideration of FASB Statement No. 95)	7 (1.57)
Reconsideration of FASB Statement No. 115	14 (2.25)
Reporting Comprehensive Income (Reconsideration of FASB Statement No. 130)	15 (1.67)
Interim Reporting	13 (2.29)
Derecognition, Primarily Financial Assets	12 (2.71)
Accounting for Interests in Joint Ventures, Cost-Sharing Arrangements, Affiliation Agreements, and Similar Arrangements with Unconsolidated Entities	9 (1.75)
Equity Method Accounting, Procedures	17 (2.57)
Definition of the Going-Concern Concept	20 (2.88)
FASB Codification/Simplification The subject of standards overload encompasses a number of separate but related issues including: An increase in the volume and sources of standard-setting activity The lack of retrievability of all the accounting rules on a particular subject The complexity and detail of accounting standards Disclosure overload.	5 (1.75)

*The survey form was made available at http://www.fasb.org. Listing and scope descriptions are from that form. In addition, this table summarizes the rankings by FASB members, as reported in "Summary of Responses to Section C Ranking of Future Agenda Priorities" (p. 7) of "Summary of Reponses to Annual FASAC Survey" (November 2001), as well as scores which are scattered throughout the report, on various pages.

Requirement A: Your Ranking

1. First assess your analysis of each topic in Table 5.12.1 in terms of the 1, 2, or 3 ranking described in the case. Then rank-order the topics.
2. Compare and contrast your assessments relative to those reported for the FASB, as well as the examples of where the Board members appear to differ from both FASAC and prior FASAC members.

Requirement B: Strategy-Related Considerations

The FASB has its stated basis for setting priorities, as described earlier in this case (see key terms and glossary as well). Apply those criteria to each topic and determine whether it is possible to assess which took priority in setting the rankings depicted in Table 5.12.1.

The instructions to the survey also indicate to respondents that the FASB always must consider the available resources in making agenda decisions and believes that it is not desirable to have projects on the agenda that are inactive for long periods of time. In addition, the Board considers the opportunity to work jointly on projects with the International Accounting Standards Board (IASB) to meet the goal of achieving convergence. Thus, the instructions advise, Council's views should be tempered by consideration of all of these factors. Do any of these considerations mitigate the effect of the key criteria set forth for the setting of FASB priorities? Do you believe such mitigation is appropriate and how should these additional considerations influence FASB standard setting, if at all?

Key Terms and Glossary

alternative solutions FASB 89, Par. 124 explains "The second factor considered is the potential for developing an alternative solution--whether one or more alternatives that will improve the relevance, reliability, and comparability of financial reporting are likely to be developed."

cost-benefit relationship FASB 89, Par. 117 elaborates on a setting in which this idea of relative costs and benefits is applied: "In addition to those views, the most frequently cited reason for discontinuing the supplementary disclosures was that the benefits derived from presenting that data had not been sufficient to justify the costs incurred." The Board notes an example of a disclosure considered in isolation as not being " unduly burdensome."

equity method of accounting FAS 133, Par. 455 states "Under the equity method of accounting, the investor generally records its share of the investee's earnings or losses from its investment. It does not account for changes in the price of the common stock…"

going concern concept FIN 39, Par. 48 states "as a general rule, accounting should reflect what is expected to occur in the normal course of business and protection in bankruptcy is not pertinent when the probability of bankruptcy is remote."

pervasiveness of the issue FASB 89, Par. 123 explains "The first factor considered is the pervasiveness of the problem to be addressed. A determination is made concerning (a) the extent to which an issue is troublesome to users, preparers, auditors, or others, (b) the extent to which practice is diverse, and (c) the likely duration of the problem (that is, is it transitory or will it persist)."

practical consequences FASB 89, Par.126 explains "The last factor considers practical consequences, namely, whether an improved accounting solution is likely to be generally acceptable and whether not addressing a particular subject might cause others to act, that is, the SEC or Congress."

technical feasibility FASB 89, Par. 125 explains "The third factor addresses the technical feasibility of a project, that is, the extent to which a technically sound solution can be developed or whether the project under consideration should await completion of other projects."

Further Readings

Beresford, Dennis R. 1993. "Frustrations of a Standards Setter," *Accounting Horizons* 7, no. 4, pp. 70-76.

Leisenring, James J. and L. Todd Johnson. 1994. "Accounting Research: On the Relevance of Research to Practice," *Accounting Horizons*, 8, no. 4, pp. 74-79.

Financial Executives International and National Investor Relations. 2001. "Best practice" guidelines for earnings releases (April): see http://www.fei.org.

Upton Jr., Wayne S. (former FASB staff member). 2001. *Special Report, Business and Financial Reporting, Challenges from the New Economy* (the New Economy Report). April --available on the FASB web site (www.fasb.org/new_economy/.html).

Wallace, Wanda A. 2001, forthcoming. "Contrarians or Soothsayers? An historical consideration of the dissents to Statements of Financial Accounting

Griffin, Paul A. 1987. *Research Report: Usefulness to Investors and Creditors of Information Provided by Financial Reporting*, Second Edition (Stamford, Connecticut: Financial Accounting Standards Board, 1987).

May, Robert G. and Gary L. Sundem. 1976. "Research for Accounting Policy: An Overview," *The Accounting Review*, 51, no. 4, pp. 747-763.

Tandy, Paulette R. and Nancy L. Wilburn. 1992. "Constituent Participation In Standard-Setting: The FASB's First 100 Statements," *Accounting Horizons* 6, no. 2, pp. 47-58.

Standards," *The CPA Journal*, December.

Zeff, Stephen A. 1987. "Leaders of the Accounting Profession: 14 Who Made A Difference," *Journal of Accountancy* 163, no. 5, pp. 46-71.

Zeff, Stephen A. 1986. "Big Eight Firms and the Accounting Literature: The Falloff In Advocacy Writing," *Journal of Accounting, Auditing and Finance* 1 (New Series), 2, pp. 131-154.

Zeff, Stephen A. 1972. "Chronology of Significant Developments in the Establishment of Accounting Principles in the United States 1926-1972," *Journal of Accounting Research* 10, no. 1, pp. 217-227.

"We should not lose the substance by grasping the shadow, but often the shadow helps us grasp the substance.

The same may be said of the role of acounting in business. Just as culture affects and is affected by language, business affects and is affected by accounting. In his satirical article on clothes, "Sartor Resartus" (The tailor retailored), Thomas Carlyle states, "Society is founded upon cloth," and "…Man's earthly interests, 'are all hooked and buttoned together, and held up, by clothes.'" [1834, p. 51]. Indeed, is it not true that business is founded upon accounting? Without accounting how could we hook and button our interests together?"   - Yuji Ijiri

[Source: Theory of Accounting Measurement, Studies in Accounting Research no. 10 (Sarasota, Fla.: American Accounting Association, 1975), p. 189; Ijiri cited Thomas Carlyle, Sartor Resartus: The Life and Opinion of Herr Teufelsdrockh (1834), edited by C.F. Harrold (Odyssey Press, 1937).]

Notes

Notes

Notes

Notes

Notes